T0270915

The Black–Scholes–Merton Model as an Idealization of Discrete-Time Economies

This book examines whether continuous-time models in frictionless financial economies can be well approximated by discrete-time models. It specifically looks to answer the question: In what sense and to what extent does the famous Black–Scholes–Merton (BSM) continuous-time model of financial markets idealize more realistic discrete-time models of those markets? While it is well known that the BSM model is an idealization of discrete-time economies where the stock price process is driven by a binomial random walk, it is less known that the BSM model idealizes discrete-time economies whose stock price process is driven by more general random walks. After recounting the foundations of discrete- and continuous-time models of financial markets, David M. Kreps develops the general theory of convergence of discrete-time models to their continuous-time limits, both in mathematical and economic terms. The exposition lowers the entry barriers to the literature of financial mathematics for less-technical readers, while providing a fuller understanding of the connections between BSM and nearby discrete economies.

David M. Kreps is the Adams Distinguished Professor of Management, Emeritus, at the Stanford Graduate School of Business. He has been honored with many awards, including the John Bates Clark Medal by the American Economic Association in 1989 and the John J. Carty Award for the Advancement of Science by the National Academy of Sciences in 2018.

Econometric Society Monograph Series

Editors:

Andrea Prat, Columbia University
Stéphane Bonhomme, University of Chicago

The Econometric Society is an international society for the advancement of economic theory in relation to statistics and mathematics. The Econometric Society Monograph series is designed to promote the publication of original research contributions of high quality in mathematical economics and theoretical and applied econometrics.

Books in the Series

Continued on page following the index

The Black–Scholes–Merton Model as an Idealization of Discrete-Time Economies

David M. Kreps
Stanford University, California

CAMBRIDGE
UNIVERSITY PRESS

CAMBRIDGE
UNIVERSITY PRESS

University Printing House, Cambridge CB2 8BS, United Kingdom

One Liberty Plaza, 20th Floor, New York, NY 10006, USA

477 Williamstown Road, Port Melbourne, VIC 3207, Australia

314-321, 3rd Floor, Plot 3, Splendor Forum, Jasola District Centre, New Delhi - 110025, India

79 Anson Road, #06-04/06, Singapore 079906

Cambridge University Press is part of the University of Cambridge.

It furthers the University's mission by disseminating knowledge in the pursuit of education, learning and research at the highest international levels of excellence.

www.cambridge.org
Information on this title: www.cambridge.org/9781108486361
DOI: 10.1017/9781108626903

© David M. Kreps 2019

First published 2019

A catalogue record for this publication is available from the British Library

ISBN 978-1-108-48636-1 Hardback
ISBN 978-1-108-70765-7 Paperback

Contents

Preface

I began this monograph (which, at the time, was a nascent paper) with the objective of understanding how and how well continuous-time models of economic phenomena – and in particular models that employ Brownian motion – compare with "near by" discrete-time models. We know that the comparisons can sometimes be strained; see, for instance, Fudenberg and Levine (2009) and Sadzik and Stacchetti (2015). So, it seemed to me, a general theory connecting the two types of models ought to be available.

I still believe that such a general theory is available. But I quickly discovered that it is difficult, and so to build my intuition, I did what any faculty member in a school of management would do: I began to look at "case studies." In particular, I began with the connections between discrete- and continuous-time models of financial markets and, in particular, the connections between the famous Black–Scholes–Merton[1] theory of pricing contingent claims by arbitrage and discrete-time models – the seminal reference is Cox, Ross, and Rubinstein (1979) – that, in the limit, "converge" to the Black–Scholes–Merton (BSM, for short) model. The scare quotes around "converge" signify that the point of the exercise is to understand what convergence means in this context and, in particular, to understand how general is this convergence.

In the course of studying these issues, I first discovered that, in some regards, BSM is the economic "limit" of more discrete-time models than I had originally thought – developing a precise statement of what this means is one of the main points of this monograph – and then that, while this fact was not known by me and, seemingly, is not well known by many of colleagues in the field of Finance, it is well known to scholars – primarily mathematicians who specialize in probability – who are members of the community of so-called Financial Mathematicians. I believe that what is known to this community of scholars should be well-known more broadly to financial economists, and so I embarked on writing an exposition of those ideas *in the simplest possible settings* and in a single, unified presentation, so they would be accessible to mainstream financial

---

[1] It is common in the literature to refer to the Black–Scholes theory, the Black–Scholes Option Pricing Model, and the Black–Scholes Formula. But the history of these ideas supports giving equal credit to Robert Merton. Hence, in this monograph, I refer to the Black–Scholes–Merton model and theory.

economists. This monograph is the result.

To be clear, "in the simplest possible setting" does not mean "in a simple setting." The limit is the BSM model of an economy, which is mathematically a complex thing. And, to give precise limiting results, I must employ some mathematically sophisticated concepts and results, among which are weak convergence of probabilities on spaces of functions, the classic functional central limit theorem of Donsker, and the Skorohod Representation Theorem. Many mainstream financial economists (and economists more generally) will not find this an easy read, although as each of these tools is introduced, I provide analogies to results on the real line that most readers will know.

At the same time, this is not an archive of everything known on these issues. To make this more accessible, I do not give general results, nor do I pose the results in the mathematically most pleasing settings. (In particular, experts will be dismayed that I conduct business in $C[0,1]$ rather than in $D[0,1]$.) My hope is that the exposition will bring less-technical readers along to (at least) a good understanding of the connections between BSM and near by discrete-time economies.

Website

While I hope and expect that this monograph contains only a few errata, it is inevitable that there are some. I may have missed pertinent references, about which readers will want to know. There are several questions and conjectures left open, which (I hope) I or others will resolve. And, of course, work on the topics discussed here is ongoing. For these reasons, a public website has been created at the URL *discrete2continuous.stanford.edu* at which you can find supplementary materials of these sorts. I recommend visiting this website, to see what is posted there, as you read this book. (If you discover errors or typos, or if you wish to suggest additional references, and in particular if you can resolve some of the questions I've left open, please email me at kreps@stanford.edu.)

Acknowledgements

While preparing this manuscript, I benefited from both technical assistance and comments by a number of colleagues. Ayman Hindy and Chi-fu Huang deserve special mention, as they provided both technical assistance and comments, and also kept me working on this with questions that I at first couldn't answer (and some that I still can't). Dimitri Vayanos read very carefully through the entire manuscript and made many suggestions that greatly improved the final version. Walter Schachermayer was both generous and invaluable on technical aspects, most significantly concerning Proposition 5.1b, but concerning many other matters, as well. Assistance as well from David Aldous, Rama Cont, Darrell Duffie, Hans Föllmer, Michael Harrison, Friedrich Hubalek, Jean-Luc Prigent, and Ruth Williams is gratefully acknowledged. Two excellent anonymous reviewers provided further assistance.

Jeff Ely was initially the Econometric Society Monograph Series editor handling this book; midstream, Andrea Pratt took over. I am grateful to both of them for the expeditious handling of the process. Karen Maloney was the acquisition editor for Cambridge University Press; she, and her editorial assistant Rachel Blaifeder, had to deal with an author who has a well deserved reputation for intransigence when it comes to book production; they did so with grace and patience. Although this book is not within his normal purview in terms of subject matter, David Tranah of CUP was very helpful concerning some the technical details related to production. Adam Hooper did an excellent job coordinating production, and copyeditor Anne Valentine exhibited a combination of flexibility to the author's desires where it made sense and strength in insisting on flexibility from the author when that was required. The book is significantly improved in style and readability through her efforts.

Dedication

The economic ideas in this monograph are due to a number of authors, and acknowledgements are given as appropriate. But the basic insight about how these questions can be approached is due to Stephen A. Ross, whose untimely death removed from financial economics one of the giants of the field. I dedicate this monograph to his memory.

1. Introduction

Ever since Arrow's (1964) classic paper, "The Role of Securities in the Optimal Allocation of Risk-Bearing," economists have recognized that a relative handful of financial securities, traded in dynamic fashion, can give far-sighted consumers the opportunity to fit their consumption plans more closely to a complete-markets ideal than might at first be imagined. Criticisms of this perspective are well known, focusing perhaps most of all on the extreme level of foresight about future prices that is required; recall that, in Radner's (1972) "equilibria of plans, prices, and price expectations," individual consumers must have accurate expectations of concerning future equilibrium prices. These same basic ideas have been adopted as foundational to asset-pricing theory in finance, where dynamic trading in a few securities is held to determine, by arbitrage, the prices of many options and other types of contingent claims.

Perhaps the ultimate expression of this idea comes from the literature dealing with the Black–Scholes–Merton (BSM) model of securities markets (Black and Scholes, 1973; Merton, 1973a). In this literature, and in particular in Harrison and Kreps (1979) and Harrison and Pliska (1981, 1983), continuous trading in two assets, a bond (with a certain interest rate) and a stock whose probabilistic law is geometric Brownian motion, is "shown" to provide markets that are complete with regard to all well-behaved contingent claims that are written on the full history of the stock price. The scare quotes around "shown" are there because this story is more nuanced and complex than is this commonly held 30-second version of what is, in fact, shown (see Chapter 3).

To come to the amazing conclusion that markets are complete requires deep mathematics and, in particular, a model of information flow that is hard (at least, for me) to comprehend, as well as trading strategies that are hard to imagine. (To synthesize, say, a European call option requires an infinite volume of trade.) But Sharpe (1978) and Cox, Ross, and Rubinstein (1979) provide a discrete-time, discrete-state analog: There are two securities, a bond with a certain interest rate and a stock, which trade, one against the other, at a discrete list of times. As long as the stock's next trading-time relative price, given today's price, has only two possible values – the so-called binomial case – markets are complete. And if one looks at a particular sequence of these binomial economies, where trading is allowed (in each economy) at a discrete number of times, but more and more frequently along the sequence, the sequence of economies "converges to" the BSM model. While the limit results are not trivial, the mathematics is not that difficult. In a sense, then, one can regard the BSM model as an *idealization* of discrete-time binomial models with frequent trading, in the same sense that the model of perfect competition is an idealization of markets in which market participants have some, but very limited, market power.[1] This provides a better sense of what sort of information flow is entailed – albeit a very special flow of information – and it provides a reasonable case that modeling trading strategies with infinite trading volumes is "close to" what happens with much less outrageous trading strategies. (Both "converges to" and "close to" need formal, exact statements, which is the reason for the scare quotes. This is the topic of Chapter 4.)

However, as in the case of recent work concerning continuous-time models and their discrete-time (asymptotic) analogs,[2] there is a seeming problem: If the (discrete-time) stock-price process has not two but three (or more) possible next-time values, even if the limiting stock price converges in the standard probabilistic sense to the BSM model, markets are incomplete and many contingent claims are not priced by arbitrage. One can still employ arbitrage arguments, but the arbitrage bounds on simple contingent claims that are implied remain wide as the security price process converges to BSM. Either one must put into the economy a more securities ($n-2$ more "independent" securities, if the greatest number of next-time prices is n), or resort to pricing arguments that involve Sharpe ratios (Cochrane and Saa-Requejo, 2000), or gain-loss ratios (Bernardo and Ledoit, 2000) to show that the BSM model is a proper idealization of these discrete-time models, as trading becomes more frequent.

I say "seeming problem," because the problem is more apparent than real. Consider, for instance, the following model of a market with two securities. Both securities trade at times $t = 0, 1/400, 2/400, \ldots, 399/400$. The first security is a bond with, for convenience, zero interest rate: Its price at each time t is 1, and at time 1 it pays the bearer 1. The second security is a stock whose prices at different times t (and whose terminal value at time 1) are constructed as follows: For a sequence of four-hundred

---

[1]   See, for instance, Novshek (1985).

[2]   See, for instance, Fudenberg and Levine (2009) and Sadzik and Stacchetti (2015). The issues that arise in those papers are different from the issues addressed here; I'll briefly discuss their work in the final chapter.

independent and identically distributed random variables $\tilde{\zeta}_k$, where each $\tilde{\zeta}_k$ has distribution given by

$$\tilde{\zeta}_k = \begin{cases} 0.075, & \text{with probability } 2/9, \\ 0, & \text{with probability } 5/9, \text{ and} \\ -0.075, & \text{with probability } 2/9, \end{cases}$$

the price of the stock at time $t = k/400$ is given by

$$\tilde{S}(k/400) = \exp\left[\sum_{j=1}^{k} \tilde{\zeta}_j\right],$$

where $\tilde{S}(0) = 1$ with certainty and, at time 1, the terminal value of the stock (the dividend it pays, say), is $\tilde{S}(1)$ (that is, $\tilde{S}(400/400)$, defined as above). In words, the stock price is a geometric random walk, where each step has positive probability of going up, down, or staying the same. The theory of such things is developed in detail in Chapter 2, but I trust that most readers will be aware of the following fact about this simple model of a two-asset security market: Because there are only two financial securities and, at each time, three ways the stock price can evolve, trading in the two securities will not permit the construction of many contingent claims. In particular, if we look at archetype contingent claim for this literature – a European call option with exercise price 1 – the range of prices at time 0 for the call option that are consistent with the price processes of the stock and bond is quite wide; in fact, one can compute that range to be from 0 up to approximately 0.5954.

However, suppose that a consumer living and trading in this two-security world wishes to synthesize the call option. She starts at time 0 by buying 0.69145 shares of the stock and selling 0.30906 bonds, for a net cost to her of 0.38239; these are the opening positions that she would take were she living in the world of BSM (where the bond has interest rate 0 and the stock is geometric Brownian motion for a standard zero-drift, unit-infinitesimal-variance Brownian motion). Subsequent to taking this opening position, at each time $t = k/400$ for $k = 1, \ldots, 399$, she rebalances her portfolio, changing her stock holding to the level she would hold in the BSM world as a function of the price of the stock, financing any required purchases of stock by selling bonds, and using the proceeds of any sale of stock to buy bonds. How does she fare?

This depends on the realized sequence of stock prices. Using simple Monte Carlo methods, I simulated sequences of stock prices and this trading strategy, with remarkable results, at least for anyone who believes that, in this trinomial world, a consumer can't get close to synthesizing the call option: Figure 1.1 shows the results of 500 simulations, where the final value of the consumer's portfolio is graphed against the final stock price. This is very, very close to synthesizing the call option.

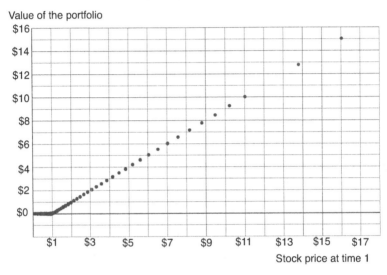

Figure 1.1. Scatter plot of stock price versus value of a portfolio that imperfectly synthesizes a European call option with exercise price 1, using the trinomial (tilde) model for $n = 400$. This shows the results of 500 rounds of simulation.

This is not perfect synthesis of the call option. But when we return to this example, we'll see that a more realistic set of "arbitrage bounds" on the price of the call option, generated by constructing dynamic hedges from the stock and bond, is more on the order of 0.38239 plus or minus 0.02. Because we have two financial securities and, at each time, three possible next positions, markets are incomplete. But they come close to being complete. Going back to Arrow's original insight that frequent trading in a few financial securities can substantially complete markets, perhaps, in this trinomial world, this insight still is substantially valid.

This is not my discovery. The community of scholars (primarily probabilists) who work in the field of financial mathematics have shown that, in a mathematical sense, the incompleteness of markets for this discrete-time trinomial model (and many more models besides) asymptotically vanishes as trading becomes more frequent; Figure 1.1 comes as no surprise to them.

This stream of literature is largely under-appreciated by mainstream scholars in finance and economic theory, perhaps because this literature has significant entry barriers in terms of mathematical sophistication. In this monograph, I try to lower those barriers enough so that mainstream economists are not surprised by Figure 1.1, but, instead, understand what can (and cannot) be said along these lines in terms of mathematics. And I try to put the mathematical results on a sound footing in terms of what they say about economics.

I first review the basic foundations of this literature. The story I wish to tell – how, how well, and when the BSM model idealizes discrete-time trading models with frequent trading – doesn't begin until Chapter 4, more than 50 pages in. Many readers will already know the material covered in Chapters 2 and 3 (concerning discrete-time and continuous-time models, respectively). But I think it helps to present a unified version of the full story, beginning with the theory in discrete and continuous time, separately.

Proofs

Throughout, I try to provide detailed and solid proofs. I do not prove everything; in particular, for deep mathematical results (e.g., the uniqueness of an equivalent martingale measure for BSM, Donsker's Theorem, the Skorohod Representation Theorem), I cite sources where the results can be found. But, with one exception, when it comes to results that are specific to the story I want to tell, I provide details. (The exception is the very complex proof of Proposition 5.1b, for which I provide a sketch and then a reference.) For the most part, a reader who is well versed in real and convex analysis should be able to follow what goes on. But the proofs – especially those that invoke Taylor's Theorem – are tedious. Readers who want to get the gist of this theory can safely skip the details, although I hope they will skim the proofs to get a sense of the logical flow being employed.

Website

A public website at the URL *discrete2continuous.stanford.edu* contains a variety of supplementary materials, including a list of errata (as they are discovered), further pertinent references (as they are suggested), and (I hope) notes on the resolution of some of the questions left open in this monograph. I suggest that readers visit the website to see what is there.

2. Finitely Many States and Times

The Explicit Model

The objects of study in this monograph are dynamic models of financial markets under uncertainty. The theory is relatively straightforward when there are finitely many states and trading times, so I'll begin with a *somewhat* general treatment. We study a model that is specified explicitly by the following items 1 through 5.

1. There is underlying uncertainty. The set of states of nature is denoted Ω, with typical element ω. The set Ω is finite. We let G denote the field of all subsets of Ω.

The term *field* is used in anticipation of the term σ-*field*, commonly used when Ω is infinite. In the context of finite Ω, a field F is a collection of subsets of Ω that is closed under (finite) unions, intersections, and the taking of complements and that includes Ω. An equivalent characterization of a field F for a finite set Ω is a partition of Ω; write $F(\omega)$ for the cell of the partition that contains ω. The field F then consists of all finite unions of cells of the partition together with the empty set.[1] In this equivalent characterization, the cells $F(\omega)$ are the "finest" events distinguished by the field of events. The specific field G is constructed from the discrete partition: Every $A \subseteq \Omega$ is a member of G or, equivalently, $G(\omega)$ is $\{\omega\}$. If A is an event – that is, a subset of Ω – we write $A \in F$ when A is in the field F. And if f is a function with domain Ω, we say that f is measurable with respect to F, denoted $f \in F$, if f is constant on every cell of the partition of Ω that generates F or, equivalently, if, for every z in the range of the f, $f^{-1}(z) = \{\omega : f(\omega) = z\} \in F$.

2. A probability measure P on Ω is given, with $P(\{\omega\}) > 0$ for all $\omega \in \Omega$. Expectation with respect to P is denoted by $\mathbf{E}[\cdot]$.

3. Economic activity takes place through time, beginning at time 0 and ending at time 1. Besides times 0 and 1, economic activity is possible at a finite sequence of times; these times (including times 0 and 1) are ennumerated $t_0 = 0, t_1, \ldots, t_{L-1}, t_L = 1$ in ascending order; that is, $t_\ell > t_{\ell-1}$ for $\ell = 1, \ldots, L$.

---

[1]   At the start of the Appendix, I show that this is an equivalent characterization.

a. Consumption takes place *only* at time 1. There is a single consumption good. Throughout, X denotes R^Ω, the set of real-valued functions on Ω, and is called the *space of contingent* or *consumption claims*.

b. Publicly available information at each time t_ℓ is given by the field of events G_{t_ℓ}. These fields are progressively (weakly) finer: $A \in G_{t_{\ell-1}}$ implies $A \in G_{t_\ell}$. G_0 is the trivial field $\{\{\Omega\}\}$ and $G_1 = G$ is the field of all subsets of Ω.

The statement that the fields are successively finer is equivalent to: For $t > t'$, the partition that generates $G_{t'}$ is made up of unions of the cells that generate the partition for G_t. Equivalently, $G_t(\omega) \subseteq G_{t'}(\omega)$ for all ω. The term for an increasingly (weakly) finer sequence of fields, $\{G_t; t \in T\}$, is a *filtration*.

4. A finite set of $1 + I$ financial securities is given, indexed by $i = 0, 1, \ldots, I$. Each security pays a dividend in the single consumption good at time 1 that can depend on ω; the dividend paid by security i in state ω is denoted by $S_i(1, \omega)$. Security 0, called the *bond*, pays 1 in every state of nature; $S_0(1, \omega) = 1$ for all ω.

5. These securities trade at times $T := \{t_0 = 0, \ldots, t_{L-1}\}$. The equilibrium (relative) price of security i at time $t \in T$ and in state ω, measured in terms of the price of the bond, is $S_i(t, \omega)$ (where the dependence on ω is often suppressed). That is, the bond is the numeraire, or $S_0(t) \equiv 1$ for all t.

For each $t \in T$, $S(t) \in G_t$; that is, security prices at each time $t \in T$ are measurable with respect to the information G_t. Since G_0 is assumed to be trivial, this means that $S(0)$ is deterministic; there is no uncertainty about initial prices.

How general is the above? The finiteness of Ω is central to the analysis of this chapter; generalizing to infinite Ω is tackled *to some extent* in Chapter 3. One might prefer more than a single consumption good and that consumption takes place throughout the time interval: Both of these can be accommodated, but at a complexity cost in notation and exposition that obscures the economics of the story; to keep the economics clear, these complications are avoided. Since security prices are relative, having one security, the bond, that acts as the numeraire in all the security markets is without any serious loss of generality as long as one security always has a strictly positive price. When we get to characterizations of solutions to optimal consumption problems for expected-utility-maximizing consumers, however, having the bond pay a constant dividend in the consumption good is a restriction (having that dividend be 1 unit is not); this could be relaxed although it makes the statements of some of the results harder to comprehend. Having only a finite number of times at which economic activity takes place, and, hence, a finite horizon, is essentially a consequence of having a finite state space Ω; rather than subject you to the argument why this is so, it is easiest just to assume this.

It is also expositionally convenient to assume that all $1 + I$ securities trade against one another at every time $t \in \mathcal{T}$, but this is not necessary for the theory to go through. I'll return to this later.

It is fairly standard in the literature to assume that G_t is (simply) the field of events generated by securities' prices up to time t. Allowing G_t to contain more information is a little bit of generality that comes at almost no cost in terms of later developments. In fact, assuming that the information modeled by G_t is available to *all* consumers is unnecessarily restrictive; this remark will also be explained later.

The Questions Addressed

Readers who think in terms of general equilibrium theory may be confused by this model formulation because, in particular, security prices are given. Shouldn't equilibrium prices be endogenously derived? Of course, in general equilibrium theory they are, *but not here*. Here, (relative) prices of the financial securities are given *as part of the exogenously specified model*. And, for those exogenously given security-price processes, we ask (and answer) the following two questions:

A. Do these relative prices make sense? Could they be part of an overall (general) economic equilibrium? This is the *viability* question: Is the given model of security prices *viable*?

B. Assuming that they make sense, what do they tell us about the cost to consumers of contingent claims (members of $X = R^{\Omega}$), supposing that consumers can trade dynamically in the various securities? This question goes with the terms *synthesis* or *replication* and *arbitrage*: By trading in the given securities, which contingent claims can be precisely *synthesized* or *replicated*? And for an arbitrary contingent claim, were it to be marketed (without changing any of the prices in the model), what does *arbitrage* tell us about the (relative) prices it might command?

What Sort of Consumers?

The viability question comes first. Before we begin to think about arbitrage and the like, we need to make sure that the given security prices make sense as equilibrium prices for some economy. And, of course, "some economy" must be populated by consumers.[2] So we move to assumptions about consumers who (we assume) are candidates for living in an economy with these security prices. Begin with the three things that specify a consumer in general equilibrium theory: the consumption set; preferences; and endowment.

6. For the formal developments of *this chapter*, I follow the common practice of saying that the consumer's consumption set is the positive orthant in X, or $X_+ = [0, \infty)^\Omega$. That is, the consumer can (only) consume nonnegative contingent claims.

    I emphasize *this chapter* because, in later chapters, I allow formally for consumers whose consumption set is all of $X = R^\Omega$. This is, in part, to allow for consumers who are expected-utility maximizers with constant absolute risk averse (CARA) utility functions, but also to accommodate some technical problems that arise when Ω is infinite. *And,* I will deal in examples with expected-utility-maximizing consumers with constant relative risk averse (CRRA) utility, which includes functions of the form $u(x) = x^{1-a}/(1 - a)$ for $a \geq 1$ as well as for $u(x) = \ln(x)$. The consumption set for such consumers is not X_+ but the strict positive orthant, or $(0, \infty)^\Omega$.

    The formal results of this chapter can be adapted to these other consumption sets, albeit with some technical difficulties arising from the fact that $(0, \infty)^\Omega$ is not closed and, even after we incorporate a budget constraint with strictly positive prices, for a consumer whose consumption set is R^Ω, her (budget) feasible set is not bounded.

7. Consumers are assumed to have complete and transitive preferences over their consumption sets, which are *in addition* strictly increasing: If x and x' are two contingent claims, both feasible consumption bundles for a consumer, and if $x(\omega) \geq x'(\omega)$ for all $\omega \in \Omega$ and $x(\omega) > x'(\omega)$ for at least one ω, then the consumer strictly prefers x to x'.

    Later, we look at consumers who are expected-utility maximizers:

---

[2] If one thinks in terms of General Equilibrium Theory, the agents who trade in these markets are naturally called *consumers*. But in some contexts to follow, it is more natural to refer to *investors* or *arbitrageurs* or simply *traders*. I use all these terms interchangably, choosing whichever is the most appropriate in the given context.

For some function $u : [0, \infty) \rightarrow R$, the consumer prefers x to x' if the expected value of $u(x(\omega))$ is greater than $u(x'(\omega))$, under the consumer's (subjective) probability assessment over Ω. When we do so, I will generally assume that u is strictly increasing, continuous, and strictly concave, and that the consumer's subjective probability assessment is P. Of course, if the consumer's subjective probability assessment is strictly positive on each $\omega \in \Omega$, this combined with the assumption that u is strictly increasing gives the sort of strict monotonicity we assume in general.

8. Consumers are assumed to be endowed in two ways: A consumer may be endowed with an initial portfolio $\theta^e \in R^{1+I}$, meaning θ_i^e "shares" of security i, and she may be endowed with terminal contingent consumption $x^e \in X$. Since all securities (are assumed to) trade at time 0, let $W^e := \theta^e \cdot S(0)$; this is the consumer's initial *wealth* from her securities endowment. And we assume that $W^e S_0(1) + x^e$ is a feasible consumption bundle for the consumer: She could sell off her securities endowment, invest all the proceeds in the bond, and then sit back, content to know that at time 1, she'll receive a dividend that, added to her commodity endowment, is a feasible consumption bundle for her.

So much for how consumers are characterized within the framework of standard general equilibrium. We add to this the rules concerning consumers' ability to participate in the securities markets, beginning with the *information endowments* of the consumers.

9. Each consumer knows the information encoded by the field G_t at each time $t \in T$, no more and no less. (Allowing different consumers to have different information endowments raises a host of interesting issues. I'll discuss some of these in a bit.)

Next, we define a space of "feasible self-financing trading strategies" and two important subsets of the space of such strategies.

10. A *feasible self-financing trading strategy* is a $1 + I$-dimensional vector stochastic process $\{\theta(t) = (\theta_0(t), \dots, \theta_I(t); t \in T\}$, such that
    a. $\theta(t)$ is G_t measurable for each $t \in T$.
    b. $\theta(t_\ell) \cdot S(t_\ell) = \theta(t_{\ell-1}) \cdot S(t_\ell)$, for each $\ell = 1, \dots, L$.

    A feasible self-financing trading strategy θ is a *zero-net-investment strategy* if, in addition to be feasible and self-financing, $\theta(0) \cdot S(0) = 0$.

A zero-net-investment strategy θ is a *free lunch* if, in addition to being a zero-net-investment strategy, $\theta(t_{L-1}) \cdot S(1) \geq 0$ in all states and $\theta(t_{L-1}) \cdot S(1) > 0$ in at least one state.

The interpretation of $\theta(t)$ is that this is the portfolio held *after* trading at time t is done. Hence, condition b – the self-financing condition – says that the value of the portfolio held before trading at time $t_\ell \in \mathcal{T}, t > 0$ must equal the value held after time t_ℓ trading is done. Note, in this regard, that we are assuming that the only endowments that a consumer possesses come as an initial portfolio of securities and a time 1 contingent (consumption) claim; the consumer has no resources at intermediate times with which to augment her portfolio. And we are assuming that consumers only consume at time 1, so there is no reason (or, for that matter, opportunity) to purchase consumption goods at intermediate times.[3] We could replace = in this condition with $\leq$ – essentially, considering trading strategies that throw away value – but the combination of the bond as a safe store of value and the strictly increasing consumer preferences permits us to ignore such wasteful trading strategies.

All trading strategies we consider will be feasible and self-financing, so the language "θ is a trading strategy" implicitly means that θ is feasible and self-financing. And, for a trading strategy θ, $V(\theta, t)$ will denote the value of the portfolio of securities held according to θ at time $t \in \mathcal{T} \cup \{1\}$; that is, $V(\theta, t) := \theta(t) \cdot S(t)$ for $t \in \mathcal{T}$, and $V(\theta, 1) := \theta(t_{L-1}) \cdot S(1)$. Hence, $V(\theta, 0)$ is the initial cost of the strategy, and $V(\theta, 1)$ is the (consumption) dividend paid by the strategy.

Note that $V(\theta, t)$ is random, depending on the state of nature ω; write $V(\theta, t)(\omega)$ or $V(\theta, t, \omega)$ for the value of $V(\theta, t)$ in state ω. Because we have assumed that both security prices and trading strategies are *progressively measurable* – that is, $S(t) \in F_t$ and $\theta(t) \in F_t$ – we know that $V(\theta, t) \in F_t$.

11. A consumer with initial securities endowment θ^e and time 1 consumption endowment x^e is not necessarily able to enact all feasible self-financing trading strategies. For a given self-financing trading strategy θ:

    a. She must be able to afford her time 0 (after-market) portfolio; that is, $\theta(0) \cdot S(0) = \theta^e \cdot S(0)$ or (and saying exactly the same thing)

---

[3] These assumptions can be relaxed, but only at huge cost in notation for little gain in economic insight.

$V(\theta, 0) = W^e$.[4] This, together with 10b, constitutes the series of dynamic budget constraints facing a consumer.

b. Her trading strategy must leave her with a final contingent consumption claim that is feasible for her, or $V(\theta, 1) + x^e \in X_+$.

c. She might face other constraints on trading strategies that she is allowed to construct; for example, she may face borrowing constraints.

However, if she does face any "extra" constraints, as recognized by 11c, those constraints *do not* preclude the following:

d. She can always access the trading strategy in which, at time 0, she sells her security endowment and purchases W^e bonds, then waits until time 1 and consumes $W^e S_0(1) + x^e$. (By definition, this strategy satisfies 11a, and by prior assumption, it satisfies 11b.)

e. And if θ is any feasible trading strategy for her, and θ' is a free lunch, then for some $\alpha > 0$, $\theta + \alpha\theta'$ is feasible for her. That is, she can augment any feasible trading strategy with a (possibly scaled-down) copy of any free lunch.

Concerning 11e, suppose θ is feasible for her. Then $V(\theta + \alpha\theta', 0) = V(\theta, 0) + \alpha V(\theta', 0)$, and $V(\theta', 0) = 0$ if θ' is a free lunch, so $V(\theta + \alpha\theta', 0) = V(\theta, 0) \leq W^e$ for this consumer. And $V(\theta + \alpha\theta', 1) = V(\theta, 1) + \alpha V(\theta', 1) \geq V(\theta, 1)$, the inequality because $\alpha > 0$ and $V(\theta', 1) \geq 0$ since θ' is a free lunch. Since $V(\theta, 1) \in X_+$, so is $V(\theta + \alpha\theta', 1)$.

That is, saying she can augment a feasible trading strategy with a (scaled copy of a) free lunch in no way compromises restrictions 11a or b. The import of 11e is: If she faces borrowing constraints and the like, those constraints do not bind on the addition of a (possibly scaled down copy of any) free lunch. The scale parameter α is a nod toward possible credit limits facing the consumer; she can implement any free lunch on some reduced scale, however much it is reduced, as long as it is not reduced to 0.

Think of a consumer who sees a free lunch but needs to borrow money (sell some bonds) to take advantage. Even if she cannot borrow funds sufficient to take advantage on a very large scale, 11e says she can find a willing lender at some small scale. One might worry that, to convince the lender, she must reveal her strategy, which would then leak out. This

---

[4] We could have $\leq$ in place of $=$, but because the bond is a safe store of value and preferences are strictly increasing, a consumer would never choose an initial portfolio whose value is less than the value of her endowment.

could be a worry if her strategy is either based on private information or is fantastically clever. But we've assumed that every consumer knows precisely $\{G_t; t \in T\}$ at each time $t \in T$, which partially ameliorates this concern.

Viability $\iff$ No Free Lunches $\iff$ Pricing Kernel $\iff$ Equivalent Martingale Measure

This is probably a good place to recap the basic plot. We are given in points 1 through 5 a model of a securities market: a finite state space; a set of trading times; a model of the information flow at each trading time; a finite set of securities with a distinguished security, indexed by 0 and called the bond; and relative (allegedly) equilibrium prices of the securities.[5] For this model, we ask: Is this model viable? Can it be supported as a general equilibrium, in the general sense of Radner's (1972) equilibrium of plans, prices, and price expectations, for some population of reasonable consumers? Points 6 through 11 establish the definition of "reasonable," with the most important pieces being: Consumers have strictly increasing preferences, and if there are free lunches out there, consumers can access them on a strictly positive scale.

With this, we can state the first and fundamental result:

Proposition 2.1. *The following four conditions for a securities market model specified as in points 1 through 5 are equivalent.*

a. *The model is **viable**, in the sense that it is consistent with a general equilibrium (of plans, prices, and price expectations; see Radner, 1972) for a specification of consumers who satisfy points 6 through 11.*

b. *No free lunches can be constructed within the model.*

c. *There exists a strictly positive set of state-contingent prices – that is, a function $p^* : \Omega \to (0, \infty)$ – such that, for each security i, time $t \in T$, and state of nature ω,*

$$S_i(t, \omega) = \frac{\sum_{\omega' \in G_t(\omega)} p^*(\omega') S_i(1, \omega')}{\sum_{\omega' \in G_t(\omega)} p^*(\omega')} . \tag{2.1}$$

*(Financial market theoriest often use the term **pricing kernel** for p^*.)*

---

[5] We are also given a reference probability distribution P on Ω, but beyond being strictly positive, P plays no role when Ω is finite.

d. *A strictly positive probability measure P^* on Ω exists under which $\{(S(t), G_t); t \in \mathcal{T}\}$ is a vector martingale: That is, for each $i = 1, \ldots, I$ and time $t_\ell \in \mathcal{T}$,*

$$S_i(t_\ell) = \mathbf{E}^*\left[S_i(t_{\ell+1})\middle|G_t\right] \tag{2.2a}$$

or, equivalently

$$S_i(t) = \mathbf{E}^*\left[S_i(1)\middle|G_t\right], \tag{2.2b}$$

where $\mathbf{E}^*[\cdot]$ denotes expectation with respect to P^*.

A strictly positive probability measure P^* that turns $\{S(t); t \in \mathcal{T}\}$ into a martingale over the filtration $\{G_t; t \in \mathcal{T}\}$ is called an *equivalent martingale measure*, where *equivalent* relates to the requirement that P^* is strictly positive. The condition that a stochastic process is a martingale over a given (discrete) filtration is typically written in the form (2.2a), involving two consecutive times. But when the martingale has a "closing time" (or when the martingale can be closed, say, by the Martingale Convergence Theorem), the law of iterated conditional expectations makes the formulation in equation (2.2b) equivalent to the more common (2.2a); and (2.2b) fits best with equation (2.1).

Proof of Proposition 2.1. Condition a implies b: For the model to be viable, each consumer (and there must be at least one) has an optimal trading strategy θ^*. If a free lunch θ' exists, 11e tells us that such a consumer can access the trading strategy $\theta^* + \alpha\theta'$ for some $\alpha > 0$. But $V(\theta^* + \alpha\theta', 1) = V(\theta^*, 1) + \alpha V(\theta', 1) \geq V(\theta^*)$ on all states ω and is strictly greater on (at least) one ω. Hence, this consumer will strictly prefer $V(\theta^* + \alpha\theta', 1) + x^e$ to $V(\theta^*, 1) + x^e$. That is, if there is a free lunch available, consumers can never find optimal trading strategies, which means the model can't be viable. The contrapositive of this is *a implies b*.

Condition b implies c: Let

$$M_0 := \{x \in X : x = V(\theta, 1) \text{ for some zero-net-investment,}$$
$$\text{feasible and self-financing strategy } \theta\}.$$

In words, M_0 is the space of contingent claims that can be produced by trading (in self-financing fashion) in the securities, with zero initial investment. It is easy to verify that M_0 is a subspace of X; that is, if $x, x' \in M_0$ are produced, respectively, by θ and θ', and if α and β are real scalars, the $\alpha\theta + \beta\theta'$ is a zero-net-investment, self-financing trading strategy that produces $\alpha x + \beta x'$. And, if no free lunches can be constructed, then M_0 has no points in common with the $X_+ \setminus \{0\}$. In particular, M_0 has empty intersection with the unit simplex over Ω,

$$\Delta := \left\{ x \in X_+ : \sum_{\omega \in \Omega} x(\omega) = 1 \right\}.$$

Since M_0 is a subspace, it is closed and convex; and Δ is compact and convex. Hence, there exists a hyperplane that strictly separates the two. That is, there is a vector $p^* \in R^\Omega$ and a constant α such that $p^* \cdot m < \alpha$ for all $m \in M_0$ and $p^* \cdot z > \alpha$ for $\in \Delta$.

Because M_0 is a subspace, it must be that $p^* \cdot m = 0$ for all $m \in M_0$: Suppose by way of contradiction that, for some $m \in M_0$, $p^* \cdot m \neq 0$. Then, taking either βm or $-\beta m$, depending on whether $p^* \cdot m >$ or < 0, and sending β to ∞, one would produce a member of m_0 whose dot product with p^* would exceed any finite α. This means that $\alpha > 0$. And since the unit vector in direction ω is in Δ, p^* dotted into this unit vector, which is $p^*(\omega)$, must be $> \alpha > 0$; that is, $p^*(\omega) > 0$ for all ω.

Because $S_0(t) \equiv 1$ for all t by construction, it is evident that (2.1) holds for $i = 0$. For $i > 0$, fix a time $t \in T$ and a state of nature ω, and consider the following zero-net-investment strategy θ. Hold the null portfolio (no shares of any security) until time t. If, at time t, $G_t(\omega)$ is not realized (if information is that ω is not the true state), continue to do nothing until time 1, realizing dividend 0. But if $G_t(\omega)$ is realized, purchase one share of security i for the price $S_i(t, \omega)$ and sell $S_i(t, \omega)$ bonds. (If $t = 0$, this makes the portfolio zero-net investment. If $t > 0$, it was zero-net investment to start, and this condition makes it self-financing.) Hold this portfolio until time 1, realizing the dividend

$$V(\theta, 1)(\omega') = \begin{cases} S_i(1, \omega') - S_i(t, \omega), & \text{for } \omega' \in G_t(\omega) \text{ and} \\ 0, & \text{for } \omega' \notin G_t(\omega). \end{cases}$$

Since θ is a zero-net-investment strategy, $V(\theta, 1)$ is in M_0, so $p^* \cdot V(\theta, 1)$ must equal 0. And

$$p^* \cdot V(\theta, 1) = \sum_{\omega' \in G_t(\omega)} p^*(\omega')\big[S_i(1, \omega') - S_i(t, \omega)\big] = 0,$$

which is

$$\sum_{\omega' \in G_t(\omega)} p^*(\omega') S_i(1, \omega') = S_i(t, \omega) \sum_{\omega' \in G_t(\omega)} p^*(\omega') \quad \text{or}$$

$$S_i(t, \omega) = \frac{\sum_{\omega' \in G_t(\omega)} p^*(\omega') S_i(1, \omega')}{\sum_{\omega' \in G_t(\omega)} p^*(\omega')},$$

which is equation (2.1).

Condition c implies condition d: This is just a matter of rescaling p^* and reinterpreting equation (2.1) Define

$$P^*(\omega) := \frac{p^*(\omega)}{\sum_{\omega' \in \Omega} p^*(\omega')},$$

so P^* is a strictly positive probability. Since P^* is just a rescaled copy of p^*, it serves equally well to define a strictly separating hyperplane (once α is rescaled), and (for finite state spaces) equation (2.1), with P^* put in place of p^*, is the G_t cell-by-cell statement of (2.2b), once you recognize that $\sum_{\omega' \in G_t(\omega)} P^*(\omega')$ is $P^*(G_t(\omega))$.

Condition d implies condition a: Begin with a lemma:

Lemma 2.1. *If θ is a feasible self-financing strategy and $\{(S(t), G_t); t \in \mathcal{T}\}$ is a martingale with respect to P^*, then $\{(V(\theta, t), G_t)\}$ is a martingale with respect to P^*.*

To establish this, we must show that, for $\ell = 0, \ldots, L - 1$,

$$V(\theta, t_\ell) = \mathbf{E}^* \big[V(\theta, t_{\ell+1}) \big| G_{t_\ell} \big],$$

where $\mathbf{E}^*$ denotes expectation with respect to P^*. Now

$$V(\theta, t_{\ell+1}) = \theta(t_{\ell+1}) \cdot S(t_{\ell+1}) = \theta(t_\ell) \cdot S(t_{\ell+1}),$$

because θ is self-financing. Hence,

$$\mathbf{E}^* \big[V(\theta, t_{\ell+1}) \big| G_{t_\ell} \big] = \mathbf{E}^* \big[\theta(t_\ell) \cdot S(t_{\ell+1}) \big| G_{t_\ell} \big] = \mathbf{E}^* \left[\sum_{i=1}^{I} \theta_i(t_\ell) S_i(t_{\ell+1}) \big| G_{t_\ell} \right]$$

$$= \sum_{i=1}^{I} \theta_i(t_\ell) \mathbf{E}^* \big[S_i(t_{\ell+1}) \big| G_{t_\ell} \big] = \sum_{i=1}^{I} \theta_i(t_\ell) S_i(t_\ell) = V(\theta, t_\ell).$$

The key equalities are the third and the fourth: Exchanging the expectation and the summation is trivial, but moving $\theta_i(t_\ell)$ outside the conditional expectation is justified because $\theta_i(t_\ell)$ is measurable with respect to G_{t_ℓ}. And then the fourth equality is based on the fact that P^* is a martingale measure.

Now consider an economy consisting of a single consumer whose endowment is one bond with no contingent claim to consumption. This consumer has access to the information G_t at time t, no more and no less. She faces no additional constraints on her trading opportunities, beyond those in 11a and b, and so her trading abilities satisfy 11d and e. And her preferences over contingent claims are given by

$$x \succeq x' \quad \text{if} \quad \mathbf{E}^*[x] \geq \mathbf{E}^*[x'].$$

Since P^* is strictly positive, these preferences are strictly increasing in the sense of 7.

If she refuses to do any trading and simply consumes the dividend thrown off by her one bond, her expected utility is 1. If she engages in any trading strategy θ (that is feasible and self-financing and that satisfies 11a and b), condition d implies that $\mathbf{E}^*[V(\theta, 1)] = \mathbf{E}^*[V(\theta, 1)|G_0] = V(\theta, 0) = 1$. So she is content to stick to the strategy of holding her one bond and consuming what it produces. This is an autarchic equilibrium (no trades are undertaken); the model is viable. ∎

The details of the proof of Proposition 2.1 may hide its relatively straightforward message, so to summarize: That a implies b or, as stated in the contrapositive, that the existence of a free lunch means the model isn't viable, is simple, given the assumptions that agents can exploit free lunches and their preferences are such that they always want to do so. Getting something valuable for nothing is inconsistent with equilibrium.

That c implies d is just a renormalization and then reinterpretation of c. Of course, the modeling assumptions that the bond pays a unit dividend and is the numeraire in securities markets is what makes the reinterpretation go. But as long as some security pays a strictly positive dividend in every state of nature, this just comes down to how one defines units.

This reinterpretation is useful on two grounds. First, in examples (provided later), it makes quick work of finding all the pricing kernels that are consistent with the explicit parts of the model. Second, and key to the step of moving from d back to a, familiarity with martingale theory, combined with the self-financing property of trading strategies, tells us that a single agent with preferences that "align" with the pricing kernel has no desire to deviate from her endowment; hence, such an agent confirms (rather trivially) the viability of the explicit parts of the model.

The meat of the proposition – and what causes headaches when we move to infinite state spaces – is the step from b to c. This comes down to an application of the Strict Separation Theorem, separating what can be achieved with zero-net-investment trading strategies from the unit simplex in R^Ω: The required convexity, closedness, and compactness conditions are obvious when Ω is finite, and the fact that the two sets are disjoint is an immediate consequence of no free lunches. I can't say that moving from the strictly separating hyperplane to the pricing kernel is immediately apparent. But the steps are straightforward enough.

Two Generalizations

Two relatively cheap generalizations can be offered.

The first concerns our assumption that every security trades at every time $t \in \mathcal{T}$. As long as the bond trades in every $t \in \mathcal{T}$, one can allow securities i for $i > 0$ to trade only in some times and contingencies, as long as the event in which i trades at time t is G_t measurable. There are four things to which you must attend if this is allowed: First, feasible self-financing trading strategies must be restricted not to change the holding of security i in events where i doesn't trade. Second, and specifically, if i doesn't trade at time 0, but a consumer is endowed with some number of shares of i, she'll need to be restricted to trading strategies where she holds her endowment at least until i is traded. This will then require a reformulation of 11d. The definition of an equivalent martingale measure is most easily given in the form (2.2b). And, most significantly, the interpretation of $V(\theta, t)$ – the value of the portfolio held at time t under trading strategy θ – becomes a bit tricky: If θ involves holding i at time t in an event where i does not trade, there is no price $S_i(t)$ which can be used to value that bit of the portfolio. What one can do, in that case, and assuming there are no free lunches, is to invoke the separating hyperplane result to come up with a pricing kernel p^* and then use p^* and equation (2.1) to create a "nominal" price for i, even if it doesn't trade, and use that (notional) price to define $V(\theta, t)$.

If you follow through with this scheme, a seeming conundrum can arise: What if there is more than one p^* consistent with the explicit model?

That is, what if M_0 can be separated from Δ in more than one way? And what if the application of (2.1), when i doesn't trade, gives more than one value for $S_i(t)$, depending on which p^* is used? This takes us to issues in the second half of this chapter, so I'll leave this hanging for now.

The second generalization concerns the assumption that all consumers have access to the information flow $\{G_t; t \in \mathcal{T}\}$. In fact, one could assume that some consumers have more information and some, less. What is important here is that (allegedly) equilibrium prices are given, every consumer is a price-taker – they trade believing that they have no effect on prices – and each consumer "knows" at least what are current (and past) stock prices. As long as this is so, and as long as every consumer has the sort of strictly increasing preferences we've assumed and can supplement any feasible-for-her trading strategy with (on some scale) any free lunches that she, based on her information, can construct, then the result is: For the model to be viable, there must be an equivalent martingale measure for the stock-price process relative to the information filtration of each consumer.

On this point, note that if $\{G_t\}$ and $\{G'_t\}$ are two filtrations with G'_t finer than G_t for each t, and if $S(t)$ is G_t measurable for each t, a probability P^* that turns $\{(S(t), G'_t)\}$ into a martingale will also turn $\{(S(t), G_t)\}$ into a martingale, but not (necessarily) vice-versa. That is, the more information is impounded in the filtration that is given as part of the model, the more powerful Proposition 2.1 becomes. (This is, perhaps, most obvious if you think in terms of the no-free-lunch condition.) But this means that, if there is a best-informed consumer – one who knows at each time at least as much as everyone else put together – and if our other assumptions are met, then that consumer's information determines the nature of equivalent martingale measures for the stock-price process.[6]

Concerning this sort of generalization, the literature suggests two issues. First, a consumer who is endowed with very good information may act strategically to avoid revealing her information to others. This is a serious issue, but not in the context of a model in which consumers are price takers with regard to prices. Second, a consumer who is endowed with less good information may learn what others know

---

[6] If there is no best-informed consumer, things get messy. Think of a three-state world for which the dividend paid by the one risky asset is 2 in state 1, 2 in state 2, and 1 in state 3. Suppose there are two consumers, one of whom, at an intermediate period, knows whether or not state 1 prevails, the second knows whether state 2 prevails. In state 3, their pooled information tells us that the state is indeed state 3. But as neither knows this alone, it would be viable for the asset, at this intermediate time, to have price 1.5.

based on equilibrium prices; in the literature, this notion goes by the rubric "rational expectations equilibria." This issue presents no problems here, as we've made no distinction between information a consumer has through "endowment" and information she gains through observation. All that is needed is to be sure that the full information that a consumer possesses is modeled by her personal information filtration.

Two Examples

Before moving on to questions about replication and arbitrage, here are two canonical examples. Both involve geometric random walks.

In both examples, there are two securities, the bond and a second, risky security, called the *stock*. For a strictly positive integer n, the set of trading times is $T = \{0, 1/n, 2/n, \ldots, (n-1)/n\}$. A random variable ζ with finite support is fixed. Let Z, with typical element z, be the support of ζ. And let $q(z)$ denote the probability that $\zeta = z$. The space Ω is Z^n, with typical element $\omega = (z_1, z_2, \ldots, z_n)$; the probability of this ω is $\prod_{\ell=1}^{n} q(z_\ell)$. In words, Ω is the space of sequences of realizations of n copies of ζ, and the probability measure on Ω models n independent and identically distributed random variables, $\{\zeta_1, \ldots, \zeta_n\}$, each with distribution ζ.

For the price of the stock at time k/n, and for its dividend at time 1, define

$$B(k/n, \omega) := \sum_{j=1}^{k} z_j \quad \text{and} \quad S(k/n, \omega) = e^{B(k/n,\omega)}$$

for each $\omega = (z_1, \ldots, z_n)$. (Since there is only one security besides the bond, the subscript 1 on $S_1(\cdot)$ is suppressed.) In words, the process B is the random walk generated by the sequence of ζ_k's, and S is the corresponding geometric random walk.

The two examples differ in the distribution of the random variable ζ. "Hats" are put on all the variables in the first example:

$$\hat{\zeta}_k = \begin{cases} +1/\sqrt{n}, & \text{with probability } 1/2, \text{ and} \\ -1/\sqrt{n}, & \text{with probability } 1/2. \end{cases}$$

Hence, $\hat{B}(k/n, \omega) = \sum_{j=1}^{k} \zeta_j$ and $\hat{S}(k/n, \omega) = \exp\left[\hat{B}(k/n, \omega)\right]$. This is the canonical *binomial*-random-walk model of Sharpe (1978) and Cox, Ross, and Rubinstein (1979).

In the second example, tildes are used:

$$\tilde{\zeta}_k = \begin{cases} 1.5/\sqrt{n}, & \text{with probability } 2/9, \\ 0, & \text{with probability } 5/9, \text{ and} \\ -1.5/\sqrt{n}, & \text{with probability } 2/9. \end{cases}$$

Then $\tilde{B}(k/n, \omega) = \sum_{j=1}^{n} \tilde{\zeta}_j$ and $\tilde{S}(k/n, \omega) = \exp[\tilde{B}(k/n, \omega)]$. This is a *trinomial*-random-walk model.

In both examples, the expected value of each ζ_k is 0 and its variance is $1/n$, so the corresponding $B(1)$ has mean 0 and variance 1. We will, eventually, look at the limit of these two specifications as n approaches infinity. But, for now, we are interested in the two examples for fixed, finite n.

Both models are viable. We can verify this by finding equivalent martingale measures for each. Figure 2.1 displays the "transition picture" for each example.

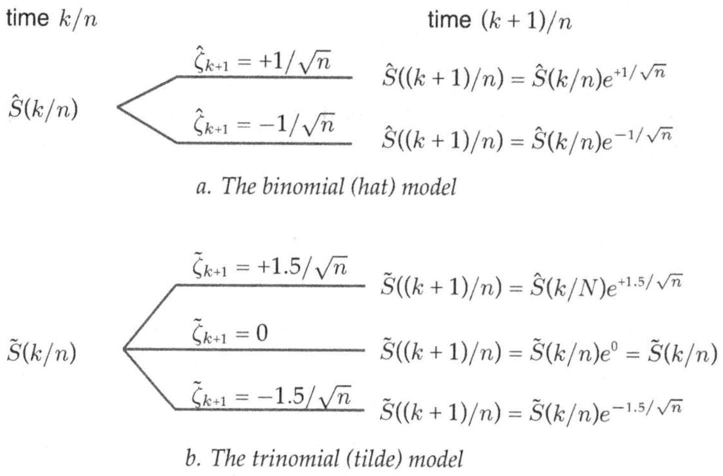

a. The binomial (hat) model

b. The trinomial (tilde) model

Figure 2.1. Transitions in the binomial and trinomial models

An equivalent martingale measure must modify the transition probabilities so that the expected value of $S((k+1)/n)$, given all of the history, equals $S(k/n)$. In the hat (binomial) model, there are two possible values for $S((k+1)/n)$ given $S(k/n)$, namely $S(k/n)e^{+1/\sqrt{n}}$ (if $\hat{\zeta}_{k+1} = +1/\sqrt{n}$) and $S(k/n)e^{-1/\sqrt{n}}$ (if $\hat{\zeta}_{k+1} = -1/\sqrt{n}$). If we let $\hat{p}^*$ be the probability of an "uptick" (the probability that $\hat{\zeta}_{k+1} = +1/\sqrt{n}$), it must be that $\hat{p}^*$ solves

$$\hat{p}^* \, \hat{S}(k/n) \exp(1/\sqrt{n}) + (1 - \hat{p}^*) \, \hat{S}(k/n) \exp(-1/\sqrt{n}) = \hat{S}(k/n),$$

or $\hat{p}^* \exp(1/\sqrt{n}) + (1 - \hat{p}^*) \exp(-1/\sqrt{n}) = 1$, whose unique solution is

$$\hat{p}^* = \frac{1}{e^{1/\sqrt{n}} + 1}.$$

That is, in the binomial model, there is at each stage a unique pair of transition probabilities that turn the stock-price process into a martingale; since the transition probabilities determine the overall probability distribution, there is a unique equivalent martingale measure.

For the trinomial model, transition probabilities $\tilde{p}_1^*$, $\tilde{p}_2^*$, and $\tilde{p}_3^*$ are required that satisfy the equation

$$\tilde{p}_1^* \, e^{+1.5/\sqrt{n}} + \tilde{p}_2^* \, e^0 + \tilde{p}_3^* e^{-1.5/\sqrt{n}} = 1 \quad \text{or} \quad \tilde{p}_1^* \, e^{+1.5/\sqrt{n}} + \tilde{p}_3^* e^{-1.5/\sqrt{n}} = 1 - \tilde{p}_2^*.$$

Since the three transition probabilities must sum to 1, if we let $\tilde{q}^*$ denote the transition probability that $\tilde{\zeta}_k = 0$ (that is, $\tilde{q}^*$ replaces $\tilde{p}_2^*$), we can take $\tilde{q}^*$ to be any value from $(0, 1)$, and then the "up-tick" and "down-tick" probabilities are

$$(1 - \tilde{q}^*)\left[\frac{1}{e^{1.5/\sqrt{n}} + 1}\right] \quad \text{and} \quad (1 - \tilde{q}^*)\left[\frac{1}{e^{-1.5/\sqrt{n}} + 1}\right],$$

respectively. (You can trust my algebra or work through the computations yourself.) In other words, we have one degree of freedom in terms of the transition probabilities at each transition; there are a lot of equivalent martingale measures for the trinomial model. And please note, the value chosen for $\tilde{q}^*$ can be different at different transitions; which includes different values of $\tilde{q}^*$ at a given time k/n with the same stock price $\tilde{S}(k/n)$ but different paths of stock prices reaching this stock price. There are a *lot* of equivalent martingale measures in the trinomial model.

What about other distributions for the ζ? The two examples should make clear the following two assertions: First, the model will be viable if and only if the support of ζ contains a strictly positive and a strictly negative value. As long as this is so, one can adjust the transition probabilities without changing the support (keeping strictly positive all transition probabilities that begin strictly positive and without adding points to the support), so that the expected value of each e^{ζ_k} is 1. And, second, there is only one way to do this if the support of ζ consists of one strictly positive and one strictly negative value. Otherwise, there will many equivalent martingale measures.

Which Contingent Claims Can Be Synthesized?

For the remainder of this chapter, assume that a viable model is fixed. Let $\mathcal{P}^*$ denote the (necessarily) nonempty set of equivalent martingale measures for the model. Let

$$M := \{x \in X : \text{For some feasible, self-financing strategy } \theta, V(\theta, 1) = x\}.$$

M is the space of *(implicitly) marketed* or *replicable* or *synthesizable* contingent claims. It is clearly a subspace of X. Moreover, we have the following multi-part corollary to Proposition 2.1. Recall that $S_0(1)$ is the element of X all of whose entries are 1.

Corollary 2.1. For a viable model:

a. $m \in M$ *if and only if* $m = m_0 + \alpha S_0(1)$, *for a scalar* α *and some* $m_0 \in M_0$. *Moreover, if* $m \in M$ *is synthesized by* θ *– that is,* $m = V(\theta, 1)$ *– then* $V(\theta, 0)$ *equals the scalar* α.

b. *And if* $m \in M$ *is synthesized by* θ *(that is,* $V(\theta, 1) = m$*), then* $V(\theta, t) = \mathbf{E}^{P^*}[m|G_t]$ *for all* $t \in T$ *and for all* $P^* \in \mathcal{P}^*$, *where* $\mathbf{E}^{P^*}$ *means expectation with respect to* P^*.

c. *Hence, if* $m \in M$ *is synthesized by* θ *and by* θ', *then* $V(\theta, 0) = V(\theta', 0)$. *In fact, for all* $t \in T$, $V(\theta, t) \equiv V(\theta', t)$.

Proof. If $m_0 \in M_0$ and $m = m_0 + \alpha S_0(1)$, the strategy that replicates m is obvious: In addition to the zero-net-investment strategy that synthesizes m_0, purchase and hold an additional α bonds. Conversely, suppose $m \in M$. Let θ be the strategy that synthesizes m, and let $\alpha = V(\theta, 0)$. The strategy θ' that is θ less α bonds is zero-net investment and has $V(\theta', 1) = V(\theta, 1) - \alpha S_0(1)$, or $V(\theta', 1) + \alpha S_0(1) = V(\theta, 1) = x$. And, of course, $V(\theta', 1) \in M_0$.

Suppose $m \in M$ is synthesized by θ and $P^* \in \mathcal{P}^*$. By Lemma 2.1, $\{V(\theta, t), G_t; t \in T\}$ is a martingale under P^*, which implies that

$V(\theta, 0) = \mathbf{E}^{P^*}[V(\theta, 1)] = \mathbf{E}^{P^*}[m]$. This is true for all $P^* \in \mathcal{P}^*$; and since $V(\theta, 0)$ is a fixed number, $\mathbf{E}^{P^*}[m]$ must be that same number for all P^*.

Part c follows from part b; for $t \in \mathcal{T}$ intermediate to 0 and 1, use the martingale property to show that $V(\theta, t) = \mathbf{E}^{P^*}[m|G_t] = V(\theta', t)$. ∎

All of this is obvious from the martingale-under-a-martingale-measure characterization of the value of any self-financing trading strategy. What is perhaps surprising is that the converse holds.

Proposition 2.2. *For a viable model, $m \in M$ if and only if $\mathbf{E}^{P^*}[m]$ is constant over all $P^* \in \mathcal{P}^*$.*

Corollary 2.2. *In the binomial model, $\mathcal{P}^*$ is a singleton, and so, for every $x \in X$, $\mathbf{E}^{P^*}[x]$ is trivially "constant" over all $P^* \in \mathcal{P}^*$. Hence, every $x \in X$ is synthesizable. Markets are complete.*

Corollary 2.1 establishes the "only if" part of Proposition 2.2. What must be shown is that, if $\mathbf{E}^{P^*}[m]$ is constant over all $P^* \in \mathcal{P}^*$, then $m \in M$. A proof is coming, but only after we widen the question.

Arbitrage Bounds on the Price of Claims

Consider the following two problem formulations:

A. Take any claim $x \in X$. Suppose we add to the existing securities a security whose dividend is x. Suppose that, while doing so, the prices of the other (given) securities don't change. What is the range of prices that x could command in the securities markets, while keeping the model viable?

B. Take any claim $x \in X$. Since Ω is finite, there is a smallest amount of consumption that x provides – $\min\{x(\omega); \omega \in \Omega\}$ – and a largest, $\max\{x(\omega); \omega \in \Omega\}$. Hence, the following two (linear) optimization problems make sense:

$$\text{Minimize } \mathbf{E}^{P^*}[m], \text{ subject to } m \geq x, m \in M, \text{ and}$$
$$\text{Maximize } \mathbf{E}^{P^*}[m], \text{ subject to } m \leq x, m \in M,$$

where P^* is any element of $\mathcal{P}^*$. Note that the choice of P^* from $\mathcal{P}^*$ is irrelevant, since for $m \in M$, $\mathbf{E}^{P^*}[m]$ is constant in P^*. Also note that writing Maximize and Minimize is appropriate; because Ω is finite and equivalent martingale measures are strictly positive, we can restrict the optimization problems to compact subsets of M, so solutions exist.[7]

These two questions are different ways of posing the question: What do the prices given by the model of security prices (and the ability to trade in those securities) tell us about possible "viable (equilibrium) prices" of an arbitrary contingent claim x?

In formulation A, imagine that x is added to the set of securities without changing the prices of the other securities. Or imagine instead that the model gives us prices of securities that we see, and while we know that a security with dividend x is also being marketed, we don't see its price. In either scenario, what price could x command in a viable equilibrium?

Formulation B is based on arbitrage considerations: If prices of the securities in the market are fixed and if $m \in M$ satisfies $m \leq x$, then either (a) $m = x$, and the market price of x (at time 0 and at any subsequent time) is given, or (b) $m < x$ in some states and the market price of x must be strictly greater than that of m, since, otherwise, buying x and selling m, and putting the proceeds (if any) into the bond creates a free lunch. The same is true on the other side. So if, for arbitrary x, we define

$$\overline{\pi}(x) := \mathrm{Min}\{\mathbf{E}^{P^*}[m], \text{subject to } m \geq x, m \in M\} \text{ and}$$
$$\underline{\pi}(x) := \mathrm{Max}\{\mathbf{E}^{P^*}[m], \text{subject to } m \leq x, m \in M\}, \tag{2.3}$$

there are two possibilities:

1. $\underline{\pi}(x) = \overline{\pi}(x)$, in which case there exist $\underline{m} \in M$ and $\overline{m} \in M$ such that $\underline{m} \leq x \leq \overline{m}$ and $\mathbf{E}^{P^*}[\underline{m}] = \mathbf{E}^{P^*}[\overline{m}]$. Since there can be no free lunches, it must be that $\underline{m} = x = \overline{m}$, and $x \in M$. And if $x \in M$, then (of course) $\underline{m} = x = \overline{m}$ are solutions to the two optimization problems, and so $\underline{\pi}(x) = \mathbf{E}^{P^*}[x] = \overline{\pi}(x)$.

2. $\underline{\pi}(x) < \overline{\pi}(x)$, in which case $x \notin M$, and the range of possible prices for x by arbitrage considerations is $(\underline{\pi}(x), \overline{\pi}(x))$.

In formulation A, it is evident that the range of prices x could command at time 0 is precisely $\{\mathbf{E}^{P^*}[x]; P^* \in \mathcal{P}^*\}$, with the obvious extension to other times. This follows because, if a security is introduced that pays dividend x without changing the prices of other securities,

---

[7] Examples can be constructed to show that solutions are not necessarily unique.

and if the model remains viable, Proposition 2.1 says that we must find martingale measures for the securities augmented by this new security. But to be a martingale measure for the augmented set implies being a martingale measure for the original set, so any martingale measure for the augmented set must be from $\mathcal{P}^*$. And if we take any P^* from $\mathcal{P}^*$ and use it to define the price process of the new security, it is a martingale measure for the augmented set.

Proposition 2.3 establishes that, for finite Ω, we get precisely the same range of prices in formulation B as we do in formulation A:

Proposition 2.3. *For a viable model and for any $x \in X$, define $\underline{\pi}(x)$ and $\overline{\pi}(x)$ by (2.3). Then either $x \in M$, so that $\underline{\pi}(x) = \overline{\pi}(x) = \mathbf{E}^{P^*}[x]$ for all $P^* \in P^*$, or $x \notin M$, in which case*

$$\underline{\pi}(x) = \inf\{\mathbf{E}^{P^*}[x]; P^* \in \mathcal{P}^*\} < \sup\{\mathbf{E}^{P^*}[x]; P^* \in \mathcal{P}^*\} = \overline{\pi}(x).$$

Please note that, in the second possibility, we write $\inf\{\mathbf{E}^{P^*}[x]; P^* \in \mathcal{P}^*\}$ and $\sup\{\mathbf{E}^{P^*}[x]; P^* \in \mathcal{P}^*\}$; while the set $\mathcal{P}^*$ is not an open set, or even relatively open in the probability simplex on Ω, it is such that the inf and sup are not attained, as the proof below makes clear.

Also, note that this proposition immediately implies Proposition 2.2: If $x \notin M$, Proposition 2.3 says that it must be that $\inf\{\mathbf{E}^{P^*}[x]; P^* \in \mathcal{P}^*\} < \sup\{\mathbf{E}^{P^*}[x]; P^* \in \mathcal{P}^*\}$. So if $\mathbf{E}^{P^*}[x]$ is constant over $P^* \in \mathcal{P}^*$, x must be in M.

Proof of Proposition 2.3. For the case where $x \in M$, the result is clear from previous discussion.

Suppose that $x \notin M$. Previous discussion establishes that $\underline{\pi}(x) < \overline{\pi}(x)$. We know that the two optimization problems have solutions; that is, there exist $\underline{m}$ and $\overline{m}$, both from M, that: (1) solve the two problems, which is to say that $\mathbf{E}^{P^*}[\underline{m}] = \underline{\pi}(x)$ and $\mathbf{E}^{P^*}[\overline{m}] = \underline{\pi}(x)$; (2) satisfy $\underline{m} \leq x \leq \overline{m}$, with a strict inequality in each case for at least one state ω and, hence, (3) $\underline{\pi}(x) = \mathbf{E}^{P^*}[\underline{m}] < \mathbf{E}^{P^*}[x] < \mathbf{E}^{P^*}[\overline{m}] = \overline{\pi}(x)$ for all $P^* \in \mathcal{P}^*$. Hence,

$$\underline{\pi}(x) \leq \inf\{\mathbf{E}^{P^*}[x]; P^* \in \mathcal{P}^*\} \leq \sup\{\mathbf{E}^{P^*}[x]; P^* \in \mathcal{P}^*\} \leq \overline{\pi}(x).$$

What must be shown is that the first and last in this string of inequalities are in fact equalities.

Suppose that $\underline{\pi}(x) < \inf\{\mathbf{E}^{P^*}[x]; P^* \in \mathcal{P}^*\}$. Let M' be the subspace generated by M and $\{x\}$; that is, $m' \in M'$ if $m' = m + \alpha x$ for $m \in M$ and some scalar α. This representation of m' is unique: If $m' = m + \alpha x = m'' + \alpha'' x$ and $\alpha \neq \alpha''$, then $(\alpha - \alpha'')x = m'' - m \in M$, contradicting $x \notin M$. And if $\alpha = \alpha''$, then m must equal m''.

Choose any scalar $\beta \in (\underline{\pi}(x), \overline{\pi}(x))$. Define $p^* : M' \to R$ by $p^*(m + \alpha x) = \mathbf{E}^{P^*}[m] + \alpha\beta$, where the choice of P^* from $\mathcal{P}^*$ obviously doesn't matter. Note that $(1, 1, \ldots, 1) \in M$, so $p^*((1, 1, \ldots, 1)) = \mathbf{E}^{P^*}[(1, 1, \ldots, 1)] = 1$.

I assert that p^* is strictly positive on any point $m' \in M'$ that is nonnegative and nonzero. Suppose, by way of contradiction, that $p^*(m + \alpha x) \leq 0$, but $m + \alpha x \geq 0$ and $\neq 0$. Clearly, α cannot be 0, for if it were $p^*(m) = \mathbf{E}^{P^*}[m]$, and $m \geq 0$ and $\neq 0$ would imply that $\mathbf{E}^{P^*}[m] > 0$. Suppose that $\alpha > 0$. Then $m + \alpha x \geq 0$ implies $-m/\alpha \leq x$ and $p^*(m + \alpha x) \leq 0$ implies $\beta \leq \mathbf{E}^{P^*}[-m/\alpha]$. But if $-m/a \leq x$ (and, since, $x \notin M$, is strictly less for at least one state),

$$\overline{\pi}(x) = \sup\{\mathbf{E}^{P^*}[\hat{m}] : \hat{m} \in M, \hat{m} \leq x\} \geq \mathbf{E}^{P^*}[-m/\alpha] \geq \beta,$$

contradicting the original choice of β as being greater than $\overline{\pi}(x)$. A symmetric argument for the case $\alpha < 0$ shows that it cannot be that $p^*(m + \alpha x) \leq 0$ for any $m + \alpha x$ that is nonnegative and nonzero.

Let $M'_0 = \{m' \in M' : p^*(m') = 0\}$; M'_0 is a (closed and convex) subspace in X. Moreover, M'_0 is disjoint from the unit simplex in X; if $x \in M'_0$ is also in the (closed and convex) unit simplex, it is nonnegative and nonzero and so would not have p^*-value 0. So we can strictly separate M'_0 from the unit simplex; by (now) familiar arguments, since M'_0 is a subspace, the separating linear functional q^* must have value 0 on M'_0. Normalize q^* so that $q^*((1, 1, \ldots, 1)) = 1$, so that it is strictly positive on the unit simplex. Of course, q^* then defines a probability measure Q^* on X, where, for all x', $q^*(x') = \mathbf{E}^{Q^*}[x']$. And $q^*(m') = p^*(m')$ for all $m' \in M'$: For any $m' \in M'$, let $m'_0 = m' - p^*(m')(1, 1, \ldots 1)$, so that $p^*(m'_0) = 0$; hence, $m'_0 \in M'_0$, which implies that $q^*(m'_0) = 0$ and (finally) $q^*(m') = q^*(m'_0) + p^*(m')q^*((1, 1, \ldots, 1)) = 0 + p^*(m') \cdot 1 = p^*(m')$. By (now) familiar arguments, Q^* is an equivalent martingale measure, which moreover satisfies $\mathbf{E}^{Q^*}[x] = p^*(x) = \beta$. This completes the proof. [8] ∎

---

[8] Of course, I could have quoted the Hahn–Banach Theorem instead of this laborious extension of p^* to all of X, but I'm committed to using separating hyperplanes whenever possible. I apologize to readers who find this overly pedantic.

Bibliographic Notes

The idea that financial assets, traded through time, can be used to "complete markets," or, at least, to synthesize claims to consumption that are not directly marketed, was first formalized by Arrow (1964). Radner (1972) and Guesnerie and Jaffray (1974) extend Arrow's original ideas for discrete-time, finite-state-space models.

In the literature of finance, the earliest general statement for finite-state-space models of "no-free-lunch if and only if pricing-kernel if and only if viability" (that is, Proposition 2.1) is (I believe) Ross (1977). But the "no-free-lunch if and only if pricing-kernel" goes back a good deal earlier, in the context of sets of gambles and the inability to arrange a set of bets that "can't lose" (which, of course, is essentially the same result); the earliest reference here of which I am aware is de Finetti (1931), with further contributions by Kemeny (1955) and Shimony (1955).[9]

To the best of my knowledge (and acknowledging my prejudices), I believe that results *in the spirit* of Propositions 2.2 and 2.3 first appeared in Harrison and Kreps (1979). However, please note the italicized modifier. In Harrison and Kreps, questions about "arbitrage bounds" on the prices of contingent claims were formulated only in first form on page 24. Issues concerning the direct synthesis of contingent claims are not addressed in Harrison and Kreps, because of difficulties that arise when Ω is infinite; see Chapter 3 for those difficulties.

For this reason, I don't know who first observed that the two problem formulations on pages 24 and 25 give the same answer when Ω is finite. So I will take the easy way out and assign this result to the category of folklore.

That said, I would be remiss not to acknowledge the important contribution of Cox and Ross (1976). Although the setting for their paper is models with infinite state spaces, it advances the notion that, if a contingent claim can be valued by arbitrage, then it can be valued by "risk-free methods." Once one is clear that useful changes of measure must preserve null sets (so, for instance, in the context of their Poisson jump processes, one changes the jump rate and not the jump size), their paper points directly at Propositions 2.2 and 2.3 and their analogs in Chapter 3.

---

[9] The term "pricing-kernel" in this earlier literature is replaced by "betting odds." I am grateful to Walter Schachermayer for pointing me to this literature.

3. Continuous Time and the Black–Scholes–Merton (BSM) Model

The (Limited) Scope of This Chapter

This chapter is primarily concerned with the classic Black–Scholes–Merton (BSM) Model.

In comparison with Chapter 2, important properties of that model are asserted, not proved. Moreover, and also in comparison with Chapter 2, many ideas are illustrated only within the specific context of BSM. In places, to develop ideas, the discussion is more general. But the point of this chapter is to understand the challenges of modeling securities markets in continuous time, rather than to develop a general theory of such things. When I can make points in the specific context of BSM, I do so.

I have two reasons for this: First, I regard continuous-time models as idealizations of discrete-time models where trading can occur rapidly. As such, developing the full general theory is something of a diversion from the points I wish to make. And, second, the mathematics required to provide a general theory of continuous-time models outbids the background of most of my intended audience. The mathematics needed to develop ideas about how continuous-time models (and the BSM model, specifically) are idealizations of discrete-time models are similarly likely to be beyond the training of many readers, and while I cannot and do not provide a complete course in what is required, I hope that, when we meet the required mathematical tools in Chapters 4 and 5, I can provide explanations sufficient to get the gist of the formal arguments. Perhaps I could do the same for what is needed to understand the general theory of continuous-time security markets, as it has been developed by financial mathematicians. But I don't believe the economic insights that emerge are worth the time, space, and effort required.

That said, the reader, whose interest is piqued by the specific focus of this chapter, should not conclude that treatments of these issues at a much broader level of generality are unavailable. A variety of excellent treatments can be consulted, with the warning that to read those treatments requires a lot more mathematics than (I hope) is required here. Some suggestions for further study are given at the end of the chapter.

The BSM Model

The BSM model concerns a securities market in the general spirit of Chapter 2, but with an infinite state space and with continuously open trading opportunities; that is, $\mathcal{T} = [0, 1)$. There are two securities, a bond with a fixed rate of interest and a risky security, the *stock*, whose price process is a geometric Brownian motion. The emphasis in the "option pricing" portion of the literature (Black and Scholes, 1973; Merton, 1973a) is on the synthesis of options via continuous trading; consumption doesn't enter the picture, although earlier work by Merton – in particular, Merton (1969) – is directed precisely at consumers solving their consumption–investment problems.

To make the transition from the models of Chapter 2 to this specific model as easy as possible, I'll formulate the BSM model for current purposes as follows. There is a probability space (Ω, F, P) on which is defined a standard Brownian motion, $\{B(t); t \in [0, 1]\}$. The σ-field generated by the Brownian motion up to time t will be denoted F_t; $F = F_1$. There are two securities, a riskless bond, which pays a constant consumption dividend of one unit at time 1, and a risky stock, which pays a state-dependent consumption dividend of $S(1, \omega) := e^{B(1,\omega)}$ in state ω. Markets are open at all times $t \in [0, 1)$ in which the stock and bond are traded against one another; the price of the stock, relative to the bond, at time t is $S(t, \omega) := e^{B(t,\omega)}$.[1]

So much for the explicit parts of the model, next come the implicit parts that describe the sorts of consumers who are meant to live in an economy with these markets and equilibrium (relative) prices. For the space X of contingent (consumption) claims, we restrict attention to F-measurable, real-valued functions on Ω. And, perhaps and especially if at some point we want to discuss consumers with expected-utility preferences that employ unbounded utility functions, we might want to impose some integrability restrictions on elements of X. It does seem natural – and directly analogous to Chapter 2 – to restrict consumers' consumption spaces to nonnegative-valued members of X, or X_+. But, for reasons that will become clear, this choice presents some problems. Endowments, however, are no problem: As in Chapter 2, consumers can be endowed with an initial portfolio of the two securities and with a claim to some (at least measurable) consumption bundle at time 1.

---

[1] Allowing for positive interest rates and for B to have a drift rate other than 0 or an infinitessimal variance other than 1 adds nothing to the story except a lot of extraneous notation.

We also need to adapt the condition that preferences are strictly increasing. With infinite Ω, and in particular with uncountably infinite Ω, we can no longer think of $P(\{\omega\}) > 0$ for all ω; instead, the natural extension of the condition that preferences are strictly increasing of Chapter 2 is: If x and x' are two feasible consumption claims for a consumer such that $P(\{x \geq x'\}) = 1$ and $P(\{x > x'\}) > 0$, then x is strictly preferred by any consumer to x'. Please note: P is some reference measure used to define the model. It is *not* necessarily the subjective probability assessment of any consumer (at least, not yet). But recall that, in Chapter 2, when assuming that each consumer had strictly increasing preferences, we assumed that each consumer's subjective probability assessment attached positive probability to each of the finitely many states. In the current context, the corresponding assumption is that each consumer's subjective probability assessment is probabilistically equivalent to P; that is, if Q is the consumer's subjective probability assessment, then $Q(A) > 0$ if and only if $P(A) > 0$, for all F measurable events A.

Next, what sorts of trading strategies can consumers employ? The notation is as before: $\theta = \{\theta(t, \omega); t \in [0, 1], \omega \in \Omega\}$ will denote a trading strategy, where $\theta(t, \omega) = (\theta_0(t, \omega), \theta_1(t, \omega))$ represents the consumer's portfolio holding of bonds and stocks (respectively, in units of the security) at time t in state ω, after any time t trading. $V(\theta, t) := \theta_0(t) + \theta_1(t) S(t)$ – we often suppress the dependence on ω – is the value process for this portfolio. Clearly, we want $\theta(t)$ to be F_t measurable for each t. But how do we express the idea that θ is self-financing? And (related to this) what sorts of restrictions should we put on how "wild" the stochastic process $\{\theta(t)\}$ can be?

Doubling Strategies

Suppose we restrict consumers to make at most a finite number of trades. To keep matters simple, we insist that consumers indicate at the outset a (countable) sequence of times $t_0 < t_1 < t_2 < \ldots < 1$ at which they might trade, with the stipulation that, at one of those times, they must proclaim that they have finished trading: Formally, besides describing what she will hold at every time $t \in [0, 1]$ (denoted by θ as before), a consumer must declare the sequence of times and a nonnegative-integer-valued random variable L, where: (1) $\theta(t)$ is F_t measurable for all t; (2) $\theta(t)$ is piecewise constant on all intervals of the form $[t_\ell, t_{\ell+1})$, (3) the event $\{L \leq \ell\}$ is F_{t_ℓ} measurable – the consumer can say, based on information she has, when she is ready to stop – and (4) $\theta(t_\ell) = \theta(t_{\ell+1}) = \ldots = \theta(1)$ on the event $\{L = \ell\}$. Then $V((\theta, L), 1)$ – the consumption dividend paid by this trading strategy – is $\theta_1(t_L)S(1) + \theta_0(t_L)$.

This restriction on feasible trading strategies may seem arbitrary, but at least it allows us to define the self-financing condition:

$$\theta(t_\ell) \cdot S(t_\ell) = \theta(t_{\ell-1}) \cdot S(t_\ell), \quad \text{for } \ell = 1, 2, \ldots$$

Unhappily, allowing consumers even this level of trading ability is too much: Consumers can construct free lunches, and so the model is not viable. The method is an adaptation of the classic doubling strategy: Suppose a gambler wishes to win $1000 at a casino where one can enter a double-or-nothing bet with probability 0.25 of doubling his money. He bets $1000 and, with probability 0.25, he retires with his $1000 in winnings. If he loses, he bets $2000. If he wins, he has recouped his original $1000 loss and made $1000 besides. This outcome – lose on round 1, then win – has probability 0.75×0.25. But with probability $(0.75)^2$, he loses the first and the second bet, in which case he bets $4000, so that if he wins, he has covered his losses of $1000 and $2000 and has an additional $1000. And so forth. With probability 1, he'll win, eventually. So he is bound to make his $1000 and, I emphasize, he does so making only a finite number of bets.

Of course, this is unrealistic on two grounds: First, while the number of bets required is finite with probability 1, it is unbounded across states of nature. Second, this requires that he can, if necessary, continue to make ever larger bets, bets that grow in size exponentially. In reality, a gambler is unlikely to be able to access those sorts of resources.

In the context of the BSM model, the analogous doubling strategies are more complex to describe, but the principles are the same. For the sequence $t_0, t_1, t_2, \ldots$, let $t_0 = 0, t_1 = 1/2, t_2 = 3/4$, and so forth. At time $t_0 = 0$, sell one bond and buy one share of stock. ($S_1(0) = 1$, so this is zero-net investment.)

At time $1/2$, if $S_1(\frac{1}{2}) \geq 2$ so that $V(\theta, \frac{1}{2}) \geq 1$, transfer all wealth into the bond, declare "no more trades," and wait for time 1. Note that $P(\{S(\frac{1}{2}) \geq 2\}) = P(\{B(\frac{1}{2}) \geq \ln(2)\}) = \alpha \approx 0.002339 > 0$.

If, on the other hand, $S_1(\frac{1}{2}) < 2$, increase the quantity of stock held to $(2 - S(\frac{1}{2}))/[S(\frac{1}{2})(2^{\frac{1}{\sqrt{2}}} - 1)]$, financing the purchase of additional shares of stock by selling bonds. By the scaling properties of k Brownian motion, the probability that $B(\frac{3}{4}) - B(\frac{1}{2}) \geq \ln(2)/\sqrt{2}$ is the same as the probability that $B(\frac{1}{2}) - B(0) = B(\frac{1}{2}) \geq \ln(2) = \alpha$, so by time $3/4$, this zero-net-investment strategy provides a value of at least 1 with probability $\alpha + (1 - \alpha)\alpha$. With probability $(1 - \alpha)^2$, it has failed to do this, but then the strategy calls to scale up the bet on the stock so that, at time $7/8$, there is probability α that the strategy has made up any losses and is ahead by 1 or more, net. Just as with the classic doubling strategy, this guarantees that, after a number of portfolio revisions that are finite in number (but unbounded in ω, and requiring an unbounded level of credit[2]), a free lunch has been achieved with probability 1.

Compare with Chapter 2. In Chapter 2, with a finite number of trading times, such eventually sure-to-win strategies are unavailable; the number of times an investor can revise her portfolio is bounded. But the spirit of Assumption 11e on page 12 was that an investor, seeing the prospect of a free lunch, could obtain whatever credit is necessary to execute the free lunch. In that spirit, one can ask whether Assumption 11e invalidates the objection that doubling strategies require a lot of credit. If an investor can present a strategy that results in sure and pure arbitrage profit, why can't she raise the necessary funds? In this regard, note two differences: In Chapter 2, there was a bound to how much capital or credit might be required, that bound being the minimum value in at any of a finite number of times, in any of a finite number of states of nature, that the free-lunch portfolio could achieve. And in 11e, we assumed that if θ' is a free lunch, consumers could execute some scaled copy of θ'. As long as the consumer can, upon presenting to her banker a sure-thing free lunch plan, obtain the credit required to execute on *some* (strictly positive) level, the theory goes through. In a doubling strategy, it doesn't matter how you scale the doubling strategy; it takes an amount of credit that is unbounded in ω.[3]

Simple Trading Strategies

This, then, seems to present us with one of two (or three) options. We could restrict consumers to a number of trades that is bounded in ω, or we could restrict them to trading strategies in which the value of their portfolios never falls below some finite "credit limit." (Or we could do

---

[2] To be precise, for any positive integer M, both the event that more than M trades will be required and the event that the value of the portfolio will fall below $-M$ have *strictly positive* probability.

[3] If this does not convince you, ask your banker to bankroll a sure-thing doubling strategy, to be implemented in Las Vegas.

both.) In Harrison and Kreps (1979), which to the best of my knowledge is the first place this issue is confronted in print, the former tack is taken. In most of the subsequent literature, the second tack is taken. There are good reasons from a mathematical perspective to take the second tack, but I don't think those reasons are so convincing as economics, for reasons to be discussed. So, at least for now, I follow the first line of attack.

Definition. A *simple trading strategy* is a self-financing trading strategy in which the portfolio held changes in composition only at a (pre-specified) finite list of times, $t_0 = 0 < t_1 < \ldots < t_L < 1$.

The self-financing condition is obvious: $\theta(t_{\ell-1}) \cdot (1, S(t_\ell)) = \theta(t_\ell) \cdot (1, S(t_\ell))$, for each $\ell = 1, 2, \ldots, L$. And the final dividend paid, $V(\theta, 1)$, is $\theta(t_L) \cdot (1, S(1))$. Note that, if we permit consumers to access any simple trading strategy, we do not insist on "no more than ten-thousand trades" or "no more than one-billion trades"; the consumer can trade as many times as she likes, as long as she specifies in advance that she won't trade more than L times, for some finite L.

A *simple free lunch* is a simple trading strategy θ such that $\theta(0) \cdot (1, S(0)) = 0$ (or, since $S(0) = 1$, that $\theta_1(0) = -\theta_0(0)$) and $V(\theta, 1) \geq 0$ with probability 1 and > 0 with positive probability. (It is worth observing, however, that in a simple free lunch, no lower bound on the $V(\theta, t)$ is implied. To execute a simple free lunch, the consumer may need to be able access unbounded amounts of credit.)

As long as we are restricting consumers to simple trading strategies, the mathematical difficulties of treating models that are more general than the specific BSM economy are reduced. So, for the next several sections, work with the following direct generalization from Chapter 2. There is a probability space (Ω, F, P) on which are defined I stochastic processes $S(t) = (S_1(t), \ldots, S_I(t))$ for $t \in [0, 1]$. These represent (for $t < 1$) the prices of I financial securities, relative to a riskless bond (security 0, with a price of 1, relative to itself); for $t = 1$, $S_i(1)$ is a consumption dividend paid by security i; the bond pays 1 in all states of nature. A filtration $\{F_t; t \in [0, 1]\}$ is given, and $S(t)$ is F_t measurable. An equivalent martingale measure for this system is a probability measure P^* on (Ω, F) that is probabilistically equivalent to P, such that $\{S_i(t); i = 1, \ldots, I\}$ is a vector martingale with respect to P^* and the filtration $\{F_t\}$.

In this setting, simple self-financing trading strategies, simple zero-net-investment trading strategies, simple free lunches, and consumers are all defined as before. In particular (and despite the possible requirement of unbounded resources), we assume that a consumer can add to her trading strategy a simple free lunch, if she can find one. And, then, the question is: How much of the following "wished-for-proposition" is true?

A "Wished-for" Proposition. *The following three conditions are equivalent:*

a. *The model is viable, where consumers are restricted to simple trading strategies (but can execute any simple free lunch in addition to whatever else they are doing).*

b. *No simple free lunches are available.*

c. *An equivalent martingale measure for the model exists.*

Of course, a will imply b or, more in the spirit of the proof, not b implies not a: If a simple free lunch is available, if consumers can do the same in addition to whatever else they are planning, and if their preferences are strictly increasing in the manner above, no strategy is best for them; whatever they plan to do, they can do better. So the model is not viable.

Furthermore, c implies a, with exactly the sort of construction used in the proof of Proposition 2.1. First, prove Lemma 2.1 adapted to this context.

Lemma 3.1. *If θ is a simple, self-financing trading strategy, the value process of θ, including the terminal (dividend) value $V(\theta, 1)$, forms a martingale under any equivalent martingale measure.*

In particular, if θ is a simple trading strategy and P^* is an equivalent martingale measure, then $\mathbf{E}^{P^*}[V(\theta, 1)] = V(\theta, 0)$. It is in this step that the limit on the number of trades is used: You prove that $\mathbf{E}^{P^*}[V(\theta, t_\ell+1)|F_{t_\ell}] = V(\theta, t_\ell)$ for $\ell = 0, 1, \ldots, L$, where the convention $t_{L+1} = 1$ is employed. This works because, over each interval, the composition of the portfolio is unchanging, so the value of the portfolio over the interval – a linear combination of martingales under P^* – is itself a martingale under P^*. The self-financing condition bridges across consecutive intervals, which proves Lemma 3.1.[4]

As in the proof of Proposition 2.1, we can construct an autarchic equilibrium with a single consumer whose preferences are given by the

---

[4] This strategy works admirably for the doubling strategy except for the very last step; you can't get $\mathbf{E}^{P^*}[V(\theta, 1)|F_{t_\ell}] = V(\theta, t_\ell)$ for any integer ℓ. If this is not clear to you, try to write out a proof and you'll see the problem.

expectation of claims with respect to this equivalent martingale measure. For this consumer, sticking with her endowment is as good as anything else she can do; the model is viable.[5]

This leaves moving from b to c. For the BSM model specifically, this is not a problem. It turns out, as a purely mathematical result, an equivalent martingale measure for the BSM model exists. Informally, this equivalent martingale measure amounts to adjusting the drift of the underlying Brownian motion B from 0 to $-1/2$. Formally, this equivalent martingale measure P^* can be described by its (strictly positive) Radon–Nikodym derivative

$$\frac{dP^*}{dP}(\omega) = \frac{1}{e^{B(1,\omega)/2+1/8}}.$$

(The Radon–Nikodym derivative is a nonnegative-valued function on the underlying probability space Ω such that, for any measurable event A, $P^*(A) = \mathbf{E}[\mathbf{1}_A \, dP^*/dP]$, where $\mathbf{E}[\cdot]$ indicates expectation with respect to P, and $\mathbf{1}_A$ denotes the indicator function of A. It exists because P^* is absolutely continuous with respect to P; that is, if $P(A) = 0$, then $P^*(A) = 0$; see, for instance, Royden (1968, p.238). Because it is strictly positive, P^* is equivalent to P. And – a fact that will be needed later – in this particular case, this Radon–Nikodym derivative is square-integrable with respect to P.)

In fact – and a good deal harder to prove – P^* defined by this Radon–Nikodym derivative is the unique equivalent martingale measure for P; see Harrison and Kreps (1979) for a proof. Uniqueness enters the story shortly.

So, in the specific context of BSM, c is true, which implies a, which implies b. But we'd like to know if the wished-for proposition transcends this specific context. And, in general, it does not.

---

[5] It may be worth observing that Lemma 3.1, as proved in the previous paragraph, holds for any martingale measure; equivalent to P or not. But for the one consumer's preferences to be strictly increasing, we need P^* to be equivalent to P. Also, if we are constructing this autarchic economy, we must restrict the set of contingent consumption claims X so that the consumer is able to evaluate all of them with this expectation; X can be no larger than the space of claims that are finitely integrable with respect to P^*. Since P^* is not the primitive – the primitive measure is P – this raises technical issues we must address.

Föllmer's Example

To get a sense of the difficulties in generalizing Proposition 2.1 to infinite state spaces, consider the following single-risky-security model of a securities market, which I believe was first posed by Föllmer (1978).

The first security is the usual bond, paying a dividend 1 in all states of nature and acting as the numeraire in the securities markets.

The second security is risky. Let Ω by a probability space on which is defined a single, exponentially distributed random variable τ. That is, $P(\tau \leq t) = 1 - e^{-t}$. Then the price process for the risky security is given by

$$S(t, \omega) = \begin{cases} 1 - t, & \text{if } t < \tau(\omega), \text{ and} \\ 1 + \tau(\omega), & \text{if } t \geq \tau(\omega). \end{cases}$$

Or, in words, the stock price drifts down at rate 1 until the "Poisson" arrival time τ, at which point it rises by 2τ and, thereafter, stays fixed.

This model admits no simple free lunches. A careful argument that this is so can be constructed using induction on the number of trading times in the trading strategy, but let me give (only) the intuition here. To make money in this market, you must either be long in the stock (before τ) and hope that τ happens, or you must short the stock (again, before τ; once τ happens, no portfolio will change its value) and hope that τ doesn't happen. But you can guarantee neither: While you are short, τ could happen and you lose money; while you are long, τ may not happen and you lose money. So, whatever you do, as long as you do something that might make you money, there is positive probability that you will lose money. And once you lose money, you can never guarantee that you can recoup your losses. If you lose money because τ has happened while you were short in the stock, you can't change the value of your position. While if you lose money because τ hasn't happened while you were long in the stock, whatever you do, there is positive probability that you will lose even more.

However, this model does not admit an equivalent martingale measure. To be an equivalent measure, the shape of the sample paths for S must be preserved: Each path drops at rate 1 until it jumps up twice the amount it has lost and stays fixed. Consider how fast the jumps must occur (if no jump has occurred) over the time interval $[t, t + h]$, if the jump rate is going to create a martingale. The loss, if there is no jump, is $-h$. The gain, if there is a jump, is (for small h) approximately $2t$. So, to turn this into a martingale, if λ is the probability of a jump over this interval, we need $-h(1 - \lambda) + \lambda 2t = 0$, or $\lambda = h/(2t + h)$. In terms of jump *rates*, the rate of a jump around time t must be $1/2t$. But this is impossible; it implies that a jump must occur in any interval $[0, \epsilon)$ (because $\int_0^\epsilon (1/2t)dt = \infty$ for all $\epsilon > 0$). To make this a martingale, τ must equal 0 with probability 1. But then the measure isn't equivalent to the original measure.

To recap: No simple free lunches, but no equivalent martingale measure, either.

However, consider the following zero-net-investment trading strategy θ^n for positive integer n. At time 0, buy n bonds and sell n shares of stock. Hold this portfolio until time $1/n$, then liquidate and hold bonds to the end. This strategy provides the following dividend

$$V(\theta^n, 1) = \begin{cases} 1, & \text{if } \tau > 1/n, \text{ and} \\ -2, & \text{if } \tau \leq 1/n. \end{cases}$$

And the probability that $\tau \leq 1/n$ is $1 - e^{-1/n} \approx 1/n$. This isn't a free lunch – it gives a negative result with positive probability – but, for large n, it comes close: For an initial net investment of 0, you make 1 with probability (roughly) $(n - 1)/n$ at the risk of losing 2 with probability $1/n$.

Generalizing Proposition 2.1: The Fundamental Theorem of Asset Pricing (FTAP)

Föllmer's example shows that moving from no simple free lunches to the existence of an equivalent martingale measure can fail when Ω is infinite, but it doesn't say what goes wrong in the proof. Recall how the proof went in Chapter 2: We construct the space M_0 of all claims that can be generated by a zero-net-investment trading strategy, note that no free lunches implies that M_0 is disjoint from the unit simplex in the space of claims, and then apply the (Strict) Separating Hyperplane Theorem to generate a "pricing kernel" that, when normalized, becomes the equivalent martingale measure.

If, in the context of a general continuous-time model (with simple trading strategies only), we could produce a suitably continuous and strictly positive pricing kernel p^* that separates M_0 from the "unit simplex," we'd have no problem normalizing it to create an equivalent martingale measure. By suitably continuous, I mean that if we define the equivalent martingale measure from p^* by $P^*(A) = p^*(\mathbf{1}_A)/p^*(\mathbf{1}_\Omega)$, for each measurable event A, then P^* should be a σ-additive measure. And suitably strictly positive is: If $P(A) > 0$, then $p^*(\mathbf{1}_A) > 0$. Once we have these things, showing that P^* so defined is a martingale measure is a straightforward exercise in the definition of a conditional probability: First, since M_0 is a subspace, the argument used in Chapter 2 shows directly that $p^*(m) = 0$ for all $m \in M_0$. Then, for any t, F_t measurable event A, and security i other than the bond, constuct the zero-net-investment strategy in which nothing happens until time t. At time t, if $\omega \notin A$, nothing happens, ever. But if $\omega \in A$, purchase a share of security i and sell $S_i(t, \omega)$ bonds, holding that portfolio until time 1. The resulting contingent consumption claim is $\left[S_i(1, \omega) - S_i(t, \omega)\right] \cdot \mathbf{1}_A(\omega)$. Since this claim is in M_0, it must have p^* value 0. But, given how P^* is defined from p^* (and given enough continuity so we can define the required integrals), this means that, for all $A \in F_t$,

$$\mathbf{E}^{P^*}[S_i(1)\mathbf{1}_A] = \mathbf{E}^{P^*}[S_i(t)\mathbf{1}_A],$$

which is the defining characteristic of $S_i(t) = \mathbf{E}^{P^*}[S_i(1)|F_t]$.

So, it all comes down to the application of the Separating Hyperplane Theorem. And that is where things can fall apart. First, all this talk about p^* being suitably continuous means that we need to put into the story a suitable topology for the space X. "Natural" candidates would be one of the L^p topologies; that is, $X = L^p(\Omega, F, P)$ for $1 \le p \le \infty$. But, except for the sup-norm (or L^∞) topology, the positive orthant isn't "solid," it contains no open subsets. And for L^∞, the dual space of continuous linear functionals is not limited to L^1. So the Hahn–Banach Theorem – the Separating Hyperplane Theorem in this setting – either doesn't (yet) apply (for $p < \infty$) or doesn't give us what we want.

At this point, two paths are open. We can choose $X = L^p(\Omega, F, P)$ for $p < \infty$, or $X = L^\infty(\Omega, F, P)$. The choice $p < \infty$ makes for a much easier and straightforward theory; the choice $p = \infty$ leads to some interesting mathematics. I don't believe, at least not for present purposes, that the virtues of $p = \infty$ are worth the cost. (And, in any case, in the canonical BSM model, $S(1)$ is unbounded; I hasten to add that extensions for unbounded security prices have been developed within the L^∞ general framework.) So I'll proceed with $p < \infty$ and, to fix matters, with $p = 2$ specifically. (The theory for other $p < \infty$ is entirely similar.)

To keep the discussion concrete, I will assume that Ω is a complete and separable metric space and that F is the Borel σ-field on Ω.[6] Let $X = L^2(\Omega, F, P)$, the space of square-integrable (with respect to P), F measurable functions on Ω. Assume that for each security i, $S_i(t) \in X$ (that is, the price of any security is square-integrable with respect to P. Let $\mathcal{X}$ be the unit simplex in X plus everything that lies above the unit simplex:

$$\mathcal{X} = \{x \in X : x \geq 0, \mathbf{E}^P[x] \geq 1\}.$$

Of course, $\mathcal{X}$ is convex. And it is bounded away from the origin: Jensen's inequality tells us that $\mathbf{E}^P[x^2] \geq (\mathbf{E}^P[x])^2 \geq 1$, and so $(\mathbf{E}^P[x^2])^{1/2} \geq 1$. But, as already noted, $\mathcal{X}$ is not *solid* in the L^2 topology; it contains no open set. So, to fix that:

Definition 3.1. *The model of securities and their prices is **viable** as a model of economic equilibrium if there is some convex and open set $\mathcal{O} \subseteq X$ such that $\mathcal{X} \subseteq \mathcal{O}$ and $M_0 \cap \mathcal{O} = \emptyset$, where M_0 is the space of contingent claims in X that result from simple, self-financing, and zero-net-investment trading strategies.*

I'll deal with the justification for this definition in a moment, to the extent that it can be justified. But let me give the (probably obvious) punchline:

Proposition 3.1. *The model of securities and their prices is viable as a model of economic equilibrium (according to the definition just provided) if and only if there is an equivalent martingale measure P^*, whose Radon–Nikodym derivative with respect to P, dP^*/dP, is square integrable with respect to P and, of course, is strictly positive.*

Proof. If $M_0 \cap \mathcal{O}$ is empty, since M_0 and $\mathcal{O}$ are convex and $\mathcal{O}$ is open, there is a nontrivial *continuous* linear functional that separates them: That is, a continuous linear function $p^* : X \to R$ and a scalar α such that $p^*(m) \leq \alpha$ for all $m \in M_0$ and $p^*(x) \geq \alpha$ for all $x \in \mathcal{O}$ (see, for instance, Luenberger, 1969, p. 133). As noted earlier, since M_0 is a subspace, it must be that $p^*(m_0) = 0$ for all $m_0 \in M_0$.

Because p^* is nontrivial, there is some $x \in X$ such that $p^*(x) \neq 0$. Choosing either x or $-x$, and calling it $\hat{x}$, we can assume that $p^*(\hat{x}) > 0$.

---

[6] For BSM, let Ω be $C[0, 1]$ with the sup norm, and let P be Weiner measure. For Föllmer's example, Ω can be $[0, \infty)$ with the Euclidean metric; the interpretation is that $\tau(\omega) = \omega$.

Now let A be any F-measurable set in Ω such that $P(A) > 0$, and consider the contingent claim $(1/P(A))1_A - \epsilon\hat{x}$. $(1/P(A))1_A \in \mathcal{X}$, so for sufficiently small $\epsilon > 0$, $(1/P(A))1_A - \epsilon\hat{x} \in \mathcal{O}$. Hence, $p^*((1/P(A))1_A - \epsilon\hat{x}) \geq \alpha \geq 0$, which implies that $p^*(1_A) > 0$.

Since $p^*(1_\Omega) > 0$, we can normalize p^* so that $p^*(1_\Omega) = 1$. And continuous linear functions in $L^2(\Omega, F, P)$ take the form $p^*(x) = \mathbf{E}^P[p^*x]$, where now $p^* \in L^2(\Omega, F, P)$, $\mathbf{E}^P[p^*] = 1$, and $\mathbf{E}^P[p^*1_A] > 0$ for all $A \in F$ such that $P(A) > 0$. (Of course, $\mathbf{E}^P[p^*1_B] = 0$ for all $B \in F$ such that $P(B) = 0$.) So, defining $P^*(A) = \mathbf{E}[p^*1_A]$ for all $A \in F$, P^* is a probability distribution on Ω that is equivalent to P, with square-integrable Radon–Nikodym derivative p^*.

We've already given the argument that shows that P^* turns each S_i into a martingale.

This leaves the converse half: If there exists an equivalent martingale measure P^* whose Radon–Nikokym derivative with respect to P is square-integrable with respect to P, then there exists an open set $\mathcal{O} \subseteq X$ such that $\mathcal{X} \subseteq \mathcal{O}$ and $M_0 \cap \mathcal{O} = \emptyset$. (Our informal arguments given previously haven't shown this – quite – because we've changed the definition of viability.) But this is easy. Let p^* denote the Radon–Nikodym derivative dP^*/dP and define $\mathcal{O} = \{x \in X : \mathbf{E}[p^*x] > 0\}$. Since p^* defines a continuous linear functional, $\mathcal{O}$ is open. And since p^* is strictly positive, any $x \in \mathcal{X}$ has $\mathbf{E}[p^*x] > 0$, so $x \in \mathcal{X}$ implies $x \in \mathcal{O}$. ∎

What justification can be offered for this definition of viability? The idea is that economic equilibrium in any economy is inconsistent with some level of "almost free lunches," where an almost free lunch is a claim that is within some small distance of an "absolute free lunch." When we look at the set $\mathcal{X}$ – that is, claims that are on or above the unit simplex in X – we are looking at claims that not only are going to raise the utility of any consumer but, because these claims are strictly bounded away in norm from the origin, will raise the utility of consumers by some amount bounded away from 0 – at least if the consumer's utility function is uniformly continuous around the origin. Imagine for $\mathcal{O}$ we take all elements of X that are within ϵ of some x in $\mathcal{X}$, for some small ϵ. Then a claim in $\mathcal{O}$ is nearly a claim – is no more than ϵ away from a claim – that will certainly raise consumers' utilities by some discrete amount. Surely (this justification goes), for any given set of consumers, there is ϵ small enough but still greater than 0, so that the existence of such an almost free lunch upsets the equilibrium. Hence, we have the definition of viability.

The problem with this is that claims that are "close" to $\mathcal{X}$ in L^2 can have very large strictly negative consumption on some states, as long as the probability of those states is very, very small. As long as we conceive of consumers having X_+ as their consumption set, this justification doesn't hold water.

If, however, we imagine that consumers have convex and continuous preferences defined on *all* of X (that are strictly increasing), this argument would make perfect economic sense. In fact, if consumers are of this sort, the definition given in this chapter is equivalent to the definition given in Chapter 2. In one direction: Suppose the model is viable in the sense of Chapter 2. Then there is some consumer (of this sort) who can find a simple trading strategy θ^* that provides her with a best consumption claim x^*. In this case, let $\mathcal{O} = \{x \in X : x + x^* \succ x^*\}$. Continuity of her preferences implies that $\mathcal{O}$ is open. Convexity of her preferences implies that $\mathcal{O}$ is convex. The strictly increasing property of her preferences implies that $\mathcal{X} \subset \mathcal{O}$. And, of course, $M_0 \cap \mathcal{O} = \emptyset$; if $m \in M_0 \cap \mathcal{O}$, then $x^* + m$ is both affordable and strictly preferred to x^*. (We do need here an assumption that this consumer can finance m in addition to whatever else she is doing.) Conversely, if the model is viable in the sense of this chapter's definition, we can produce p^* and use it to define a consumer's preferences as being represented by the expectation of any claim under P^*; this makes the model viable per the definition of Chapter 2, just as was done in Chapter 2.

It is probably worth observing that *truncated doubling strategies* – that is, doubling strategies that stop after some finite number of bets – give a small probability (only) of a loss, combined with a probability close to one of a definite gain. That is, if θ^* is a doubling strategy for BSM and θ^{*N} is θ^* but stopped after N bets, then $V(\theta^{*N}, 1) \to x^* \in \mathcal{X}$ with probability 1. Proposition 3.1, and the fact that the BSM admits an equivalent martingale measure with a square-integrable Radon–Nikodym derivative, tells us that while this gives us convergence almost surely, the size of the losses in θ^{*N} are so large that we don't get convergence in L^2.

"Arbitrage Pricing" by Viability Arguments

Continuing our attempts to replicate the results of Chapter 2, we turn to issues of "pricing by arbitrage" and "synthesis of contingent claims" for models that are viable.

We'll continue with the general framework outlined on the bottom of page 34: We have I risky assets and the bond, markets are open at all $t \in [0,1)$, consumers are restricted to simple trading strategies, and claims (and the prices of all assets) are square-integrable. We assume the model is viable in the sense of the Definition 3.1, so we know that at least one equivalent martingale measure exists, with a Radon–Nikodym derivative relative to P that is square-integrable. And we let $\mathcal{P}^*$ denote the set of all such equivalent martingale measures.

What can we say about the "arbitrage price" of a (square-integrable) claim x? Recall the first way we operationalized this question back on page 24:

A. Take any claim $x \in X$. Suppose we add to the existing securities a security whose dividend is x. Suppose that, while doing so, the prices of the other (given) securities don't change. What is the range of prices that x could command in the securities markets, while keeping the model viable?[7]

The answer is clear. If, for some $P^* \in \mathcal{P}^*$, the price of x at time 0 is $\mathbf{E}^{P^*}[x]$ and, more generally, if its price process is given by $S_x(t) = \mathbf{E}^{P^*}[x|F_t]$, then P^* is an equivalent martingale measure for the augmented set of securities, and the model (with x having these prices) remains viable. Conversely, if $S_x(t)$ is a price process for this claim and if the augmented model is viable, an equivalent martingale measure Q^* must exist for the full (augmented) model. But if Q^* is an equivalent martingale measure for the full augmented model, it is as well for the original model (without security x); hence, $Q^* \in \mathcal{P}^*$. We conclude that

> For a claim x, the range of prices it can command, given a viable model of other securities whose prices don't change with the introduction of x, is $\{S_x(t) = \mathbf{E}^{P^*}[x|F_t] : P^* \in \mathcal{P}^*\}$, where $\mathcal{P}^*$ is the set of equivalent martingale measures for the original viable model.

Recall the earlier claim that, for the BSM model, $\mathcal{P}^*$ is singleton, the one equivalent martingale measure we identified is the only equivalent martingale measure for that model. This is a mathematical fact. This means that every security whose dividend is x (if x is square-integrable) has a unique price consistent with the prices given by the BSM model. We do need to be careful in this extraordinary claim: Recall that, in the BSM model, the σ-field F is the σ-field generated by the Brownian motion

---

[7] Or, equivalently, suppose that a security whose dividend at time 1 is x is being bought and sold in a viable market where the prices of the $I + 1$ securities we know about have prices given by our model. What prices for this security are consistent with the prices we see?

through time 1. Implicit in this is that x is F measurable. So what we're saying is: Any contingent claim whose value (dividend) at time 1 is a function of the history of the Brownian motion – which is equivalent to, is a function of the history of the stock price – is "priced by viability-defined arbitrage."

"Arbitrage Pricing" by Synthesis

Now consider the second formulation of "arbitrage pricing" given on pages 24–5 as well as the question addressed by Proposition 2.2: Suppose we have a viable model, so we know that at least one equivalent martingale measure exists. Let $\mathcal{P}^*$ be the set of all equivalent martingale measures. Let M be the space of contingent claims that can be synthesized out of the securities in the model, in the sense that $m \in M$ if $m = V(\theta, 1)$ for some simple self-financing portfolio θ; M_0, as before, is the set of all $m \in M$ such that m is a zero-net-investment claim. What can we say about M?

It is clear that all three parts of Corollary 2.1 hold: (a) $m \in M$ if and only if $m = m_0 + \alpha S_0(1)$ for some scalar α and $m_0 \in M_0$. (b) If $m \in M$ is generated by θ, then $V(\theta, t) = \mathbf{E}^{P^*}[m|F_t]$ for all t and all $P^* \in \mathcal{P}^*$. (c) Hence, if $m \in M$ is synthesized by both θ and θ', $V(\theta, t) \equiv V(\theta', t)$.

Do results analogous to Propositions 2.2 and 2.3 hold? Define

$$\bar{\pi}(x) := \inf\{\mathbf{E}^{P^*}[m], \text{subject to } m \geq x, m \in M\} \text{ and}$$
$$\underline{\pi}(x) := \sup\{\mathbf{E}^{P^*}[m], \text{subject to } m \leq x, m \in M\}.$$

Is it true that (a) $m \in M$ if and only if $\bar{\pi}(x) = \underline{\pi}(x)$, and (b) $\bar{\pi}(x) = \sup\{\mathbf{E}^{P^*}[x]; P^* \in \mathcal{P}^*\}$ and $\underline{\pi}(x) = \inf\{\mathbf{E}^{P^*}[x]; P^* \in \mathcal{P}^*\}$?

Some parts of these statements still work:

- If $x \in M$, then $\mathbf{E}^{P^*}[x] = V(\theta, 0)$ for every $P^* \in \mathcal{P}^*$, where θ is the simple strategy that synthesizes x. So $\bar{\pi}(x) = \underline{\pi}(x)$.

- And if $m \geq x$, then $\mathbf{E}^{P^*}[m] \geq \mathbf{E}^{P^*}[x]$ for any $P^* \in \mathcal{P}^*$.[8] Since $\mathbf{E}^{P^*}[m]$ is constant over $P^* \in \mathcal{P}^*$, this implies that if $m \in M$,

---

[8]   Be careful here: If $m \geq x$ for all $\omega \in \Omega$, then the expected value of m would be at least as large as the expected value of x under *any* measure on Ω for which the integrals make sense. But in this context, thinking about m and x being in $L^2(\Omega, F, P)$, the statement $m \geq x$ is really the statement that $P(\{\omega \in \Omega : m(\omega) \geq x(\omega)\}) = 1$. So $m \geq x$ implies the same inequality for the two expectations taken with respect to any measure absolutely continuous with respect to P. This, of course, includes all $P^* \in \mathcal{P}^*$.

$\mathbf{E}^{P^*}[m] \geq \sup \{\mathbf{E}^{Q^*}[x] \; ; \; Q^* \in \mathcal{P}^*\}$, for all $P^* \in \mathcal{P}^*$. Therefore,

$$\overline{\pi}(x) = \inf \{\mathbf{E}^{P^*}[m] : m \geq x\} \geq \sup \{\mathbf{E}^{Q^*}[x] \; ; \; Q^* \in \mathcal{P}^*\}.$$

Similarly, $\underline{\pi}(x) \leq \inf \{\mathbf{E}^{Q^*}[x]; Q^* \in \mathcal{P}^*\}$.

However, the other "halves" of Propositions 2.2 and 2.3 do not hold: Even if $\overline{\pi}(x) = \underline{\pi}(x)$, m may not be synthesizable with a simple self-financing strategy. And $\overline{\pi}(x)$ may be strictly greater than $\sup \{\mathbf{E}^{Q^*}[x]; Q^* \in \mathcal{P}^*\}$, with a similar strict inequality on the other side.

The BSM model provides examples. As already noted, for the BSM model, $\mathcal{P}^*$ is singleton; only one equivalent martingale measure exists. So take, for instance, the prototype contingent claim: The European call option on the price of the stock, with exercise price 1, or

$$x_C(\omega) = \max \{0, S(1, \omega) - 1\}.$$

Suppose we could synthesize this claim with a simple trading strategy. Then, for this trading strategy, there is some time $t_L < 1$ after which (until time 1) its composition does not change; it holds some amount θ_0' of bond and some amount θ_1' of stock, where both θ_0' and θ_1' are F_{t_L} measurable. This pays the dividend $\theta_0' + \theta_1' S(1)$ at time 1. But no value of $S(1)$ (in $(0, \infty)$) is precluded (with probability 1) at time $t_L < 1$, so it must be that θ_0' and θ_1' are such that $\theta_0' + \theta_1' S(1) = \max \{0, S(1, \omega) - 1\}$ for all $S(1) \in (0, \infty)$: In particular, it must be that $\theta_0' + \theta_1' S(1) = 0$ for all $S(1) < 1$. This implies that $\theta_1' \equiv 0$, and therefore that $\theta_0' \equiv 0$, in which case $\theta_0' + \theta_1' S(1) \neq \max \{0, S(1, \omega) - 1\}$ for $S(1) > 1$.[9]

As for the bounds created by $\overline{\pi}(x)$ and $\underline{\pi}(x)$: Let x° be the contingent claim

$$x^\circ(\omega) := \begin{cases} S(1, \omega), & \text{if } S(1, \omega) \leq 1, \\ 1, & \text{if } 1 \leq S(1, \omega) \leq 100, \\ 101 - S(1, \omega), & \text{if } 100 \leq S(1, \omega) \leq 101, \text{ and} \\ 0, & \text{if } S(1, \omega) > 101. \end{cases}$$

This is less complicated than it may seem: x° has value 0 for very high values of $S(1, \omega)$; it is bounded above by 1 and below by 0; it equals 1 for

---

[9]   A slightly more complex version of this argument works for any x that is a function (only) of $S(1)$ but not a conditionally affine function of $S(1)$, conditional on F_t, $t < 1$.

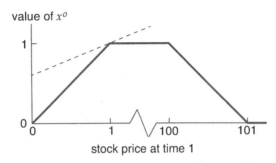

Figure 3.1. *The claim* x^o. The claim x^o is the heavy line. The dashed line gives an over-approximating portfolio (see text).

$S(1)$ between 1 and 100; it rises linearly on $[0, 1]$, and it falls linearly on $[100, 101]$. (It is designed to be continuous to head off speculation that what is about to happen is an artifact of a discontinuity). See Figure 3.1.

I assert that $0 = \underline{\pi}(x^o) < \mathbf{E}^*[x^o] < \overline{\pi}(x^o)$, where $\mathbf{E}^*$ is expectation with respect to the unique equivalent martingale measure.

- The argument that $0 = \underline{\pi}(x^o)$ is the easier of the two: For any simple self-financing strategy θ, there is a last time $t_L < 1$ that θ trades. Let its final composition be denoted (θ_0, θ_1) where both θ_0 and θ_1 are F_{t_L} measurable functions. The problem is that, whatever is the value of $S(t_L)$, there is positive probability that, at time 1, the stock price will be very close to 0 and positive probability that it will be very, very large. The dividend paid by x^o as $S(1)$ approaches 0 is $S(1)$, while the final value of the portfolio is $\theta_0 + \theta_1 S(1)$, which approaches θ_0 as $S(1)$ approaches 0. Hence, to ensure that this portfolio finishes below x^o with probability 1, $\theta_0 \leq 0$ is required. And the value of x^o as $S(1)$ approaches infinity is 0. So to ensure that this portfolio finishes below x^o in the event that $S(1)$ is very large, we must have $\theta_1 \leq 0$. And if θ_0 and θ_1 are both less than or equal to 0, the value of the dividend paid by the portfolio is ≤ 0. Hence, taking the expectation of $\theta_0 + \theta_1 S(1)$ (where, remember, θ_0 and θ_1 are both random, but both ≤ 0), we get a nonpositive value. Of course, the portfolio of no stocks and no bonds gives dividend 0, less than or equal to x^o in every state, so $\underline{\pi}(x^o) = 0$. And $\mathbf{E}^*[x^o] > 0$, so we have the first inequality, that $\underline{\pi}(x^o) < \mathbf{E}^*[x^o]$.

- As for the upper bound: Suppose θ is a simple strategy that majorizes x^o; that is, $V(\theta, 1) \geq x^o$. Let t_L be the last time that

θ changes composition, and let θ_0 and θ_1 be the (F_{t_L} measurable) composition of θ at that time. It must be that $\theta_1 \geq 0$; otherwise, for very large values of $S(1)$, $V(\theta, 1)$ would be less than x^o. It must be that $\theta_0 \geq 0$; otherwise $V(\theta, 1) < x^o$ for values of $S(1)$ that are very close to 0. And it must be that $\theta_0 + \theta_1 \geq 1$; otherwise $V(\theta, 1) < x^o$ for values of $S(1)$ in a neighborhood of 1. In other words, the value of the portfolio, as a function of $S(1)$ (and conditional on F_{t_L}) is an affine function of $S(1)$ with a nonnegative slope and that passes at or above $(1, 1)$, the shape of which must be (at least) the dashed line in Figure 3.1. The dashed line that applies will depend on θ_0 and θ_1, which in turn will depend on information available at time t_L. But if we compute the conditional expectation (with respect to P^*) of $\theta_0 + \theta_1 S(1) = V(\theta, 1)$, conditional on F_{t_L}, this conditional expectation will be greater than $\mathbf{E}^*[x^o]$ by *at least* $\mathbf{E}^*[\mathbf{1}_{\{S(1)>101\}}|F_{t_L}]$, where $\mathbf{1}_{\{S(1)>101\}}$ is the indicator function of $\{S(1) \geq 101\}$. Hence, when we compute the unconditional $\mathbf{E}^*[\theta_0 + \theta_1 S(1)]$, it exceeds $\mathbf{E}^*[x^o]$ by at least (and, in fact, more than) $\mathbf{E}^*[\mathbf{1}_{\{S(1)>101\}}] > 0$.

Simple trading strategies are too limiting. Abusing mathematical terminology, the space of simple trading strategies is incomplete, so that working with simple trading strategies only is like trying to do analysis only with rational numbers. [10]

These examples are constructed from the fact that, with simple trading strategies, trading stops some set time before time 1. But it isn't only time 1; think of examples similar to the ones above, but where the contingent claim is a function of $S(t)$ for some time t. Being unable to trade as time approaches t will raise the same problems. (Being able to trade at time t itself will be "too late.") This suggests that we should look at trading strategies that (are allowed to) trade continuously.

If we want to incorporate continuous trading into the model so as to get results like Propositions 2.2 and 2.3, we face three challenges.

- Restrictions must be imposed sufficient to prevent doubling strategies and other ways that might make otherwise sensible models nonviable.

---

[10] At least, at this point, one can hope that this is so: While M may be less than X in the BSM model, one can hope that M is suitably dense in X. Note: "Suitably" is not simply a throw-away here, as shown by the discussion just finished concerning gaps between, say, $\inf\{\mathbf{E}^{P^*}[x^o] : P^* \in \mathcal{P}^*\}$, $\underline{\pi}(x^o)$, and $\overline{\pi}(x^o)$. The astute reader will recognize that this connects to the subtitle of this monograph.

- But, at the same time, permitted trading should be rich enough to "fill in" the holes left by simple trading strategies.

- And – this challenge is perhaps not as easy to anticipate as the first two – we need to define what self-financing means with continuous trading.

We already have an inkling of one way to meet the first challenge: Insist that $V(\theta, t)$ is uniformly bounded below, representing (say) a credit limit. But what of the second and third challenges?

The Financial-Gains Integral

Consider a simple self-financing trading strategy θ, for $I + 1$ assets, which trades at times $t_0 = 0, t_1, \ldots, t_L < 1$. Let $t_{L+1} = 1$. The strategy begins with an investment of funds $\theta(0) \cdot (1, S(0)) = V(\theta, 0)$. Thereafter, when it trades, it neither puts fresh funds into nor takes funds out of the portfolio, which is the self-financing condition. Hence, if we know $V(\theta, t_\ell)$ for $\ell = 0, 1, \ldots, L$, we can compute

$$V(\theta, t_{\ell+1}) = V(\theta, t_\ell) + \sum_{i=1}^{I} \theta_i(t_\ell) \cdot \left(S_i(t_{\ell+1}) - S_i(t_\ell)\right).$$

This is just an accounting identity: The increase in value of the portfolio is just the sum over the securities of how much each gained (or lost) in value, times the number of securities in the portfolio. The "financial gain" term for the bond is 0, because the bond's price is the constant 1; hence, when we compute the change in value, we can start with $i = 1$ instead of with $i = 0$. And, if we take any time $t \in [0, 1]$ intermediate to some pair of trading times t_ℓ and $t_{\ell+1}$, the same formula works for computing $V(\theta, t)$ from $V(\theta, t_\ell)$ and the financial gains $S_i(t) - S_i(t_\ell)$. But then, assuming the securities price processes are suitably "differentiable," we can iterate on this accounting identity to get

$$V(\theta, t) = V(\theta, 0) + \sum_{i=1}^{I} \int_0^t \theta_i(t) dS_i(t). \tag{3.1}$$

In words, the value of the portfolio at any time t is the sum of the financial gains that have accrued from holdings in each asset, which can be computed as the integral of moment-by-moment financial gains on each asset times the moment-by-moment holding of that asset. And we can skip the bond in this sum, since it produces no financial gains.

That, of course, assumes that no funds go into or come out of the port-folio except at time 0; that is, it assumes that the portfolio is self-financing. But – and please pay close attention, because this is a hugely important and convenient "trick" – for any portfolio strategy for the risky securities $\{\theta_i(t); t \in [0,1], i = 1, \ldots, I\}$, we can make this a self-financing trading strategy for the risky securities *plus the bond* by paying for any purchases of the risky securities with the bond and storing the proceeds of any sales in the bond. *That is, any trading strategy $\{\theta_i(t); t \in [0,1], i = 1, \ldots, I\}$ for the I risky securities can be made self-financing by suitable trades in the bond. And since the financial-gains integral (3.1) doesn't include a calculation for financial gains or losses on the portfolio's bond holding – because the bond's price never changes – for **any** trading strategy $\{\theta_i(t); t \in [0,1], i = 1, \ldots, I\}$ for the I risky securities, the integral (3.1) describes the value process for a self-financing trading strategy, the risky-securities holdings of which are given by $\{\theta_i(t); t \in [0,1], i = 1, \ldots, I\}$.*

Of course, this is only an accounting identity, which works because the bond's price never changes. If a trading strategy for the I risky assets $\{\theta_i(t); t \in [0,1], i = 1, \ldots, I\}$ is specified, the bond holding at each moment is determined by the self-financing requirement. We can write down what that holding must be at each time t using the financial-gains integral. Since

$$\theta_0(t) + \sum_{i=1}^{I} \theta_i(t)S_i(t) = V(\theta, t) = V(\theta, 0) + \sum_{i=1}^{I} \int_0^t \theta_i(t)dS_i(t),$$

it must be that

$$\theta_0(t) = V(\theta, 0) + \sum_{i=1}^{I} \int_0^t \theta_i(t)dS_i(t) - \sum_{i=1}^{I} \theta_i(t)S_i(t). \tag{3.2}$$

What a boon this is for defining continuous trading and, simultaneously, incorporating the self-financing condition into the story. *Any portfolio strategy for the risky assets is okay, as long as the strategy, together with the given risky-security price processes, allows for a meaningful definition of the financial-gains integral.*

In fact, this is not so easy or straightforward as it may seem. Take the case of the BSM model, with one risky security ($I = 1$) whose evolution is geometric Brownian motion. This price process has infinite variation over every nontrivial time interval – Brownian motion moves "a lot" – so defining what is meant by dS, the differential of geometric Brownian motion or, perhaps more to the point, the *stochastic integral* $\int_0^t \theta(t)dS(t)$, requires some nontrivial mathematics. It can be, and is done, using the Itô theory of stochastic integration. But consider: For Itô differentials, the product rule says that $d(\theta_1 S_1) = \theta_1 dS_1 + S_1 d\theta_1 + dS_1 d\theta_1$, where the subscript 1 is used to denote the stock; subscript 0 will denote the bond. And if both θ_1 and S_1 are Itô processes, the term $d\theta_1 dS_1$ is *not* 0. Now use (3.2) to derive $d\theta_0$; it is

$$d\theta_0 = \theta_1 dS_1 - d(\theta_1 S_1) = \theta_1 dS_1 - \theta_1 dS_1 - S_1 d\theta_1 - dS_1 d\theta_1 = -S_1 d\theta_1 - dS_1 d\theta_1,$$

or $d\theta_0 + S_1 d\theta_1 = dS_1 d\theta_1$. The left-hand side of this equation, seemingly, is the momentary change in the bond holding times (implicitly) the unit price of the bond , plus the momentary change in the stock holding, times the price of the stock. *Doesn't self-financing mean that, at all points, this should be 0?* Because if it is an expression of the self-financing condition, we'd need $dS_1 d\theta_1$ to be 0, and, in general, this isn't true.

The point is: We can express the self-financing condition as $dV = \theta_1 dS_1$, which is (essentially) what is happening with the financial-gain integral way of doing business. Or we can express it as $d\theta_0 + S_1 d\theta_1 = 0$, which *seems* to be saying that the purchase of bonds and stock nets to 0. But, for stochastic integrals of the Itô type, if θ_1 is an Itô integral with a nontrivial Brownian component – which it is, in BSM – the two ways of expressing "self-financing" are not the same.

It turns out, as a consequence of how the Itô integral is defined – and more generally, how stochastic integrals are usually defined – that the financial-gain way of doing business is economically correct. The reason is that Itô integrals are forward looking: $\theta_1 dS_1$ is "defined" over a small interval of time from t to $t + h$ as the value of $\theta_1(t)$ times $S_1(t+h) - S_1(t)$. You fix the portfolio at the start of the interval, and accrue the financial gain over what happens after that. In contrast, $S_1 d\theta_1$ is defined as $S_1(t)$ times the difference $\theta_1(t + h) - \theta(t)$; you get to backdate the value of the trade you make to the price that prevailed at the start of the interval. Economically, that's cheating, which is why the financial-gain integral is "correct."

In the BSM Model, with Continuous Trading, Markets Are Complete

This, then, is the basic story in the literature of financial mathematics:

- First, the absence of "free lunches," suitably defined, is shown to imply the existence of an equivalent martingale measure, suitably generalized. The standard technology for doing this – for proving what is known in the literature as the Fundamental Theorem of Asset Pricing, or FTAP – is different from what happens in Proposition 3.1. Instead of taking $X = L^2(\Omega, F, P)$, it is typical that $X = L^\infty(\Omega, F, P)$. The notion of a "free lunch" from Chapter 2 is replaced by "a free lunch with vanishing risk," or a sequence of strategies that are, in the limit, a free lunch, and where any possible loss approaches 0 uniformly along the sequence. And, then, it is shown that "no free lunches with vanishing risk" implies the existence of a generalization of the notion of an equivalent martingale measure, involving notions of local martingales and sigma-martingales.[11] The math gets a bit thick in places, and the reader must consult other sources – I give references at the end of the chapter – to see how it all goes, but that's the spirit of the exercise.

- Then, using the general theory of stochastic integrals for martingales and semi-martingales, the space of "marketed securities" M is defined as the space of all (well-behaved) contingent claims x that can be written as an initial investment plus a stochastic integral with respect to the price process. In other words, x is an initial investment plus the integral of financial gains from a self-financing investment strategy, where integrands are restricted so that (a) the stochastic integrals make sense and (b) free lunches are avoided.

In the case of the simple BSM model, as well as for substantial generalizations, *every* (well-behaved) contingent claim x is marketed. Roughly, the logical chain is as follows: For any (well-behaved) claim x, $\mathbf{E}^{P^*}[x|F_t]$ is a martingale under the probability measure P^* (assuming integrability of x, which is one of the technical conditions.) Conversely, any martingale can be viewed as the conditional-expected-value process of its value at time 1. Hence, "markets are

---

[11] Conversely, Delbaen and Schachermayer (1994) show that if the price process is not a semi-martingale, then a free lunch with vanishing risk can be constructed using a sequence of simple trading rules. So, in a fundamental sense, the space of semi-martingales is the right space of stochastic processes for modeling financial markets.

complete" if and only if every martingale over the filtration generated by the original security prices can we written as a stochastic
integral with respect to those prices; that is,

$$V_x(t) = \mathbf{E}^{P^*}[x] + \int_0^t \theta(u)dS(u).$$

This property – that every martingale over the filtration generated
by a (vector) martingale can be written as a stochastic integral of
the original martingale – has been extensively studied in the mathematics literature, where it is called the Martingale Representation
Theorem. And the Martingale Representation Theorem is connected
to the uniqueness of equivalent martingale measures for the original
measure P. This gives the complete-markets result for the simple
BSM model discussed here as well as for substantial generalizations
of that model.

Editorial: Continuous-Time Trading as an Idealization

As mathematics, all this works. And there is a very substantial
literature that generalizes in many directions. But, in terms of economic
insights, I'm skeptical about what is learned *directly* from this theory.

As with any model – or at least, any model that is meant to say something about the real world – what we have here is a simplification and
stylization of reality. The question is: How far from the real world is
it? And when you come to conclusions through analysis of your model,
do you understand which assumptions in the model are driving those
conclusions?

Perhaps the most "mysterious" part of BSM is the nature of the
Brownian filtration. How general is this as a model of information flows
in the real world? Of course, we know of instances when there are sharp
breaks in expectations about future economic activity, something that
BSM misses. But is the flow of information in the BSM model a reasonable
model of information flows in "normal times?" And, because the key
result that markets are complete derives from the Martingale Representation Theorem: How special a result is this? What is the *economic* intuition
for this crucial result from mathematics?

It is also true that assumptions contained within the model are, at
least, economically suspicious. The elimination of doubling strategies is
a bit ad hoc, but overall it seems economically reasonable: At least, I don't

believe that I could convince my local bank to provide me with the funds required to carry out a doubling strategy in Las Vegas.

On the other hand, think of what sort of trading strategies are required to, say, synthesize the European call option, $x_C(\omega) = \max\{0, S(1, \omega) - 1\}$. The trading strategy that synthesizes this contingent claim has $\theta_1(t) = \Phi\big([\ln(S(t) + (1 - t)/2]/\sqrt{1 - t}\big)$, where $\Phi(\cdot)$ is the cumulative distribution function of a standard (mean 0, variance 1) Normal variate. That's not a simple formula, but it is not difficult to see that, for $t < 1$, it is differentiable in $S(t)$ and t. Which, since $S(t)$ has unbounded variation, implies that $\theta_1(t)$ will have unbounded variation. In other words, to synthesize the call option, the consumer must generate an infinite total trading volume. Perhaps that's a reasonable modeling conceit. But it is a lot to swallow.

Put it this way: We've assumed that there are no transaction costs, whatsoever. In terms of synthesizing contingent claims, if there are transaction costs on buying and selling securities, the theory won't be nearly as neat. But, for a fixed simple trading strategy, at least, the total transaction cost incurred goes to 0 as the level of transaction costs goes to 0. Hence, we can view our developments, insofar as we do not progress beyond simple trading strategies, as being a theory of "almost synthesis," as the level of transaction costs approaches 0. But if the total trade volume is infinite, it doesn't matter how small the transaction costs are. If transaction costs are positive, they completely overwhelm what the trading strategy is attempting to accomplish.

I'm not saying that the BSM model is a bad model of the real world. But there are reasons for doubt or, at least, skepticism. One way to build confidence in the model is to answer the question: Does the BSM model give economically similar answers to models of securities markets that we can understand more readily? Or, put a bit more operationally: Which models of security markets have economically meaningful properties – and what are those properties – that are similar to those of BSM?

Note that this second formulation of the question provides us with two tasks. We must identify economically meaningful properties to use as tests, and then we need to test with those properties, to see which models (that are easier to comprehend) come close to BSM.

Here, at last, we have arrived at the point of this monograph. The plan is to see to what extent the BSM model is an idealization of models in which markets are open only at a discrete set of times, but where trading opportunities recur rapidly. The broader the class of discrete-but-

rapid-trading models that are idealized by BSM, and the more economically meaningful ways this is true, the greater faith we can have in the
lessons that can be drawn from the BSM model.

Bibliographic Notes

Seminal references for models of continuous-time dynamic trading
are Merton (1971, 1973b, 1977). Of particular note in this regard is the
Merton (1977) paper, which presents the first description of how, in the
context of the BSM economy, an investor can synthesize contingent claims
written on the history of the stock price by trading dynamically in the
stock and bond. Also, the conundrum discussed on page 50 – which of
two "obvious" but inconsistent ways to express the self-financing condition – is first resolved in Merton (1971).

In terms of the history of more formal and complete developments,
it is easiest to separate the two pieces described by the bullet points on
pages 51–3:

- *The Fundamental Theorem of Asset Pricing, or FTAP*; or how one justifies
  the existence of an equivalent martingale measure (or a generalization
  of same) and thereby permits stochastic integration and the use of the
  financial-gains integral: As discussed, the literature on this bifurcates
  based on whether one takes $X = L^p(\Omega, F, P)$ for $p < \infty$ or $p = \infty$. The
  first approach, taken here, is simpler. Harrison and Kreps (1979) take
  this approach, more or less: They work with the definition of viability
  used in Chapter 2, but assume consumers have consumption sets that
  are all of X and that are continuous and convex in addition to being
  strictly increasing. That, as we noted, is equivalent to the definition
  of viability in this chapter. For a detailed treatment of this approach,
  see Stricker (1990).

  The alternative approach, with $X = L^\infty(\Omega, F, P)$, is significantly
  more complex, as (in the end) it involves an extension of the classic
  Hahn–Banach Theorem. The first (and, I am allowed to say, fairly
  primitive) paper on the subject is Kreps (1981). Important steps in
  improving and generalizing the result are due to Dalang, Morton,
  and Willinger (1990), concerning discrete parameter (but infinite Ω)
  models, and a series of papers by Delbaen and Schachermayer for the
  continuous-time case. The seminal paper in this series is Delbaen and
  Schachermayer (1994); see also Delbaen and Schachermayer (2006) for
  both the basic "plot" and a complete account of the steps in developing

this approach.

- Harrison and Pliska (1981, 1983) are the seminal references concerning the use of the financial-gains integral and the theory of stochastic integration for semi-martingales to find the "full" space of marketed claims and, in cases like BSM, to show that markets are complete. The first paper connects market completeness to the Martingale Representation Theorem; the second paper connects these two equivalent properties to uniqueness of equivalent martingale measures.

The reader interested in pursuing these details in depth is probably best off consulting a unified treatment of the subject, of which there are many. With apologies to authors whose books and monographs I do not list, among the books I know best (at different levels), besides Delbaen and Schachermayer (2006), are Duffie (2001), Karatzas and Shreve (2014), Shreve (2004), and Williams (2006). Also, for a more complete development of the history of these ideas, see Schachermayer (2010).

4. BSM as an Idealization of Binomial-Random-Walk Economies

In this chapter, we examine the path set first by Sharpe (1978) and Cox, Ross, and Rubinstein (1979), a path that is, I believe, almost universally employed when first "explaining" BSM to students. We take the binomial random walk (or hat) models from Chapter 2 and ask: For large n, which means rapid trading opportunities at times $t = 0, 1/n, 2/n, \ldots, (n-1)/n$, in which economically relevant senses are the binomial-random-walk economies similar to BSM? One answer can be given immediately: In each of the binomial-random-walk economies, markets are complete, which is also true of BSM. That, of course, is not a convergence result: Markets in the binomial-random-walk economy for $n = 2$ are complete, and yet one wouldn't say the $n = 2$ economy is similar to the BSM economy.

For a convergence result, we begin with Cox, Ross, and Rubinstein (1979). In BSM and in each of binomial-random-walk economies, a consumer can synthesize the classic European call option with exercise price 1: $x_C(\omega) = \max\{0, S(1, \omega) - 1\}$. My notation here is poor, as these are separate economies, with separate state spaces; to be clearer about things, I'll use (for the time being) a superscript n for the nth binomial-random-walk economy, and no extra markings for BSM. (Since the binomial-random-walk economies for different n are the only discrete-time economies I'll consider in this chapter, for the balance of the chapter I drop the hats and refer simply to "the nth economy"; it should always be understood in this chapter that this means "the nth binomial-random-walk economy.") So Cox, Ross, and Rubinstein compare

$$x_C^n(\omega^n) := \max\{0, S^n(1, \omega^n) - 1\} \text{ for large } n \text{ with}$$

$$x_C(\omega) := \max\{0, S(1, \omega) - 1\}.$$

Let θ^n be the trading strategy in the nth economy that synthesizes x_C^n, and let θ be the trading strategy that synthesizes x_C. They prove that

$$\lim_{n \to \infty} V^n(\theta^n, 0) = V(\theta, 0),$$

where V^n is the value process in the nth discrete-time economy. In words, the initial investment required to synthesize x_C^n converges as $n \to \infty$ to the initial investment needed to synthesize x_C.

It is generally believed that this convergence result is not limited to the call option, and our first task is to answer the question: *For which contingent claims x is it true that the initial investment required to synthesize x in the nth economy approaches the initial investment required to synthesize x in BSM?*

One State Space

The question just posed doesn't quite make sense: The "natural" state spaces for the discrete-time economies are different from what is "natural" for BSM, and since contingent claims are functions from the (respective) state spaces to the real line, writing x for a contingent claim means different things for different n and in the limit. We first of all must find a way to identify claims in one economy with claims in another economy.

One way we might do this is to identify claims as specific functions of the price processes. For instance, for the European call option with exercise price 1, we first define $C_1 : [0, \infty) \to [0, \infty)$ by $C_1(r) := \max\{0, r - 1\}$ and then, for each n (and in the limit), identify x_c^n as $C_1(S^n(1, \omega))$. However, a different way of doing business, while a bit more challenging at first, will facilitate proofs: We put all the economies on a common state space, Ω. Then a contingent claim x – a function from Ω to R – is a single well-defined thing. And we can do this – we can conduct our business on a common state space Ω – by having, for each n and in the limit, *different probability measures P^n and P on Ω.*

The common space we use is $C[0, 1]$, the space of continuous functions from $[0, 1]$ to the real line. Write ω for a member of $C[0, 1]$ – that is, ω is a continuous function from $[0, 1]$ to R – and write $\omega(t)$ as the value of the function ω at time t, for $t \in [0, 1]$. Endow $\Omega = C[0, 1]$ with the sup-norm topology; that is, the distance between two continuous functions ω and ω' is $\max\{|\omega(t) - \omega'(t)|; t \in [0, 1]\}$. With respect to this measure of distance (or norm), Ω is a complete separable metric space. Let F be the Borel σ field on Ω and, for $t \in [0, 1]$, let F_t be the Borel σ field generated by the value of ω from time 0 to time t.

The next step is to put probability distributions P and P^n on this space. For P, we use Wiener measure, where we identify ω as a path of the underlying Brownian motion; hence, $S(t, \omega) = e^{\omega(t)}$ under P.

As for the P^n: Go back to the binomial random walk $\{B^n(k/n); k = 0, 1, \ldots, n\}$ used in defining the nth economy. For each n, there are 2^n "paths" that are possible for this random walk, and P^n will give each one of those paths probability $1/2^n$. I put "paths" in scare quotes because the random walk is only defined at times k/n for $k = 0, 1, \ldots$; to turn the random walk "path" into an element of $C[0, 1]$, use linear interpolation between the path's values at consecutive times k/n and $(k + 1)/n$. P^n, then, is the discrete probability measure with 2^n elements in its support, each one a "zig-zag" path that, over each time interval k/n to $(k + 1)/n$, either increases linearly by $1/\sqrt{n}$ or decreases linearly by that amount. And the price of the stock in the nth economy at time t is given by the same formula $S(t) = e^{\omega(t)}$, but now with respect to the probability measure P^n.

To be very pedantic here: A single function $S : C[0, 1] \to C[0, 1]$ is fixed. Given $\omega \in C[0, 1]$, $S(\omega)$ is the function from $C[0, 1]$ defined by $(S(\omega))(t) := e^{\omega(t)}$. Viewing S this way, as a function from $C[0, 1]$ to $C[0, 1]$, makes it natural to write $(S(\omega))(t)$ or $S(\omega)(t)$ for the value of the function $S(\omega)$ at time t, emphasizing that $S(\omega)$, like ω, is an element of $C[0, 1]$. We sometimes write things this way, but we also write $S(t, \omega)$, which is consistent with the notation in earlier chapters, to mean the same thing. The difference between the nth economy and the n'th economy, and the difference between the nth economy and the BSM economy, derives *entirely and only* from the probability measures they variously prescribe over $C[0, 1]$.

Readers for whom this sort of construction is new are likely to find it difficult to comprehend at first. I apologize, but given where we are going, this way of doing business pays huge dividends later on. If you find this difficult to comprehend at first, please work with this construction until you get the idea.

$C[0,1]$ versus $D[0,1]$

At the other end of the readership spectrum, readers familiar with the literature of financial mathematics will likely wince at my use of $C[0, 1]$ instead of $D[0, 1]$. (If you struggled with the previous section, it might be a good idea to skip this one.) To explain, elements of $D[0, 1]$ are functions from $[0, 1]$ to the real line that are right-continuous and have left limits. [1]

---

[1] A lot of the theory of these things depends on pieces of probability that were first

Most of the literature conducts its business in $D[0,1]$.

Of course, $C[0,1]$ is a subspace within $D[0,1]$, but working in $D[0,1]$ gives us the ability to include more security-price processes. For instance, let $\{z(t); t \in [0,1]\}$ be a Poisson process with uniform downward drift, but with jumps up of size 1 at Poisson arrival times with arrival rate 1. Suppose we have a market in which there is a single stock, whose price process is $e^{z(t)}$. Readers may recall the Cox and Ross (1976) paper, which worked with stock-price processes of this sort. (Föllmer's example also has this general character, but with a jump size that approaches 0 for early jumps; it is that small jump size early on that causes the difficulties we saw.) Or we could think of a stock-price process that is, for the most part, a geometric Brownian motion, but with discrete jumps at Poisson arrival times. The sample paths of the stock price (or the log of the stock price) are not continuous. But they do live in $D[0,1]$.[2]

Everything we do in this chapter could be conducted if we had $\Omega = D[0,1]$ instead of $C[0,1]$. But, because Brownian motion has continuous sample paths, as long as we limit our discussion to BSM, it isn't necessary to use $D[0,1]$. And working with $D[0,1]$ presents a complication, a completely surmountable complication, but a nonetheless a complication that makes the subject less penetrable. Imagine, for instance, that we wanted to show results about the convergence of discrete-time economies to the economy based on a Poisson process sketched in the previous paragraph. Prices in the nth discrete-time economy are realized at times $0, 1/n, 2/n, \ldots$. We form a discrete-time stochastic process z^n that, at time k/n, equals $z^n((k-1)/n) - 1/n$ with probability $(n-1)/n$ or $z^n((k-1)/n) + 1$ with probability $1/n$. And $S^n(k/n) = e^{z^n(k/n)}$. As $n \to \infty$, this stock-price process "converges" to $S(t) = e^{z(t)}$ from last paragraph. And results of the sort we are about to show for the nth binomial economies versus BSM will hold. But, in this extension, measuring distance between sample paths – which we will see is important – cannot be done using the sup-norm topology. Roughly put, $S(t)$, if it jumps at all, jumps are times t for irrational t with probability 1. $S^n(k/n)$

---

developed by French mathematicians. So if you've seen the expression *càdlàg* used in a paper on these matters, this is short for *continue à droit, limite à gauche*, which is French for right continuous, with left limits.

[2] In Chapter 6 we discuss both the Cox and Ross model and the hybrid that combines geometric Brownian motion with the Cox–Ross model, at which point formal analysis requires us to move from C to D.

jumps only at rational times t. So if we measured distance with the sup norm, a path that jumped at time, say, $\pi/4$, would be very far from the same path with a jump at time $3.14159/4$. The "right" way to measure distance in $D[0,1]$ involves allowing slight deformations of time, so that a jump at time t is viewed as "close to" a jump of the same size at a time t', if t and t' are close together. This is done with what is called the Skorohod topology on $D[0,1]$. And, to reiterate, everything works out very nicely. But it does complicate the exposition.

Working in $C[0,1]$ does have one unfortunate feature. Recall that we placed the nth binomial random walk into $C[0,1]$ by using linear interpolation between times k/n and $(k+1)/n$. This means that the corresponding $S(t) = e^{\omega(t)}$, for paths ω in the support of P^n, will be continuous, but they will also have "momentum" over time intervals $[k/n, (k+1)/n]$: If the path of $S(t)$ starts going up immediately after $t = k/n$, it will inexorably continue to rise until time reaches $(k+1)/n$. Investors cannot take advantage of this momentum, because (we suppose) markets in the nth discrete-time economy are only open at times $t = k/n$. But, when we speak of the equivalent martingale measure P^{*n} for the nth economy – a probability measure equivalent to P^n (with precisely the same 2^n-element support in Ω) – it does not turn $\{S(t); t \in [0,1]\}$ into a martingale. Instead, it turns $\{S(k/n); k = 0,1,\ldots,n\}$ into a martingale. If we were working with $D[0,1]$ instead of $C[0,1]$, this ugliness can be avoided: Instead of making the nth binomial random walk into a continuous path by using linear interpolation, we could turn it into a path in $D[0,1]$ by saying that it says fixed over each interval $[k/n, (k+1)/n)$. On balance, however, it will help the exposition to avoid the complications that $D[0,1]$ would cause, even given this uglification concerning what is an equivalent martingale measure.

One State Space, Continued

So, we have a single state space $\Omega = C[0,1]$, a single filtration $\{F_t\}$ (where F is F_1), a sequence $\{P^n; n = 1,2,\ldots\}$ of discrete probability measures on $C[0,1]$, and one more probability measure P, Wiener measure. Let $\mathbf{E}$ denote expectation with respect to P and $\mathbf{E}^n$ expectation with respect to P^n.

In this setting, a general contingent claim is a function $x : C[0,1] \rightarrow R$. Always implicit in the term "contingent claim" is the assumption that x is F-measurable. Examples include contingent claims x that are functions of $S(1, \omega) = S(\omega)(1) = e^{\omega(1)}$; that is, functions of the final stock price. But there are also claims that are functions of the stock price at other (single) times $t \in [0, 1)$ (and which are therefore F_t measurable), claims that are functions of the stock price at a finite set of times $t_1, t_2, \ldots, t_M$, and claims which are functions of the entire path of the stock-price history; for instance, $x^{\text{MAX}}(\omega) = \max\{S(\omega)(t) = e^{\omega(t)}; t \in [0, 1]\}$, as well as a call option on x^{MAX}, or $z(\omega) = \max\{0, x^{\text{MAX}}(\omega) - 1\}$, claims that were initially investigated in Goldman, Sosin, and Gatto (1979).

Recall from Chapters 2 and 3 that there exist probabilities P^{*n} and P^*, defined on Ω, such that the following hold:

- Each P^{*n} is equivalent to P^n (has precisely the same 2^n element support), and P^* is equivalent to P.

- Under P^*, $\{S(t); t \in [0, 1]\}$ is a martingale (over $\{F_t\}$). Let $\mathbf{E}^*$ denote expectation with respect to P^*. The Radon–Nikodym derivative dP^*/dP, which we denote p^*, is (for $\Omega = C[0, 1]$) $p^*(\omega) = 1/e^{\omega(1)/2 + 1/8}$.

- Under P^{*n}, $\{S(k/n); k = 0, 1, \ldots, n\}$ is a martingale (over the discrete filtration $\{F_{k/n}; k = 0, 1, \ldots, n\}$.) Let $\mathbf{E}^{*n}$ denote expectation with respect to P^{*n}. (We will develop formulas for dP^{*n}/dP^n shortly.)

- P^* is the unique equivalent martingale measure to P. Every contingent claim x (at least, every contingent claim x that is square-integrable with respect to P) can be synthesized by self-financing trading in the stock and bond in the sense of Chapter 3. The initial investment needed to synthesize x is $\mathbf{E}^*[x]$.

- P^{*n} is the unique measure equivalent to P^n under which $\{S(k/n); k = 0, 1, \ldots, n\}$ is a martingale. Every contingent claim x can be synthesized by self-financing trading in the stock and bond in the nth economy. The initial investment needed to synthesize x is $\mathbf{E}^{*n}[x]$.

Be careful when interpreting the last two bullet points. Consider the contingent claim x given by

$$x^o(\omega) = \begin{cases} 2, & \text{if } \omega(1) \text{ is transcendental, and} \\ 1, & \text{if } \omega(1) \text{ is algebraic.} \end{cases}$$

Under P (and hence P^*), $x^o = 2$, with probability 1. So $\mathbf{E}^*[x^o] = 2$. And one "synthesizes" x^o in the BSM economy by purchasing and holding two bonds. On the other hand, under P^n for any n, and hence under all the P^{*n}, $x^o = 1$ with probability 1. So $\mathbf{E}^{*n}[x^o] = 1$ for all n; and in the nth binomial economy, one synthesizes x^o by buying and holding one bond.

It is true that we are working on a single state space and that contingent claims are functions from that state space to the real line. But, for a given probability measure on that state space, a contingent claim becomes a random variable on the probability space, and random variables do not "change" if you change their values on sets of probability 0.[3] So, under P and P^*, the function x^o as defined above is the "same" random variable as the claim that pays 2 in every state, while under P^n and P^{*n}, x^o is the same random variable as the claim that pays 1 in every state. P and P^* are mutually singular to P^n and P^{*n} for all n, so the "same" claim x^o – a given real-valued *function* on Ω – can be wildly different as *random variables* under P or P^* and any of the P^n or P^{*n}.

Generalizing Cox, Ross, and Rubinstein

In the terminology and notation developed here, Cox, Ross, and Rubinstein's classic (1979) paper shows that

$$\lim_{n \to \infty} \mathbf{E}^{*n}[x_C] = \mathbf{E}^*[x_C];$$

the initial investment required to synthesize the call option (with exercise price 1) in the nth binomial economy converges, as n goes to infinity, to the initial investment required to synthesize the call option in BSM. But the example of x^o just developed shows that this does not hold for all contingent claims. To generalize the Cox, Ross, and Rubinstein result to other contingent claims, some conditions on the contingent claim x will be required. Because x^o is discontinuous everywhere, one wonders: Is continuity of x sufficient?

This is where the sup-norm topology on $C[0, 1]$ enters the story. When we say that x is continuous, we mean that if $\{\omega_\ell : \ell = 1, \ldots\}$ is a sequence

---

[3] Readers may recognize this as the statement that a random variable on a probability space is really an equivalence class of functions on the state space, where two functions are equivalent if they agree with probability 1.

of elements of $C[0,1]$ that converge in the sup norm topology to $w \in \Omega$, then continuity of x means that $\lim_\ell x(w_\ell) = x(w)$. Suppose, for instance, that $x(w) = f(e^{w(1)}) = f(S(1,w))$ for some function $f : R \to R$; the contingent claim's value only depends on the time 1 value of the stock. This is true, for instance, for both x_C and x^o. Then, if f is a continuous function, x will be continuous. Of course, the f for x^o is massively discontinuous, while the f for x_C is continuous. Other examples of continuous contingent claims x are claims that are continuous functions of the stock price at a finite number of states and the claim x^{MAX} .

Continuity of x is not enough. But it is in the right direction:

Proposition 4.1. *If x is a bounded and continuous contingent claim,*

$$\lim_{n \to \infty} \mathbf{E}^n[x] = \mathbf{E}[x] \quad and \quad \lim_{n \to \infty} \mathbf{E}^{*n}[x] = \mathbf{E}^*[x].$$

That is, for any bounded and continuous contingent claim x, the initial investment required to synthesize x in the nth binomial economy converges to the initial investment required to synthesize x in the BSM economy.

We already know from the example x^o that discontinuities can pose problems. Here is an example to show that continuity by itself is not enough: Recall from page 22 that $\pi^{*n} = 1/(e^{1/\sqrt{n}} + 1)$ is the probability of an "uptick" for the nth binomial-random-walk model under P^{*n}. Hence, among other things,

$$P^{*n}(\{w(1) = \sqrt{n}\}) = (\pi^{*n})^n,$$

where the n outside the parentheses on the right-hand side of this equation means "raised to the power n." This is so because $w(1) = \sqrt{n}$ for only one path under P^n and P^{*n}, namely the path that has the random walk move up in value on each step. Consider the contingent claim x of the form $x(w) = f(w(1))$, where $f : R_+ \to R_+$ equals 0 for most of its arguments, but at the values $r = \sqrt{n}$, rises to the height $n/(\pi^{*n})^n$. It does this in continuous fashion: Over a very small neighborhoold of $\sqrt{n}$, the neighborhood $\sqrt{n} \pm (\pi^{n*})^{3n}/n$, it rises and then falls linearly, forming a very tall, very very thin isoceles triangle. The area of the triangle, even if its height is squared, is less than $(\pi^{*n})^n$, which obviously makes the claim finitely integrable with respect to both P and P^*. But because the spikes occur precisely at points where P^n and P^{*n} put mass $1/2^n$ and $(\pi^{*n})^n$, respectively, its expectations with respect to P^n and P^{*n} both approach ∞ as n approaches ∞.

While this example shows that unbounded and continuous claims *may* be problematic, the literature tells us that some continuous and unbounded claims, x_C, the canonical call option, and x^{MAX} are both unbounded and both "work." Perhaps Proposition 4.1 can be extended to some continuous contingent claims that, while unbounded, are not so wildly unbounded as the previous example. And, in the same spirit, perhaps Proposition 4.1 can be extended to claims that are discontinuous, but not so wildly discontinuous as x^o. Both "perhaps" are answered with "yes, it is possible," and we'll provide partial results later in this chapter. But, first, Proposition 4.1 needs a proof.

The proof of Proposition 4.1 comes down to demonstrating that $P^n \Rightarrow P$ and $P^{n*} \Rightarrow P^*$, where $\Rightarrow$ is the symbol used for *weak convergence of probability measures*. You are (almost certainly) familiar with weak convergence of probability measures on the real line, although you may not know the concept by that name. But, in this context, where all the probability measures are defined on $C[0, 1]$, $\Rightarrow$ means weak convergence of the probability measures on that space, or *functional weak convergence*. Since (I anticipate) many readers will not know what this means or how things like this are proved, the next two sections provide background. (Readers familiar with functional weak convergence and Donsker's Theorem can safely skip the next two sections.)

Weak Convergence in General

Consider the classic Central Limit Theorem, a simple version of which is: Suppose $\{z_k; k = 1, 2, \ldots\}$ is a sequence of i.i.d. random variables with mean 0 and variance 1. To match up with developments in this chapter, think concretely of $z_k = +1$ or -1, each with probability $1/2$. Look at the random variables

$$Z^n = \frac{1}{\sqrt{n}} \sum_{k=1}^{n} z_k.$$

As n goes to infinity, Z^n converges in distribution to a Normally distributed random variable with mean 0 and variance 1, which I'll temporarily label Z.

Convergence in distribution is in fact a statement about the probability *distributions* of the random variables Z^n and a standard unit Normal Z. Unlike convergence in probability or almost-sure convergence, there is no immediate requirement that the Z^n and Z live on the same probability space. Put another way, suppose μ^n is the (scaled binomial) probability distribution on R induced by Z^n and μ is the probability distribution of the standard Normal. Instead of saying that Z^n *converges in distribution to* Z, we equivalently say that μ^n *converges weakly to* μ, writing $\mu_n \Rightarrow \mu$.

What do these two equivalent statements mean? Most treatments of the Central Limit Theorem (I believe) define the phrase "convergence in distribution" in terms of the cumulative distribution functions F_n of Z^n and F of the unit Normal: F_n converges to F in this sense if $\lim_n F_n(x) = F(x)$ for every continuity point of $F(x)$ (which, for the standard Normal, is every $x \in R$).

But, from a mathematical point of view, a better way to operationalize this form of convergence is: A sequence of probability measures $\{\mu^n\}$ on R converges weakly to a probability measure μ on R if, for every function $f : R \to R$ that is bounded and continuous, $\int f(x)\mu_n(dx) \to \int f(x)\mu(dx)$. Note that we can write the same condition in terms of the random variables Z^n and Z: A sequence of real-valued random variables $\{Z^n\}$ converges in distribution to the real-valued random variable Z if, for every function $f : R \to R$ that is bounded and continuous, $E[f(Z^n)] \to E[f(Z)]$.

For real-valued random variables, the measures on R that they induce, and their cumulative distribution functions, these are equivalent ways of operationalizing (a) convergence in distribution of the random variables or (b) weak convergence of the measures or distribution functions. That is, you can use either (with an "if") as your definition of this mode of convergence, and then prove that the other is an equivalent characterization (with an "if and only if"). Moreover, $\mu_n \Rightarrow \mu$ is also equivalent to

- $\lim \sup_n \mu_n(A) \le \mu(A)$ for all closed sets $A \subseteq R$, and

- $\lim \inf_n \mu_n(B) \ge \mu(B)$ for all open sets $B \subseteq R$.

This is all for measures on the real line. But the same concepts work mathematically for measures defined on any metric space $\mathcal{S}$. (Measurability is defined relative to the Borel σ field on $\mathcal{S}$, which we denote by

$\mathcal{F}$. We'll temporarily use s to denote generic elements of $\mathcal{S}$.)

Definition. *If $\{\mu_n\}$ is a sequence of probability measures on $(\mathcal{S}, \mathcal{F})$ and μ is another probability measure on $(\mathcal{S}, \mathcal{F})$, we say that $\mu_n \Rightarrow \mu$, read as "the sequence $\{\mu_n\}$ converges weakly to μ," if for all bounded and continuous functions $f : \mathcal{S} \to R$, $\lim_n \int_{\mathcal{S}} f(s)\mu_n(ds) = \int_{\mathcal{S}} f(s)\mu(ds)$ or, written differently, $\lim_n \mathbf{E}^{\mu_n}[f(s)] = \mathbf{E}^{\mu}[f(s)]$.*

The Portmanteau Theorem for Weak Convergence of Probabilities. *The following are equivalent ways of defining weak convergence of probability measures on a metric space:*

a. $\lim_n \int_{\mathcal{S}} f(s)\mu_n(ds) = \int_{\mathcal{S}} f(s)\mu(ds)$ *for all bounded and continuous real-valued functions on $\mathcal{S}$.*

b. $\lim_n \int_{\mathcal{S}} f(s)\mu_n(ds) = \int_{\mathcal{S}} f(s)\mu(ds)$ *for all bounded and **uniformly** continuous real-valued functions on $\mathcal{S}$.*

c. $\lim \sup_n \mu_n(A) \leq \mu(A)$ *for all closed sets $A \subseteq \mathcal{S}$.*

d. $\lim \inf_n \mu_n(B) \geq \mu(B)$ *for all open sets $B \subseteq \mathcal{S}$.*

e. $\lim_n \mu_n(G) = \mu(G)$ *for all sets $G \subseteq \mathcal{S}$ whose boundary ∂G has probability 0 under μ.*

For a proof, see Billingsley (1999, Theorem 2.1).[4]

Once you've internalized this definition of weak convergence on a general metric space $\mathcal{S}$, you can anticipate what comes next: $C[0, 1]$ with the sup norm metric is a metric space, and we'll be doing things like showing that $P^{*n} \Rightarrow P^*$, on that space.

Please note: Proposition 4.1 states that for every bounded and continuous function x on Ω,

$$\lim_n \mathbf{E}^n[x] = \mathbf{E}[x] \quad \text{and} \quad \lim_n \mathbf{E}^{*n}[x] = \mathbf{E}^*[x].$$

But this is the definition of, respectively, $P^n \Rightarrow P$ and $P^{*n} \Rightarrow P^*$. Let me emphasize this: *The conclusion of Proposition 4.1 is the **definition** of functional weak convergence. If we can show that $P^n \Rightarrow P$ and $P^{*n} \Rightarrow P^*$, the*

---

[4] These characterizations of weak convergence make it clear that the concept is topological: Any equivalent metric on $\mathcal{S}$ would give the same notion of weak convergence. Indeed, a neighborhood base for the topology of weak convergence is all sets of the form $\{\mu' : | \int f_n(x)\mu'(dx) - \int f_n(x)\mu(dx)| < \epsilon \text{ for } n = 1, 2, \ldots, N\}$, for each μ, finite collection of continuous and bounded functions $f_1, f_2, \ldots, f_N$, and for strictly positive ϵ. For measures on R, this topology is metrizable, by the Prohorov metric.

conclusion of Proposition 4.1 follows definitionally. So, to prove Proposition 4.1, we need to find another way, besides verifying the definition, to show these weak convergence results.

That "other way" employs the following general result.

Theorem 4.1. Characterizations of weak convergence of measures on $C[0, 1]$. *Given a sequence of probability measure* $\{Q^n\}$ *and a "target" distribution* Q, *all on* $C[0, 1]$, *for* $Q^n \Rightarrow Q$ *to hold, it is necessary and sufficient that* a *and* b *hold:*

a. *Each finite-dimensional distribution of* ω *under* Q^n *converges to its counterpart under* Q. *That is, for each integer* L *and selection of* L *times* $t_1, t_2, \ldots, t_L$, *the joint probability distributions of* $(\omega(t_1), \omega(t_2), \ldots, \omega(t_L))$ *under the* Q^n *must converge weakly to the corresponding joint distribution under* Q.

b. *The family* $\{Q^n\}$ *must be* **tight**: *For every* $\epsilon > 0$, *there exists a compact set* K *(in* $C[0, 1]$*) such that* $Q^n(K) > 1 - \epsilon$ *for all* n.

Moreover, for a sequence of measures on $C[0, 1]$, $\{Q^n\}$, *to be tight, it is necessary and sufficient that:*

c. *For each* $\eta > 0$, *there exist an* a *and an* n_0 *such that*

$$Q^n(\{\omega : |\omega(0) \geq a|\}) \leq \eta \text{ for all } n > n_0.$$

d. *For each* $\epsilon > 0$ *and* $\eta > 0$, *there exist a* δ, $0 < \delta < 1$, *and an* n_0 *such that*

$$Q^n(\{\omega : w(\delta, \omega) \geq \epsilon\}) \leq \eta \text{ for all } n > n_0,$$

where $w(\delta, \omega) := \sup\{|\omega(t) - \omega(t')|; \ t, t' \in [0, 1], |t - t'| \leq \delta\}$ *is the modulus-of-continuity function.*

While I employ these results,[5] I do not provide a proof. For the reader who wishes to see all the details, I recommend Billingsley (1999), with the warning that these results are spread out over several chapters.[6]

---

[5] Specifically, to show $P^{*n} \Rightarrow P^*$, I show a and b; b is shown using c and d.

[6] While it is far from a demonstration that c and d are necessary and sufficient for tightness, or why tighness is required for weak convergence, the following example taken from Billingsley provides some intuition: Let Q be the probability measure on $C[0,1]$ that assigns probability 1 to the path $\omega^0(t) = 0$ for all t. And let Q^n be the probability measure on $C[0,1]$ that assigns probability 1 to the path $\omega^n(t) = nt$ for $0 \leq t \leq 1/n$, $= 2 - nt$ for $1/n \leq t \leq 2/n$, and $= 0$ for $t \geq 2/n$. (That is, ω^n is an isoceles triangle over the

Before moving on, here is a useful corollary to the characterization of tightness in $C[0, 1]$ provided by c and d:

Corollary 4.1. *Suppose the sequence of measures* $\{Q^n\}$ *on* $C[0, 1]$ *is tight. Then for every* $\eta > 0$ *there exist* $A > 0$ *and* n_0 *such that*

$$Q^n\left(\{\omega : \sup\{|\omega(t)|; t \in [0, 1]\} \leq A\}\right) > 1 - \eta, \quad \text{for all } n > n_0.$$

In words, "most" of the paths ω are uniformly (in the Q^n) bounded: For $\eta > 0$, a (larger-the-smaller-is-η) set $[-A, A]$ can be found such that, under all the Q^n, the probability that $\omega(t)$ ever exits the set $[-A, A]$ is η or less. The proof is simple: Split η into two. Apply condition c to find an a such that, with probability less than $\eta/2$, under any Q^n ($n \geq n_0$ for some n_0), ω starts more than a away from 0. Then pick $\epsilon = 1/10$, say, and use condition d to produce a δ and an n_0' such that, for all $n \geq n_0$, the Q^n probability that $w(\delta, \omega) \geq 1/10$ is less than $\eta/2$. But then, for each Q^n ($n \geq \max\{n_0, n_0'\}$), the probability of a path that ever reaches a distance greater than $A = a + 0.1(1 + 1/\delta)$ from 0 is less than η.

Donsker's Theorem

Billingsley provides a proof of the following classic result:

Donsker's Theorem. *Take any i.i.d. sequence of random variables* $\{z_k\}$, *such that each* z_k *has mean 0 and variance 1. For each* n *and* $k = 0, 1, 2, \ldots, n$, *define*

$$Z^n(k/n) = \frac{1}{\sqrt{n}} \sum_{j=1}^{k} z_k.$$

Turn each path of the "process" $\{Z^n(k/n); k = 0, 1, \ldots, n\}$ *into a continuous function on* $[0, 1]$ *by linearly interpolating between consecutive values, and let*

---

range $[0, 2/n]$ with height 1, and is 0 otherwise.) Since $f(\omega) := \max\{\omega(t); t \in [0, 1]\}$ is a continuous linear functional on $C[0, 1]$, $Q^n[f(\omega)] = 1$ for all n, and $Q[f(\omega)] = 0$, it is clear that Q^n does not converge weakly to Q. But all finite-dimensional distributions of the Q^n converge to the corresponding finite-dimensional distribution of Q. The problem is a violation of condition d: Because the moduli of continuity of ω^n do not converge, they can get far from ω^0 quickly (and return quickly), which presents insuperable problems for bounded and continuous functions on $C[0, 1]$ such as f. For more intuition, see the last three paragraphs of the proof of the subsection *Extending the proof* ... in Billingsley (1999, pp. 99ff).

Q^n be the probability distribution on $\Omega = C[0, 1]$ induced by this process. Then $Q^n \Rightarrow P$, where P is Wiener measure on $C[0, 1]$.

So, in particular, for our binomial-random-walk economies, $P^n \Rightarrow P$.

Donsker's Theorem is the functional version of the Central Limit Theorem. By the standard Center Limit Theorem, in the setting of Donsker's Theorem, we know that the probability distribution of $Z^n(1)$ converges weakly to the unit Normal distribution, which is the distribution of Brownian motion at time 1. And, for any $t \in [0, 1]$, it only takes a slight tweak on the standard Central Limit Theorem to show that the distribution of $Z^n(t)$ converges weakly to a Normal with mean 0 and variance t, which is the distribution of Brownian motion at time t. Indeed, using the "independent increments" properties of Brownian motion and random walks, it is not that hard to show (and should appeal to your intuition) that for any finite collection of times $t_1, t_2, \ldots, t_L$, all between 0 and 1 (inclusive), the joint distribution of $\left(Z^n(t_1), Z^n(t_2), \ldots, Z^n(t_L) \right)$ converges weakly to the joint distribution of Brownian motion at those times. I'm not claiming that the proof of these things can be written down in one line or two; the fact that, for most times $t \in [0, 1]$, $Z^n(t)$ will be on one of the linearly interpolated pieces makes for (at least) some complications. But, with an understanding of the Central Limit Theorem, these consequences should be intuitive.

That's the first step in proving that $Q^n \Rightarrow P$. The second step is to show tightness of $\{Q^n\}$, which is done using the characterization of tightness given by conditions c and d of Theorem 4.1. Showing that condition c holds is trivial in this case: $\omega(0) = 0$ with Q^n-probability 1. The hard work is in showing condition d; see Billingsley (1999), if you must.

Proof of Proposition 4.1

We aim to show that $P^n \Rightarrow P$ and $P^{*n} \Rightarrow P^*$. The first is a direct implication of Donsker's Theorem, so nothing more is needed. As for $P^{*n} \Rightarrow P^*$: This may seem intuitively obvious to some readers (if so, apply your "intuition" to the Pötzelberger–Schlumprecht example of Chapter 7), but it still requires a proof.

The first thing to do is to show convergence of the finite-dimensional distributions. Here, I only prove that the distribution of $\omega(1)$ under P^{*n} converges to the distribution of $\omega(1)$ under P^*, the latter being a Normal distribution with mean $-1/2$ and variance 1. The same proof technique works to show that the distribution of $w(t)$ under P^{*n} converges to its distribution under P^*, for all t. Then, using independent increments, one proves that the distribution of $w(t') - w(t)$ under P^{*n} converges to its distribution under P^*, for all t', t such that $t' > t$. This result is then strung together finitely many times to get convergence of the finite-dimensional distributions.

To show that the distribution of $w(1)$ under P^{n*} converges to its distribution under P^* requires a slightly fancier version of the Central Limit Theorem, Lindeberg's Central Limit Theorem (CLT) for Triangular Arrays (see Billingsley, 1995, Section 2).[7] Recall that, for the random-walk models, we used ζ_k for the scaled (by $1/\sqrt{n}$) step in the random walk. To denote that we are working with the nth model, put on a superscript n; since we are only working with the binomial-random-walk model in this chapter, omit the hat. Then (to refresh memories), we have that, for $k = 1, \ldots, N$, $w(k/n) - w((k-1)/n) = \zeta_k^n$ under P^{*n} has the distribution

$$\zeta_k^n = \begin{cases} 1/\sqrt{n}, & \text{with probability } 1/(1 + e^{1/\sqrt{n}}), \text{ and} \\ -1/\sqrt{n}, & \text{with probability } e^{1/\sqrt{n}}/(1 + e^{1/\sqrt{n}}). \end{cases}$$

(Just to remind you, these are the unique probabilities that give $\mathbf{E}^{*n}[e^{\zeta_k^n}] = 1$, which is what it takes to get the stock price to be a martingale.)

It is straightforward to compute the mean of each ζ_k^n (under this distribution), denoted μ_n:

$$\mu_n := \mathbf{E}^{*n}[\zeta_k^n] = \frac{1 - e^{1/\sqrt{n}}}{(1 + e^{1/\sqrt{n}})\sqrt{n}}.$$

Let $\xi_k^n = \zeta_k^n - \mu_n$; further computation shows that the second moment of ξ_k^n (the variance of ζ_k^n) is

$$\mathbf{E}^{*n}[(\xi_k^n)^2] = \frac{1}{n}\left[\frac{4}{2 + e^{1/\sqrt{n}} + e^{-1/\sqrt{n}}}\right].$$

---

[7] We need Lindeberg's version instead of the garden-variety Central Limit Theorem because, as n changes, so do the distributions of the terms that make up the partial sums. Look at the probabilities with which $\zeta_k^n = 1/\sqrt{n}$ and $-1/\sqrt{n}$ in the next display in the text. If they were and remained 1/2 apiece, this would be a simple CLT. But they only approach 1/2 apiece in n; for any given n, there is slightly higher probability of $-1/\sqrt{n}$ than $1/\sqrt{n}$.

So if we define $\gamma_n = \sqrt{2 + e^{1/\sqrt{n}} + e^{-1/\sqrt{n}}}/2$ and let $\chi_k^n = \gamma_n \xi_k^n$, the triangular array $\{\chi_k^n \; ; \; n = 1, 2, \ldots, \; k = 1, \ldots, n\}$ satisfies the three "standard triangular array conditions":

a. Across each "row," the variables are mutually independent.

b. They have mean 0; and the sum of the second moments across each row is 1.

c. The supports of the χ_k^n shrink to 0 as $n \to \infty$.

(Condition *c* is sufficient for the general condition of Lindeberg.) Hence, by Lindeberg's Central Limit Theorem for Triangular Arrays, the distributions of $Z^n := \sum_{k=1}^n \chi_k^n$ under P^{*n} approach the standard Normal distribution. But, since $\gamma^n \to 1$ as $n \to \infty$, the same is true of $Y^n := \sum_{k=1}^n \xi_i^n$. And since

$$Y^n = \sum_{k=1}^n \left[\xi_k^n - \frac{\left(1 - e^{1/\sqrt{n}}\right)}{\left(1 + e^{1/\sqrt{n}}\right)\sqrt{n}} \right] = \omega(1) - \frac{\sqrt{n}(1 - e^{1/\sqrt{n}})}{1 + e^{1/\sqrt{n}}}, \quad \text{and}$$

$$\lim_{n \to \infty} \frac{\sqrt{n}(1 - e^{1/\sqrt{n}})}{1 + e^{1/\sqrt{n}}} = -\frac{1}{2},$$

the last by a simple Taylor series argument, we know that the sequence of distributions of the $\omega(1)$ under the probability distributions P^{*n} approach a Normal with mean $-1/2$ and variance 1, which is the distribution of $\omega(1)$ under P^*.

As stated earlier, this proof can be used in a relatively straightforward fashion (invoking independent increments along the way) to show convergence of all the finite-dimensional distributions.

Finally, we must show that the probability distributions $\{P^{*n}\}$ are tight. We could attempt to show this directly, following the methods of Billingley (1999) in his proof of Donsker's Theorem. But, for this model, there is an easier, indirect way, using the "compact set" characterization of tightness. We start with a lemma:

Lemma 4.1. *A strictly increasing function* $\rho : (0, 0.5) \to (0, 1)$ *exists such that:*

a. $\lim_{\epsilon \to 0} \rho(\epsilon) = 0$,

b. *for any event A, if* $P(A) \le \epsilon$, *then* $P^*(A) \le \rho(\epsilon)$, *and*

c. *for every ϵ there exists an $n(\epsilon)$ such that if $n \geq n(\epsilon)$ and $P^n(A) \leq \epsilon$, then $P^{*n}(A) \leq \rho(\epsilon)$.*

Before proving and then using Lemma 4.1, let me explain what it is saying. Suppose we have two probability measures, Q and Q^* on a space (Ω, F), where Q^* is absolutely continuous with respect to Q. It is not difficult to show, for this one pair of probabilities, that for any sequence of measurable sets $\{A_n\}$, $\lim_n Q(A_n) = 0$ implies $\lim_n Q^*(A_n) = 0$. (Use the Radon–Nikodym derivative dQ^*/dQ.) Hence, for one pair of probabilities Q and Q^*, the existence of a function ρ that satisfies conditions a and b is obvious. The lemma says that, in our context, *one* function ρ can be chosen that works simultaneously for P and P^* as well as for *all* the P^n and P^{*n}, for large enough n, where "large enough" can depend on ϵ. This uniformity is the point.

Proof of Lemma 4.1. First construct the function ρ. For $\epsilon \in (0, 0.5)$, let z_ϵ be the (negative) real number such that $P(\{\omega(1) \leq z_\epsilon\}) = \epsilon$. That is, z_ϵ is the value such that the cumulative probability of a standard (mean 0, variance 1) Normal at z_ϵ is ϵ. And let $\rho(\epsilon) = P^*(\{\omega(1) \leq z_\epsilon + 1\})$. Obviously, $\rho(\epsilon)$ takes a value between 0 and 1, ρ is a continuous and strictly increasing function of ϵ and, since $\lim_{\epsilon \to 0} z_\epsilon = -\infty$, $\lim_{\epsilon \to 0} \rho(\epsilon) = 0$.

   Now consider the following "maximization" problem:

Maximize over all measurable events $A \in \Omega$ $P^*(A)$, subject to $P(A) \leq \epsilon$.

Since $P^*(A) = \mathbf{E}\left[p^*(\omega)\mathbf{1}_A\right]$ (where p^* is shorthand for dP^*/dP), it is evident that a solution to this problem is the set A of P-probability ϵ on which p^* is largest. But we know that $p^*(\omega) = 1/e^{\omega(1)/2+1/8}$, and so this set A is the set of paths that give the smallest values of $\omega(1)$; that is, the set of all paths such that $\omega(1) \leq z_\epsilon$. Since we took $\rho(\epsilon)$ to exceed $P^*(\{\omega(1) \leq z_\epsilon\})$, we know that for any event A such that $P(A) \leq \epsilon$, it must be that $P^*(A) \leq \rho(\epsilon)$.

   For the P^{*n}: For the time being, let p^{*n} denote dP^{*n}/dP^n. This Radon–Nikodym derivative, defined on the 2^n points in the support of P^n, is easily computed. For ω one of those 2^n paths, write $u(\omega)$ for the number of upticks in the path ω and $d(\omega)$ for the number of downticks. Of course, $\omega(1) = (u(\omega) - d(\omega))/\sqrt{n}$. And, since $u(\omega) + d(\omega) = n$ (for the

n th binomial model), we have

$$u(\omega) = \left[\sqrt{n}\,\omega(1) + n\right]/2 \quad \text{and} \quad d(\omega) = \left[n - \sqrt{n}\,\omega(1)\right]/2.$$

Recall that the probability of an uptick under P^{*n} is $\pi^{*n} = 1/(1+e^{1/\sqrt{n}})$, which is less than one-half. Under P^n, the probability of an uptick is, of course, $1/2$. So

$$\begin{aligned} p^{*n}(\omega) &= \frac{\left[\pi^{*n}\right]^{u(\omega)}\left[1 - \pi^{*n}\right]^{d(\omega)}}{(1/2)^n} \\ &= \frac{\left[\pi^{*n}\right]^{\left[\sqrt{n}\,\omega(1)+n\right]/2}\left[1 - \pi^{*n}\right]^{\left[n-\sqrt{n}\,\omega(1)\right]/2}}{(1/2)^n}, \end{aligned} \tag{4.1}$$

for each of the 2^n paths in the support of P^n. Since $\pi^{*n} < 1/2$, it is evident that $p^{*n}(\omega)$ is a decreasing function of $\omega(1)$. Please note: The previous sentence has two parts. First, $p^{*n} = dP^{*n}/dP^n$ is a function of $\omega(1)$; two paths leading to the same final value of ω give the same value for the Radon–Nikodym derivative. And, second, p^{*n} is a *decreasing* function of $\omega(1)$.[8]

Now look at the maximization problem:

Maximize over all measurable events $A \in \Omega$ $P^{n*}(A)$, subject to $P^n(A) \le \epsilon$.

The solution consists of the one path that has no upticks (that is, such that $\omega(1) = -\sqrt{n}$), the n paths with a single uptick, and so forth, adding in paths until the probability of all the paths added into the set is just below ϵ. (Since all paths under P^n have equal probability $1/2^n$, there is no "knapsack" problem about filling the quota ϵ. For ϵ smaller than $1/2^n$, the only sets A that satisfy the constraint $P^n(A) \le \epsilon$ are P^n-null sets, and all of those are solutions. But for a given $\epsilon > 0$, for sufficiently large n, there are P^n-non-null sets that satisfy the constraint, and the solution is as we've described.) Let $A_n(\epsilon)$ be an event that solves this maximization problem (for large enough n). Of course, $P^n(A_n(\epsilon)) \le \epsilon$; I assert that $\lim_{n\to\infty} P^n(A_n(\epsilon)) = \epsilon$: Suppose to the contrary that along some subsequence n', $P^{n'}(A_{n'}(\epsilon)) < \epsilon - \delta$ for some $\delta > 0$. For n' so

---

[8]   Pay careful attention to these two statements; once you understand them, the rest of the proof is straightforward. And keep these statements in mind when, in Chapter 5, the equivalent martingale measure associated with the Esscher Transform is introduced for more general random-walk models.

large that $1/2^{n'} < \delta$, we can stick another path into $A_{n'}(\epsilon)$ without vi-
olating the required constraint, and, of course, this increases the $P^{*n'}$
probability of the (augmented) set. And so, since (a) $A_n(\epsilon)$ consists of
paths of lowest $\omega(1)$, (b) the distribution of $\omega(1)$ under P^n converges to
its distribution under P, and (c) the distribution of $\omega(1)$ under P has a
continuous distribution function, in the limit it consists of all paths with
$\omega_1 \leq z_\epsilon$. But then the convergence of the distribution of $\omega(1)$ under P^{*n}
to the distribution of $\omega(1)$ under P^* implies that, for large enough n,
$\lim_n P^{*n}(A_n(\epsilon)) = \lim_n P^{*n}(\{\omega(1) \leq z_\epsilon\}) = P^*(\{\omega(1) \leq z_\epsilon\}) \leq \rho(\epsilon)$.
This completes the proof of the lemma.   ∎

Lemma 4.1 allows us to finish the proof of Proposition 4.1. Donsker's
Theorem shows that $P^n \Rightarrow P$, so the "second half" of Prohorov's Theorem
(Billingsley, 1968, Theorem 6.2) ensures that the family $\{P^n\}$ is tight. The
sequence $\{P^n\}$ is tight if (and only if), for every $\epsilon > 0$, there is a compact
set $K \subset C[0,1]$ such that $P^n(K) \geq 1 - \epsilon$ for all n. So let K_ℓ be a
compact set (in $C[0,1]$) such that $\tilde{P}^n(K_\ell) \geq 1 - 1/\ell$, and let K_ℓ^C be the
complement of K_ℓ. The lemma tells us that $\tilde{P}^{*n}(K_\ell^C) \leq \rho(1/\ell)$ for all
sufficiently large n; we can enlarge K_ℓ^C as necessary to make this true
for all n while keeping K_ℓ compact (we need to take the union of the
original K_ℓ with finitely many other compact sets), and since $\rho(1/\ell) \to 0$
as $\ell \to \infty$, the family $\{P^{*n}\}$ is tight.

The rest of the proof of Proposition 4.1 is immediate. Since $P^n \Rightarrow P$
and $P^{*n} \Rightarrow P^*$, the definition of weak convergence is that, for any
bounded and continuous contingent claim x, $\lim_{n \to \infty} \mathbf{E}^n[x] = \mathbf{E}[x]$ and
$\lim_{n \to \infty} \mathbf{E}^{*n}[x] = \mathbf{E}^*[x]$. Or, to translate the second half of this in terms
appropriate to this context, the sequence of initial investments required to
synthesize any bounded and continuous contingent claim in the nth binomial economy converges to the initial invessment required to
synthesize the claim in BSM.   ∎

Unbounded and Discontinuous Contingent Claims

What of "mildly" discontinuous or unbounded contingent claims?
I preface this section with the question: Does it really matter? If we
have the result for bounded and continuous claims, isn't that sufficient
from an economic perspective? I think that a good economic case can
be made that Proposition 4.1 is "good enough." Claims that promise to

pay more than, say, a quintillion dollars, are unlikely to do so. And while we haven't established the real purchasing power of our numeraire, whatever it is, we can probably find upper and lower bounds on payoffs that exclude nothing that is economically relevant. Indeed, modeling the price of the stock as being unbounded above – while it does make for some simple formulae – is unrealistic; perhaps we could rebuild BSM (and the binomial-random-walk models) so that there is an absorbing barrier at some fantastically large number.

As for discontinuities, at least some discontinuous functions can be approximated to any desired degree by continuous functions. If consumer preferences are continuous, getting a contingent claim that is arbitrarily close to some ideally desired but otherwise discontinuous claim is probably good enough.

But, at the same time, formal results for unbounded and mildly discontinuous contingent claims are available. For instance:

Proposition 4.2.

a. *Suppose x is a continuous contingent claim such that*

$$|x(\omega)| \leq \sum_{N=-M}^{M} \alpha_N e^{N\omega(1)} = \sum_{N=-M}^{M} \alpha_N S(1,\omega)^N, \qquad (4.2)$$

for a positive integer M and for positive scalars α_N. Then x is square-integrable with respect to both P and P^*, and

$$\lim_{n \to \infty} \mathbf{E}^n[x] = \mathbf{E}[x] \quad \text{and} \quad \lim_{n \to \infty} \mathbf{E}^{*n}[x] = \mathbf{E}^*[x].$$

b. *Fix a finite set of times $t_1 < t_2 < \ldots < t_k$ and, for $j = 1, \ldots, k$, intervals in R_+, $\rho_1, \ldots, \rho_k$. That is, each ρ_j is a subset of R of the form $[\underline{r}_j, \overline{r}_j]$, where $\underline{r}_j \leq \overline{r}_j$, where the interval can instead be open, or half-open and half-closed, and where, if the interval is open on the right-hand side, $\overline{r}_j = \infty$ is permitted. Let A be the event where the stock price at time t_j is in ρ_j for each $j = 1, \ldots, k$, and let x be the contingent claim that pays 1 if $\omega \in A$ and 0 otherwise. For any such contingent claim x,*

$$\lim_{n \to \infty} \mathbf{E}^n[x] = \mathbf{E}[x] \quad \text{and} \quad \lim_{n \to \infty} \mathbf{E}^{*n}[x] = \mathbf{E}^*[x].$$

Proposition 4.2*b* is simple to prove. The proof follows from the fact that the finite-dimensional distributions converge weakly, and at the limit (of geometric Brownian motion), all finite-dimensional cumulative distribution functions are everywhere continuous. Note that the class of contingent claims covered by this corollary has economic significance: It is the set of "Arrow–Debreu" contingent claims for a broad class of events.

Proving Proposition 4.2*a*, on the other hand, takes a fair bit of work, which is left for the appendix. But the intuition is easily supplied. Go back to the example that begins on page 63, showing that continuity of x is not enough. The example is rigged so that the values of $x(\omega)$ (which depend on $\omega(1)$ only) spike to an enormous height for $\omega(1) = \sqrt{n}$. The probability that $\omega(1) = \sqrt{n}$ under P^{*n} (and under P^n) goes to 0 as n goes to infinity, but x is so high that the product of the probability that $\omega(1) = \sqrt{n}$ times the height of x goes to infinity. But, at the same time, the spike happens rapidly, in a neighborhood of diameter that goes to 0 even more rapidly than the height of the spike goes to infinity, so that against the distribution of $\omega(1)$ under P^*, the integral of these spikes is finite.

The condition in Proposition 4.2*a* allows for claims x that are unbounded, but their "unboundedness" is controlled: it is less than a polynomial in $S(\omega(1))$. Integrated against P^* or P^{*n} for any n (as well as against P and P^n for any n), this bound means that the contribution to the overall integral of extreme events (ω such that $\omega(1)$ is extreme) vanishes. And then, Proposition 4.1 can be extended to Proposition 4.2*a* by "cutting off" x at those extreme events. The reader who wishes to see how this is done formally can consult the appendix.

But one caveat should be added: Compare the contingent claims x_C – the standard European call option – with x^{MAX}, the claim that pays the maximum value of the stock price over the time interval from 0 to 1. The first of these is obviously covered by Proposition 4.2*a* but the second is not. A different result, not provided here, based on the distribution of the maxima of binomial random walks, is required to cover the case of x^{MAX}.

Convergence of Solutions to the Consumer's Problem: Formulation

While Proposition 4.1 (and the extensions just given) provides substantial justification for thinking that BSM is an economically valid idealization of the binomial-random-walk economies for large n, we can go further. Suppose we take a consumer and place her in one of these economies. Imagine that she is an expected-utility maximizer, with a well-behaved utility function u. Specifically, suppose that u is continuously differentiable, strictly increasing, and strictly concave. How does she fare (asymptotically) in the discrete-time economies, relative to how she fares in the continuous-time limit?

Three immediate issues to resolve are: Is the consumer constrained to consume nonnegative amounts? As an expected-utility maximizer, her subjective probability assessment matters: What is it? And what is the nature of her initial endowment?

In terms of a constraint that she consume only nonnegative quantities, three cases are found in the literature: (a) The consumer is allowed to consume negative quantities – that is, the constraint $x \geq 0$, where x is her consumption bundle, is not imposed – and u is defined on $(-\infty, \infty)$. (b) The consumer is constrained to choose a bundle x that satisfies $x \geq 0$ (with probability 1), and u's domain of definition is $[0, \infty)$, where $u(0)$ is finite. (For instance, consider $u(x) = x^{1/2}$.) (c) The domain of definition of u is $(0, \infty)$, as is the case where $u(x) = \ln(x)$ or $= x^{1-a}/(1 - a)$ for $a > 1$. In such cases, the consumer effectively faces the constraint $x > 0$ with probability 1. (As long as she begins with strictly positive wealth, which we always assume, she has no problem meeting this constraint.)

I deal *only* with Cases a and b in what follows. Most of what follows can be adapted to Case c, at least as long as $\lim_{x \to 0} u(x) = -\infty$ for that case, which is true concerning the CRRA examples just given. But this third case requires special arguments (essentially, variations on the arguments employed for Case a), and dealing with this case significantly clogs the exposition. (Dealing with two cases is bad enough, although I believe the value from providing these two cases justifies the complications in exposition.) So, in what follows, when I speak of the consumer's problem without $x \geq 0$ being imposed, it is implicit that u's domain of definition is $(-\infty, \infty)$; when dealing with the consumer's problem with $x \geq 0$ being imposed, u's domain of definition is implicitly $[0, \infty)$, *with*

$u(0)$ *a finite number.* (I do allow $u'(0) = \infty$, as is the case for $u(x) = x^{1/2}$, for instance.)

Notation for the range of derivatives of u is needed, so define

$$\underline{u}' = \lim_{x \to \infty} u'(x) \quad \text{and} \quad \overline{u}' = \begin{cases} \lim_{x \to -\infty} u'(x), & \text{if } x \geq 0 \text{ is not imposed, and} \\ +\infty, & \text{if } x \geq 0 \text{ is imposed.} \end{cases}$$

(The definition of $\overline{u}'$ when the nonnegativity constraint is imposed is artificial, but it is what works with formulas to be developed.)

As for the consumer's (subjective) probability assessment, we assume that in the nth binomial economy, her subjective assessment is P^n, and in the BSM economy, it is P.

Her endowment can consist of an initial portfolio of securities as well as claims to time 1 consumption. Since markets are complete in all these economies, the exact composition of her endowment doesn't matter, only its market value at the outset. (If she has an endowment of time 1 consumption, she can effectively sell it at time 0.) So, to simplify notation, assume (wlog) that her endowment has a time-0 market value of $W_0 > 0$ bonds.

Because markets are complete, both in BSM and in the discrete-time, binomial-random-walk economies, the consumer can purchase any contingent claim (for consumption purposes) that she can afford. Hence, in the nth discrete-time economy, she seeks to

Maximize $\mathbf{E}^n[u(x)]$, subject to $\mathbf{E}^{*n}[x] \leq W_0$ and, perhaps $x \geq 0$.

In the BSM economy, she seeks to solve a similarly formulated problem, with the n's removed.

In the discrete-time economies, the support of P^n is finite. (It has 2^n members.) So issues of integrability do not arise. They could arise in the BSM economy, so we arbitrarily assume that, in the BSM economy, the consumer is restricted to consumption claims that are square-integrable with respect to P. (Since dP^*/dP is square integrable with respect to P, this ensures that x is integrable with respect to P^*.)

The questions to be answered are: If x^{*n} is the solution to her problem in the nth binomial-random-walk economy, and if x^* is the solution to her problem in BSM, does x^{*n} approach x in any meaningful sense? Is $\lim_n \mathbf{E}^n[u(x^{*n})] = \mathbf{E}[u(x^*)]$?

Existence and Characterization of Solutions for Discrete-Time Economies

To answer these questions, we first discuss existence of solutions to the consumer's problem and characterize solutions, when they exist. For the binomial-random-walk economies, where $X = R^\Omega$ is essentially finite,[9] this is more or less a standard result when $x \geq 0$ is imposed; when $x \geq 0$ is not imposed, there is a bit of work to do.

Proposition 4.3. *Consider the problem:*

> *Maximize* $\mathbf{E}^n[u(x)]$, *subject to* $\mathbf{E}^{*n}[x] \leq W_0$ *and, as desired,* $x \geq 0$,

for a utility function u that is strictly increasing, strictly concave, and continuously differentiable and for $W_0 > 0$.

a. *Necessary and sufficient conditions for x^{*n} to be the solution to this problem are that $\mathbf{E}^{*n}[x^{*n}] = W_0$ and, for some strictly positive multiplier λ^{*n} and for each of the 2^n paths ω that have positive probability under P^n,*

$$u'(x^{*n}(\omega)) \leq \lambda p^{*n}(\omega),$$

where p^{*n} is the Radon–Nikodym derivative dP^{*n}/dP^n given by equation (4.1) on page 73, and equality is required unless (a) $x^{*n}(\omega) = 0$ and (b) the constraint $x \geq 0$ is imposed.

b. *A solution, if it exists, is unique.*[10]

c. *If the constraint $x \geq 0$ is imposed, a solution exists. If $x \geq 0$ is not imposed, a solution exists if and only if*

$$\frac{\overline{u'}}{\left(1 - \pi^{*n}\right)^n} > \frac{\underline{u'}}{\left(\pi^{*n}\right)^n}. \tag{4.3}$$

---

[9] "Essentially" is necessary here, as $\Omega = C[0, 1]$ is certainly not finite. But the support of each P^n is finite, and that is what matters.

[10] That is, $x^*(\omega)$ is uniquely defined for the paths ω that have positive probability.

While standard general proofs (for instance, Kreps, 2013, Proposition 3.5) can be cited for the case where $x \geq 0$ is imposed,[11] it may be helpful to sketch the full proof.

Suppose x is advanced as a solution and, for two paths ω and ω', both with positive probability, $u'(x(\omega))/p^{*n}(\omega) > u'(x(\omega'))/p^{*n}(\omega')$. Since all paths have the same probability under P^n, an increase in $x(\omega)$ of size $\epsilon/p^*(\omega)$ and a balancing decrease in $x(\omega')$ of size $\epsilon/p^*(\omega')$, for sufficiently small ϵ, will increase expected utility while holding fixed $\mathbf{E}^{*n}[x]$. So if this variation is possible, x cannot be a solution. Such a variation is possible as long as $x(\omega') > 0$ or if $x \geq 0$ is not imposed; it is not possible only if $x(\omega') = 0$ *and* $x \geq 0$ is imposed.

Hence, if $x \geq 0$ is not imposed, the terms $u'(x^{*n}(\omega))/p^{*n}(\omega)$ must be equal for all paths with positive probability; let λ^{*n} be the common value of $u'(x^{*n}(\omega))/p^{*n}(\omega)$.

If $x \geq 0$ is imposed, the terms $u'(x^{*n}(\omega))/p^{*n}(\omega)$ must be equal for all paths where $x^{*n}(\omega) > 0$ – let λ^{*n} be this common value – while for any paths ω that have $x^{*n}(\omega) = 0$, we must have $u'(x^{*n}(\omega))/p^{*n}(\omega) \leq \lambda^{*n}$. This implies necessity of the first-order conditions in part a; sufficiency follows from the concavity of u (and the linearity of the constraint) by the usual means; see the proof of Proposition 4.4 in the Appendix for details if you wish.

Part b of the proposition, uniqueness of the solution, follows from the strict concavity of u in the standard fashion.

If the constraint $x \geq 0$ is imposed, standard compactness-of-the-feasible-set arguments shows that a solution must exist. But when $x \geq 0$ is not imposed, part c asserts that inequality (4.3) is necessary and sufficient for a solution. Taking necessity first, fix n. It is clear from the first-order condition $u'(x^*(\omega)) = \lambda^{*n}p^{*n}(\omega)$ that $x^*(\omega)$ will be decreasing in $p^{*n}(\omega)$. We know that $p^{*n}(\omega)$ is minimal for the one path $\overline{\omega}$ that has only upticks, so that $\overline{\omega}(1) = \sqrt{n}$, in which case $p^{*n}(\overline{\omega}) = (2\pi^{*n})^n$. And we know that $p^{*n}(\omega)$ is maximal for the path $\underline{\omega}$ that has only downticks, or $\underline{\omega}(1) = -\sqrt{n}$, in which case $p^{*n}(\underline{\omega}) = (2(1-\pi^*))^n$. (In fact, we know that $p^{*n}(\omega)$ in general is a function (only) of $\omega(1)$ and is decreasing in $\omega(1)$;

---

[11] Of course, if the nonnegativity constraint is imposed, $\overline{u'} = \infty$; since $\underline{u'} < \infty$, (4.3) holds automatically. Condition (4.3) has force only when $x \geq 0$ is not imposed, which fits with the fact that we know a solution must exist when $x \geq 0$ is imposed. See the "solution-finding machine" that is described starting on the next page for the logic behind this.

hence, we know that, at the optimal solution, $x^{*n}(\omega)$ is an increasing function of $\omega(1)$.) Combining this with the first-order conditions for solutions at these two extreme paths, the existence of a solution with multiplier λ implies that

$$\frac{u'\left(x^*(\overline{\omega})\right)}{(2\pi^{*n})^n} = \lambda^{*n} = \frac{u'\left(x^*(\underline{\omega})\right)}{(2(1-\pi^{*n}))^n}.$$

Of course, since u is concave, $u'(x^*(\overline{\omega})) > \underline{u}'$, and $u'(x^*(\underline{\omega})) < \overline{u}'$, so if we have a solution, it must be that

$$\frac{\underline{u}'}{(2\pi^{*n})^n} < \lambda^{*n} < \frac{\overline{u}'}{(2(1-\pi^{*n}))^n}. \tag{4.4}$$

Hence, (canceling the common terms 2^n), if (4.3) does not hold, a solution cannot exist.

On the other hand, (4.3) is sufficient to guarantee existence of a solution: Let v be the inverse function to u'. Since u' is strictly decreasing and continuous, so is v. Consider the following "machine" for finding a solution. Assume that (4.3) holds. For all λ that satisfy inequality (4.4) and for each of the 2^n paths ω with positive probability, define

$$\chi^{*n}(\lambda,\omega) = \begin{cases} 0, & \text{if } \lambda p^{*n}(\omega) > u'(0) \text{ and } x \geq 0 \text{ is imposed, and} \\ v(\lambda p^{*n}(\omega)), & \text{otherwise.} \end{cases}$$
$$\tag{4.5}$$

And define $\mathcal{W}^n(\lambda) := \mathbf{E}^{*n}\left[\chi^{*n}(\lambda,\omega)\right]$.

The restriction of λ to the range in (4.4) together with the strict concavity of U ensures that, for each ω, χ^{*n} is well defined. Regardless of whether $x \geq 0$ or not is imposed, if $\lambda > \underline{u}'/(2\pi^{*n})^n$, then $\lambda p^{*n}(\omega) > \underline{u}'$ for all ω. And, by a similar argument, for all λ in the range in (4.4), $\lambda p^{*n}(\omega) < \overline{u}'$ for all ω. If $x \geq 0$ is *not* imposed, this means that $\lambda p^{*n}(\omega)$, the argument of v in the definition, is the derivative of u for some value of x and, of course, that value is unique. While if $x \geq 0$ is imposed, either $\lambda p^{*n} \leq u'(0)$, so for some (unique) $x \geq 0$, $u'(x) = \lambda p^{*n}$, or $\lambda p^{*n} > u'(0)$ and the "default" value $\chi^{*n}(x) = 0$ is mandated.

Moreover, for each ω, $\lambda \to \chi^{*n}(\lambda,\omega)$ is decreasing and continuous, and it is strictly decreasing when $\chi^{*n}(\lambda,\omega)$ is given by $v(\lambda p^{*n}(\omega))$ (since v is strictly decreasing). Hence $\lambda \to \mathcal{W}^n(\lambda)$ is decreasing, and it is strictly decreasing whenever, for some ω, $\chi^{*n}(\lambda,\omega) = v(\lambda p^{*n}(\omega))$.

Now consider the values of $W^n(\lambda)$ as λ approaches its upper and lower bounds. As it approaches its lower bound, for $\omega = \bar{\omega}$, $\lambda p^{*n}(\bar{\omega})$ approaches $\underline{u}'$, and so $\chi^{*n}(\lambda, \bar{\omega})$ approaches ∞. Since $\bar{\omega}$ has positive probability, $W^n(\lambda)$ also approaches ∞. On the other side: (a) If $x \geq 0$ is not imposed, then a similar argument shows that $\chi^{*n}(\lambda, \underline{\omega})$ approaches $-\infty$, so $W^n(\lambda)$ approaches $-\infty$. (b) If $x \geq 0$ is imposed, the upper bound on λ is $+\infty$. So for all ω, $\lambda p^{*n}(\omega)$ approaches infinity. If $u'(0)$ is finite, then for large enough λ, $\chi^{*n}(\lambda, \omega) = 0$ for all ω; while if $u'(0) = \infty$, $\chi^{*n}(\lambda, \omega)$ approaches 0 for each ω, and so $W^n(\lambda)$ approaches 0.

But then: (a) If $x \geq 0$ is not imposed, $W^n(\lambda)$ ranges from $-\infty$ to $+\infty$ in continuous fashion. (b) And if $x \geq 0$ is imposed, $W^n(\lambda)$ ranges from 0 to $+\infty$ continuously. By the Intermediate Value Theorem, in either case, there is a λ such that $W^n(\lambda) = W_0$. (Recall that $W_0 > 0$.) Moreover, this λ is unique; this follows from the fact that $\chi^{*n}(\lambda, \omega)$ is strictly decreasing in λ whenever it is given by $v(\lambda p^{*n}(\omega))$, and if $W^n(\lambda) = \mathbf{E}[\chi^{*n}(\lambda, \omega)] = W_0 > 0$, this must be so for at least one ω. This unique λ is, of course, λ^{*n}.

Putting everything together, because λ^{*n} satisfies $W^n(\lambda^{*n}) = W_0$, $x^{*n}(\omega) := \chi^{*n}(\lambda^{*n}, \omega)$ satisfies all the conditions sufficient for a solution to the consumer's problem, which completes the proof. ∎

The details in this "machine" for generating a solution may obscure its relative simplicity. The function $\chi^{*n}(\lambda, \omega)$ finds the value of consumption in state ω that satisfies the first-order conditions if λ is the multiplier. These values decline continuously as λ rises, strictly so unless $x \geq 0$ is imposed and the first-order condition gives value 0 for ω, and so the overall cost of $\chi^{*n}(\lambda, \cdot)$, which is $W^n(\lambda)$, declines continuously in λ. We look at λ over a range that (a) allows χ^{*n} to be well defined, and (b) ensures that any initial wealth level $W_0 > 0$ is hit for some λ within the range. That is all that is going on.

Existence and Characterization of Solutions for the BSM Economy

Similar results, and a similar "machine" for generating solutions, obtain for BSM, even though the space X is infinite dimensional,[12] with one complication: For the nth discrete-time economy, the existence of a

---

[12] Recall that X is the space of P-square-integrable contingent claims defined on $C[0, 1]$.

solution is guaranteed if $x \geq 0$ is imposed; if $x \geq 0$ is not imposed, a solution is guaranteed if and only if (4.3) holds. In this case, the story is not quite as cut and dried.

Proposition 4.4. *Consider the problem*

Maximize $\mathbf{E}[u(x)]$ *subject to* $x \in X$, $\mathbf{E}^*[x] \leq W_0$, *and, as desired,* $x \geq 0$,

for a utility function u *that is strictly increasing, strictly concave, and continuously differentiable, and for* $W_0 > 0$.

a. *Necessary and sufficient conditions for* x^* *to be the solution if* $x \geq 0$ *is imposed are* $x^* \in X$, $\mathbf{E}^*[x] = W_0$, *and*

$$u'(x^*(\omega)) \leq \lambda^* p^*(\omega) = \frac{\lambda^*}{e^{\omega(1)/2+1/8}} \quad P\text{-a.s.,}$$

for some $\lambda^* > 0$, *with equality if* $x^*(\omega) > 0$. *And if the constraint* $x \geq 0$ *is not imposed, then* $u'(x^*(\omega)) = \lambda^* p^*(\omega)$, P-a.s.

b. *The solution, if one exists, is unique (up to changes on* P-null sets*).*

c. *If* $x \geq 0$ *is imposed, a necessary condition for a solution to exist is that* $\underline{u'} = \lim_{x \to \infty} u'(x) = 0$. *If* $x \geq 0$ *is not imposed, this condition and, in addition,* $\overline{u'} := \lim_{x \to -\infty} u'(x) = \infty$ *are necessary. But these conditions are not sufficient.*

The proof of parts *a* and *b* is an adaptation of the proof sketched above for parts *a* and *b* of Proposition 4.3, adapted to this infinite-dimensional setting. The detailed proof is provided in the Appendix. I'll discuss part *c* here:

Observe first of all that, for the discrete-time economies, existence of a solution is guaranteed without any further conditions. But, in this case, $\underline{u'} = 0$ is necessary for a solution, *even if* $x \geq 0$ is imposed. An example illustrates why:

Suppose $\underline{u'} > 0$. Take the initial wealth W_0 and divide it into two parts. The first part provides $W_0/2$ at time 1 (by buying that many bonds). The second part is used to finance a claim ψ_n given by

$$\psi_n := \begin{cases} 0, & \text{if } \omega(1) < n, \text{ and} \\ K_n e^{\omega(1)/2+1/8}, & \text{if } \omega(1) \geq n, \end{cases}$$

where K_n is chosen so that

$$\mathbf{E}^*[K_n e^{\omega(1)/2+1/8}] = \mathbf{E}[p^*(\omega)\, K_n e^{\omega(1)/2+1/8} \mathbf{1}_{\{\omega(1)\geq n\}}]$$
$$= \mathbf{E}[K_n \mathbf{1}_{\{\omega(1)\geq n\}}] = W_0/2,$$

and where $\mathbf{1}_{\{\cdot\}}$ is the standard indicator function. We must verify that ψ_n is square-integrable with respect to P for each n, but since it is a constant times $e^{\omega(1)/2}$, this is evident. By definition, the sum of these two claims, call the sum ϕ_n, provides at least $W_0/2$ in all states. Its price is W_0, so it is is affordable. Since markets are complete, it can be synthesized from the stock and bond. And, because u is concave, for all $x > W_0/2$, $u(x) \geq u(W_0/2) + \underline{u}'(x - W_0/2)$. The expected utility derived from ϕ_n, is then $\mathbf{E}[u(\phi_n)] \geq u(W_0/2) + \mathbf{E}[\underline{u}'\psi_n]$ (since $\phi_n - W_0/2 = \psi_n$). But

$$\mathbf{E}[\underline{u}'\psi_n] = \underline{u}'\mathbf{E}[\psi_n] = \underline{u}'\mathbf{E}\big[K_n e^{\omega(1)/2+1/8}\mathbf{1}_{\{\omega(1)\geq n\}}\big]$$

$$\geq \underline{u}' e^{n/2+1/8}\mathbf{E}\big[K_n\mathbf{1}_{\{\omega(1)\geq n\}}\big] = \underline{u}' e^{n/2+1/8}W_0/2.$$

Since this goes to $+\infty$ in n, the consumer's problem can have no (finite) solution; a sequence of affordable contingent claims provides her with unbounded expected utility.

The example may be hard to disentangle, so to explain: ϕ_n is a claim that pays a very generous consumption dividend if the stock does well. The probability of the stock doing that well goes to 0, of course, but – and the key to the example – it goes to 0 a lot faster under P^* than under P. (Readers well trained in statistics may recall how fast the tail of the Normal distribution goes to 0.) Hence, this claim provides a very generous bang (measured in expected *consumption* units) for the buck (cost) where it provides a positive dividend; the bang for the buck is, roughly speaking, determined by the ratio of P to P^* where dividends accrue. If the marginal expected utility of those generous consumption dividends went to 0 fast enough – if the utility bang for the buck vanished – these claims would not be worth pursuing. But if $\underline{u}'$ is strictly bounded away from 0, the great deals that can be purchased in states where the stock price is high allow the consumer to generate unbounded amounts of utility.

This can't happen in any one of the discrete-time economies because, of course, there is a limit to how how far apart can be $P^*(\omega)$ and $P(\omega)$.

But it may be worth observing that, if $\underline{u}' > 0$, we can construct a sequence of claims $\{x_n\}$, where x_n is an affordable and nonnegative contingent claim for the nth discrete-time economy, such that $\mathbf{E}^n[u(x_n))] \to \infty$. The construction is simple: In the nth discrete-time economy, let $\bar{\varpi}^n$ denote the extreme path for that economy for which $\bar{\varpi}^n(1) = \sqrt{n}$ (that is, the path $\bar{\varpi}^n$ consists of n upticks), and then choose the claim the provides $W_0/2$ for all paths ω other than $\bar{\varpi}^n$ and otherwise "transfers" $W_0/2$ wealth to state $\bar{\varpi}^n$. This provides consumption $W_0/2 + W_0/(2P^{*n}(\bar{\varpi}^n))$ in state $\bar{\varpi}^n$, and since $P^n(\bar{\varpi}^n)/P^{*n}(\bar{\varpi}^n) = 1/(2\pi^{*n})^n$, which goes to infinity in n, this provides unbounded expected utility, as long as $\underline{u}' > 0$.

We can also see, even if $x \geq 0$ is imposed, that $\underline{u}' = 0$ is required, by examining the first-order conditions for an optimum. Suppose $x \geq 0$ is imposed and x^* is a solution for $W_0 > 0$. Let $\lambda^* > 0$ be the multiplier guaranteed by part a. Recall that $p^*(\omega) = 1/e^{\omega(1)/2+1/8}$, which is strictly decreasing in $\omega(1)$, with limit 0 as $\omega(1) \to \infty$. Since $u'(0) > 0$ (and, recall, we allow that it could be $+\infty$, to accommodate functions like $u(x) = x^{1/2}$), and since $\lambda^* > 0$ is fixed, $\lambda^* p^*(\omega) < u'(0)$ for (almost) all paths ω for which $\omega(1)$ is large enough. But this implies that for (almost) all such paths, $u'(x^*(\omega)) = \lambda^* p^*(\omega)$, and since $\lambda^* p^*(\omega)$ approaches 0 as $\omega(1)$ approaches infinity, this means, if we have a solution, that $u'(x^*(\omega))$ must approach 0 as $\omega(1)$ approaches infinity. Of course, there is positive probability under P that $\omega(1)$ exceeds any finite value, so there must be large x such that $u'(x)$ is arbitrarily close to 0. Hence, if there is a solution, $\underline{u}' = 0$ is required.

In case $x \geq 0$ is not imposed: The same argument applies to show that $\underline{u}' = 0$ is necessary for a solution. But now, in addition, we have $x^*(\omega) = \lambda^* p^*(\omega)$ for (almost) all ω, including those for which $\omega(1)$ is very large negative. As $\omega(1)$ approaches $-\infty$, $p^*(\omega) = 1/e^{\omega(1)/2+1/8}$ approaches ∞, so for a solution to exist, $u'(x)$ must (for small enough x) be arbitrarily large. That is, $\overline{u}' = \infty$.

But while $\underline{u}' = 0$ and, if $x \geq 0$ is not imposed, $\overline{u}' = \infty$, are necessary for the existence of a solution, they are not sufficient. Go back to the example we constructed for the sequence of claims $\{\phi_n\}$. In computing $\mathbf{E}[u(\phi_n)]$, we used the assumption that $\underline{u}' > 0$ to construct a lower bound that is certainly not tight. Even if $\underline{u}' = 0$ – that is, $u'(x) \to 0$ as $x \to \infty$ – it might be that $u'(x)$ goes to 0 so slowly that these claims would still generate unbounded expected utility for our investor.

This takes us, finally, to the "machine" for generating solutions to the consumer's problem, when they exist. Assume that $\underline{u}' = 0$. If $x \geq 0$ is not imposed, assume that $\overline{u}' = \infty$. For each λ in $(0, \infty)$ and each $\omega \in \Omega$, define

$$\chi^*(\lambda, \omega) = \begin{cases} 0, & \text{if } \lambda p^*(\omega) > u'(0) \text{ and } x \geq 0 \text{ is imposed, and} \\ v(\lambda p^*(\omega)), & \text{otherwise,} \end{cases}$$

$$(4.6)$$

where (recall) $p^*(\omega) = 1/e^{\omega(1)/2+1/8}$. And, *if $\chi^*(\lambda, \cdot)$ is P integrable,* define $W(\lambda) = \mathbf{E}^*[\chi^*(\lambda, \omega)]$. Because of the assumptions that $\underline{u}' = 0$ and, if $x \geq 0$ is not imposed, $\overline{u}' = \infty$, for every $\lambda > 0$, $\chi^*(\lambda, \omega)$ is (uniquely) well defined here. Moreover, $\chi^*(\lambda, \omega)$ is nonincreasing in λ and, where it is not 0, it is strictly decreasing in λ. However, there is no guarantee that it is integrable, hence the italicized caveat that $\chi^*(\lambda, \cdot)$ must be P-integrable when defining W.

The following is an immediate (almost definitional) corollary to Proposition 4.4a:

Corollary 4.2. *Suppose $\underline{u}' = 0$. If the constraint $x \geq 0$ is imposed, suppose that $\overline{u}' = \infty$. Given the utility function u and initial wealth level W_0, there is a solution to the consumer's problem for the BSM economy if and only if, for some $\lambda^* > 0$, $\chi^*(\lambda^*, \cdot)$ is P square-integrable and $W(\lambda^*) = W_0$, in which case $x^*(\omega)$ must equal $\chi^*(\lambda^*, \omega)$ P almost surely, for that λ^*.*

Obviously, there can only be one λ for which $W(\lambda) = W_0$; assuming the integrability of χ^*, W is strictly decreasing in λ where it is strictly positive.

But, we reiterate, there is no guarantee that, for a given utility function u, $\chi^*(\lambda, \cdot)$ will be integrable, let alone square-integrable, even if $x \geq 0$ is imposed (so there is no problem with values of χ^* less than 0). If $u'(x)$ goes to 0 "too slowly," v will approach ∞ "very quickly" (as its argument approaches 0). The reader is invited to work through the unhappy case where $u'(x) = 1/\ln(x)$.[13]

At the risk of over-talking this general point: One might say that the problem of existence of solutions to the consumer's problem shows that certain consumers are incompatible with the BSM model of security prices. But, I believe, this is backwards. Consumers drive equilibrium

---

[13] For more on these issues, see Kramkov and Schachermayer (1999).

prices, not the reverse. So the correct statement is that the BSM model of security prices is incompatible with certain consumers. In particular, in the BSM model, the risk premium on the stock over the bond remains constant no matter how high are stock prices. But high stock prices means a wealthier economy and so, presumably, wealthier consumers. If consumers' preferences are such that they become less risk averse – to the point where risk aversion asymptotically vanishes – as they become richer, equilibrium prices would have to reflect that, with a risk premium for the stock over the bond that decreases – and perhaps asymptotically vanishes – as the stock price goes through the roof.

Employing Proposition 4.4

It is well known that the consumer's problem in the BSM economy has a solution for CRRA and CARA utility functions. Indeed, Merton (1969) tells us what portfolio choices by the consumer solve her problem for these utility functions. These are textbook results, but Proposition 4.4 gives us easy access to those solutions. Because the case of CRRA utility functions enters the story later, I'll illustrate with them:[14] (The reader is invited to do the analysis for CARA utility, or look at the end of the Appendix, where this is done as part of the proof of a different proposition.) CRRA utility with coefficient of relative risk aversion $a > 0$ is $u(x) = x^{1-a}/(1-a)$ for $a \neq 1$ and $u(x) = \ln(x)$ for $a = 1$. For all a, then, $u'(x) = x^{-a}$, hence $v(z) = (u')^{-1}(z) = z^{-1/a}$. Hence,

$$x^*(\omega, \lambda) = v\left(\frac{\lambda}{e^{\omega(1)/2+1/8}}\right) = v\left(\frac{\lambda e^{-1/8}}{S(1)^{1/2}}\right) = \lambda' S(1,\omega)^{1/2a},$$

for another constant λ'. Now

$$\mathbf{E}^*\left[\lambda' S(1,\omega)^{1/2a}\right] = \lambda' \mathbf{E}^*\left[S(1,\omega)^{1/2a}\right] = \lambda' \exp\left(\frac{1}{8a^2} - \frac{1}{4a}\right),$$

---

[14] On page 77, I said that I would not deal with CRRA utility functions whose coefficient of relative risk aversion is $a \geq 1$. But, to illustrate how Proposition 4.4 can be employed, I proceed to do so. I assert, as I did on page 77, that Propositions 4.3 and 4.4 can be adopted to fit the case where u's domain of definition is $(0, \infty)$, at least as long as $\lim_{x \to} u(x) = -\infty$, to maintain "continuity." But I have not proved that this is so here.

by a standard formula for the expected value of moments of a log-normal random variable. This must equal W_0, which gives us

$$\lambda' = W_0 \times \exp\left(\frac{1}{4a} - \frac{1}{8a^2}\right),$$

so that

$$x^*(\omega) = W_0 \times \exp\left(\frac{1}{4a} - \frac{1}{8a^2}\right) \times S(1,\omega)^{1/2a}.$$

Hence, the value of the portfolio θ that gets this claim is $\mathbf{E}^*\left[x^*|F_t\right]$, from which we can find the portfolio strategy θ.[15] Sparing you the algebra, the result, originally derived by Merton, is that $\alpha(S(t),t)S(t) = V(\theta,t)/(2a)$; the consumer should hold $1/(2a)$ of her current wealth (the value of her portfolio) in the stock, with the rest in the bond.[16] One can also find the expected utility she receives: For $a \neq 1$, it is

$$\mathbf{E}[u(x^*)] = \frac{1}{1-a}\mathbf{E}\left[(x^*)^{1-a}\right] \quad \text{(which, after tedious algebra)}$$

$$= \frac{W_0^{1-a}}{1-a} \times \exp\left(\frac{1-a}{8a}\right).$$

Convergence of Solutions to the Consumer's Problem, Completed

The result we seek is that, under suitable conditions, if x^{*n} is the solution to the consumer's problem wealth level W in the nth discrete-time economy, and x^* is the solution for wealth level W in the BSM economy, then x^* is the limit in n of the x^{*n}. Of course, this only makes sense if the consumer's problem has solutions, so for the remainder of this section, the following is assumed.

---

[15] You can find the amount of stock held in synthesizing any claim by computing the infinitessimal variance of the portfolio-value process; since the bond holding contributes no variance, this must all come from the stock holding.

[16] The general formula derived by Merton is that the fraction of current wealth held in the stock should be $(\mu - r)/(a\sigma^2)$ where μ is the drift of the stock, in this case $1/2$, r is the interest rate, in this case 0, and σ^2 is the infinitesimal variance, in this case 1. Note the connection of this formula to the well-known Sharpe ratio $(\mu - r)/\sigma$.

Assumption 4.1. *The consumer in question has expected-utility preferences, with utility function u that is strictly increasing, strictly concave, and continuously differentiable on its domain of definition. Moreover, $\underline{u'} := \lim_{x \to \infty} u'(x) = 0$ and, if the constraint $x \geq 0$ is not imposed in the consumer's expected-utility maximization problem, $\overline{u'} := \lim_{x \to -\infty} u'(x) = \infty$.*

Per Proposition 4.4, the assumptions concerning $\underline{u'}$ and (if $x \geq 0$ is not imposed) $\overline{u'}$ are necessary for the consumer's problem to have a solution for any wealth level W (but, to reiterate, they are not sufficient). And then, by Proposition 4.3, this ensures that for each discrete-time economy and every wealth level W, the consumer's problem has a solution.

Showing that x^{*n} converges to x^* encounters an immediate difficulty, because P^n (for each n) and P are mutually singular. Solutions to the consumer's problem are defined (only) up to equivalent functions. That is, if ω is a path that has probability 0 under P^n, then we can change $x^{*n}(\omega)$ to be anything we wish and we don't change the fact that x^{*n} is a solution for the nth discrete-time economy. And when it comes to x^*, since any countable set of paths in Ω have the P-probability 0, we could take the set of all the paths that have positive probability under some P^n, change x^* to be, say, $\equiv W$ on them, and x^* would still be a solution, in the sense that it gives the consumer maximal expected utility.[17]

The best hope we have for proving a convergence result is to show convergence of $x^{*n}(\omega)$ to $x^*(\omega)$ *for specific versions of $x^{*n}(\omega)$ and $x^*(\omega)$.*[18] So that is what we do. For each value of a multiplier λ, modify slightly the "machines" given by (4.5) and (4.6) to define specific functions $\chi^{*n}(\lambda, \omega)$ and $\chi^*(\lambda, \omega)$ for each $\lambda \geq 0$ and $\omega \in \Omega$, and, when we find the values of λ that give the "right" level of initial expenditure – temporarily call them λ^{*n} for the nth discrete-time economy and λ^* for BSM – we fix $x^{*n}(\omega) = \chi^{*n}(\lambda^{*n}, \omega)$ and $x^*(\omega) = \chi^*(\lambda^*, \omega)$, and show that $\chi^{*n}(\lambda^{*n}, \omega)$ converges to $\chi^*(\lambda^*, \omega)$ for every ω.

---

[17] If the reader is concerned that dynamically synthesizing this claim might be hard – how could the consumer know "in advance" that the path will be one of those in the countable set? – other claims can be created that (a) are more easily imagined to be implemented dynamically and (b) make the same basic point.

[18] In case this language is unfamiliar to the reader: Recall that random variables on a probability space are (generally) defined only up to changes on a set of probability 0, using the reference probability. Hence, a random variable, such as x^*, is really an "equivalence class" of measurable functions on the space, where two such functions, call them $\hat{x}^*$ and $\check{x}^*$, are equivalent if the probability of the event on which they differ is 0. A *version* of a random variable is one specific measurable function chosen out of the equivalence class.

The first step is to modify (4.5) and (4.6) so that they provide a specific value of $\chi^{*n}(\lambda, \omega)$ and $\chi^*(\lambda, \omega)$, respectively, for every value of $\lambda > 0$ and $\omega \in \Omega$. To begin, define functions $f^{*n} : R \to (0, \infty)$ and $f^* : R \to (0, \infty)$ as follows:

$$f^{*n}(x) := \frac{[\pi^{*n}]^{[n + x\sqrt{n}]/2} [1 - \pi^{*n}]^{[n - x\sqrt{n}]/2}}{(1/2)^n} \quad \text{and} \quad f^*(x) := \frac{1}{e^{x/2 + 1/8}}. \tag{4.7}$$

It is probably apparent, but just in case, note that $p^{*n}(\omega) = f^{*n}(\omega(1))$ for each of the 2^n paths that have positive probability under P^n – that is, $f^{*n}(\omega(1))$ is a version of dP^{*n}/dP^n – and $p^*(\omega) = f^*(\omega(1))$ is a version of dP^*/dP.

Next, we modify (4.5) and (4.6):

$$\chi^{*n}(\lambda, \omega) = \begin{cases} 0, & \text{if } \lambda f^{*n}(\omega(1)) > u'(0) \\ & \text{and } x \geq 0 \text{ is imposed, and} \\ v(\lambda f^{*n}(\omega(1))), & \text{otherwise.} \end{cases} \tag{4.5'}$$

$$\chi^*(\lambda, \omega) = \begin{cases} 0, & \text{if } \lambda f^*(\omega(1)) > u'(0) \\ & \text{and } x \geq 0 \text{ is imposed, and} \\ v(\lambda f^*(\omega(1))), & \text{otherwise,} \end{cases} \tag{4.6'}$$

Define $\mathcal{W}^n(\lambda)$ and $\mathcal{W}(\lambda)$ for these modified definitions of the χ^{*n} and χ^*, and it should be clear that if $\mathcal{W}^n(\lambda^{*n}) = W_0$, then $\chi^{*n}(\lambda^{*n}, \omega)$ is a version of the optimal solution of the consumer's problem in the nth discrete-time economy, and if $\mathcal{W}(\lambda^*) = W_0$ (which entails the implicit assumption that $\chi^*(\lambda^*, \cdot)$ is square-integrable with respect to P), then $\chi^*(\lambda^*, \cdot)$ is a version of the optimal solution of the consumer's problem for the BSM economy.

We can finally state our convergence result.

Proposition 4.5. *Consider the problem of an expected-utility-maximizing consumer whose utility function u is strictly increasing, strictly concave, and continuously differentiable on its domain of definition, with the constraint $x \geq 0$ imposed or not. Suppose that square-integrable solutions to the consumer's problem in the BSM world exists for all initial wealth levels W in an open subinterval*

*of $(0, \infty)$. Temporarily denote these solutions by x^*_W, where the subscript W
indicates the initial wealth level for which x^*_W is a solution. Suppose as well
that these solutions x^*_W, as well as the functions $u(x^*_W)$, satisfy the inequality
(4.2) for some positive integer M and positive scalars α_N.*

From earlier results, we know the following:

a. *$\underline{u'} := \lim_{x \to \infty} u'(x) = 0$ and, if $x \geq 0$ is not imposed in the consumer's
    maximization problem, $\overline{u'} := \lim_{x \to -\infty} u'(x) = \infty$.*

b. *For each integer n, the consumer's problem in the nth discrete-time economy
    for every wealth level W has a solution with corresponding multiplier λ^{*n}_W,
    and $\chi^{*n}(\lambda^{*n}_W, \cdot)$ is a version of the solution to her problem with wealth level
    W.*

c. *For each W in the given open neighborhood, there exists λ^*_W such that
    $\chi^*(\lambda^*_W, \cdot)$ is a version of the solution to her problem in the BSM economy if
    her wealth level is W.*

Then, for all wealth levels W in this open neighborhood,

$$\lim_{n \to \infty} \lambda^{*n}_W = \lambda^*_W \qquad \lim_{n \to \infty} \chi^{*n}(\lambda^{*n}_W, \omega) = \chi^*(\lambda^*_W, \omega), \text{ for all } \omega, \text{ and}$$

$$\lim_{n \to \infty} \mathbf{E}^n \left[u(\chi^{*n}(\lambda^{*n}_W, \omega)) \right] = \mathbf{E} \left[u(\chi^{*n}(\lambda^{*n}_W, \omega)) \right].$$

Several remarks about this proposition are in order:

1. The supposition that each x^*_W and $u(x^*_W)$ satisfy inequality (4.2) is
    used to invoke Proposition 4.2 as needed.

2. The key result is that the multipliers for the discrete-time economies
    λ^{*n}_W converge to the corresponding multipliers for the BSM economy,
    λ^*_W. The two other convergence results follow easily once we show
    this. Of course, for convergence of the optimal solutions, we are
    relying on the fact that we've fixed specific versions of the solutions.

3. Note that $\chi^{*n}(\lambda^{*n}_W, \omega)$ converges to $\chi^*(\lambda^*_W, \omega)$ for *every* ω. Do not
    mistake this for almost-sure convergence: Almost-sure convergence
    is convergence with reference to a single probability measure, which
    can be extended to cases with multiple measures that are all proba-
    bilistically equivalent. But in this context, where the P^n are mutually

singular to P, it simply doesn't work. That said, since the consumption levels $\chi^{*n}(\lambda_W^{*n}, \omega)$ and $\chi^*(\lambda_W^*, \omega)$ are strictly increasing in $\omega(1)$, an easy corollary to "convergence for every ω" is that consumption levels converge in distribution.

4. The convergence of the optimal multipliers, and hence the entire proof of the proposition, is based on the following lemma:

Lemma 4.2. *The sequence of functions $\{f^{*n}\}$ defined by (4.7) approach the function f^* in the following (strong) sense: There exists a series of strictly positive numbers $\{\epsilon_n\}$ such that $\lim_n \epsilon_n = 0$ and, for each n and for x such that $|x| \le \sqrt{n}$,*

$$\left| \frac{f^{*n}(x)}{f^*(x)} - 1 \right| \le \epsilon_n \text{ or, equivalently } f^*(x)(1-\epsilon_n) \le f^{*n}(x) \le f^*(x)(1+\epsilon_n).$$
(4.8)

I will not prove Lemma 4.2 here. This is a consequence of a more general result that appears in Chapter 5. But it may help to say a word about it: Although it may not be immediately evident, dP^{*n}/dP^n can be rewritten as $\left(dP^{*n}/dP^n\right)(\omega) = \mathrm{e}^{-a_n\omega(1)-b_n}$ for constants a_n and b_n, so that $f^{*n}(x) = e^{-a_n x - b_n}$ for the same constants. This is the so-called *Esscher Transform* of P^n; see pages 102–7. Moreover, we can show that $a_n = 1/2 + o(1/\sqrt{n})$ and $\lim_n b_n = 1/8$, which makes it obvious that f^{*n} converges pointwise to f^* and, moreover, that it converges to f^* in the manner asserted in the lemma.

Proof of Proposition 4.5. In what follows, I write $\chi^*(\lambda, x)$ and $\chi^{*n}(\lambda, x)$, for $\lambda > 0$ and $x \in R$ as shorthand for $\chi^*(\lambda, \omega)$ and $\chi^{*n}(\lambda, \omega)$, respectively, for any ω such that $\omega(1) = x$.

For every wealth level W inside the open interval for which there are well-behaved solutions to the consumer's problem in the BSM economy, [19] there is a corresponding optimal multiplier λ_W^*. It is immediate from earlier analysis that λ_W^* is strictly decreasing and continuous in W.

Fix some specific W in this interval, and two other wealth levels $\underline{W}$ and $\overline{W}$ such that $\underline{W} < W < \overline{W}$ and such that, for arbitrary $\delta > 0$, $\overline{W} - \underline{W} < \delta$. Of course, $\lambda_{\underline{W}}^* > \lambda_W^* > \lambda_{\overline{W}}^*$.

---

[19] "Well-behaved" here refers to the assumption that these solutions and their utility levels satisfy (4.2).

Enlist the lemma to produce the sequence $\{\epsilon_n\}$. Without loss of generality, we can assume that the sequence is nonincreasing. Repeating the second version of (4.8), we have

$$f^*(x)(1 - \epsilon_n) \leq f^{*n}(x) \leq f^*(x)(1 + \epsilon_n), \text{ for all } x \text{ such that } |x| \leq \sqrt{n}.$$

Since λ_W^* (for the previously fixed level W) is strictly positive, we have

$$\lambda_W^* f^*(x)(1 - \epsilon_n) \leq \lambda_W^* f^{*n}(x) \leq \lambda_W^* f^*(x)(1 + \epsilon_n),$$

and since v is a decreasing function,

$$\chi^*(\lambda_W^*(1 - \epsilon_n), x) \geq \chi^{*n}(\lambda_W^*, x) \geq \chi^*(\lambda_W^*(1 + \epsilon_n), x),$$

both for all x such that $|x| \leq \sqrt{n}$.

Fix m large enough so that $\lambda_{\underline{W}}^* > \lambda_W^*(1 + \epsilon_m)$, and $\lambda_{\overline{W}}^* < \lambda_W^*(1 - \epsilon_m)$. For all $n \geq m$, since the sequence $\{\epsilon_n\}$ is nonincreasing, we have

$$\chi^*(\lambda_W^*(1 - \epsilon_n), x) \geq \chi^{*n}(\lambda_W^*, x) \geq \chi^*(\lambda_W^*(1 + \epsilon_n), x),$$

for all x such that $|x| \leq \sqrt{n}$, which implies that, for all $n \geq m$,

$$\mathbf{E}^{*n}\left[\chi^*(\lambda_W^*(1 - \epsilon_n), \omega(1))\right] \geq \mathbf{E}^{*n}\left[\chi^{*n}(\lambda_W^*, \omega(1))\right]$$
$$\geq \mathbf{E}^{*n}\left[\chi^*(\lambda_W^*(1 + \epsilon_n), \omega(1))\right].$$

But since $\lambda_{\underline{W}}^* > \lambda_W^*(1 + \epsilon_m) > \lambda_W^*$, there is some W' between $\underline{W}$ and W such that $\lambda_{W'}^* = \lambda_W^*(1 + \epsilon_m)$; applying Proposition 4.2 (since $\chi^*(\lambda_{W'}^*, \cdot)$ satisfies (4.2)) gives

$$\lim_{n \to \infty} \mathbf{E}^{*n}\left[\chi^*(\lambda_W^*(1 + \epsilon_m), \omega(1))\right] = \mathbf{E}^*\left[\chi^*(\lambda_W^*(1 + \epsilon_m), \omega(1))\right]$$
$$= \mathcal{W}^*(\lambda_W^*(1 + \epsilon_m)) = W'.$$

And, similarly, $\lim_{n \to \infty} \mathbf{E}^{*n}[\chi^*(\lambda_W^*(1 - \epsilon_m), \omega(1))] = W''$ for some W'' between W and $\overline{W}$. But, since $\underline{W}$ and $\overline{W}$ were chosen to be within δ of W, for arbitrarily small δ, this implies that

$$\lim_{n \to \infty} \mathbf{E}^{*n}[\chi^{*n}(\lambda_W^*, \omega(1))] = W. \tag{4.9}$$

Moreover, since W was arbitrarily chosen from the open interval, we know that (4.9) holds for all W in this interval.

Now suppose that $\lim_{x \to \infty} \lambda_W^{*n}$ does not exist or, if it exists, is different from λ_W^*. In particular, suppose that, along some subsequence $\{n'\}$, $\limsup_{n' \to \infty} \lambda_W^{*n'} > \lambda_W^*$. Hence there is a wealth level W' in the open interval with $W' < W$ and $\limsup_{n' \to \infty} \lambda_W^{*n'} \geq \lambda_{W'}^*$. But then, along this subsequence,

$$W = \liminf_{n' \to \infty} \mathbf{E}^{*n'}\big[\chi^{*n'}(\lambda_W^{*n'}, \omega)\big] \leq \lim_{n' \to \infty} E[\chi^{*n'}(\lambda_{W'}^*, \omega)] = W' < W,$$

where the last equality follows from (4.9). This is a contradiction. Repeating the argument on the other side, we have that $\lim_{n \to \infty} \lambda_W^{*n} = \lambda_W^*$.

That $\chi^{*n}(\lambda_W^{*n}, \omega)$ converges to $\chi^*(\lambda_W^*, \omega)$ for each ω follows from the $\lambda_W^{*n} \to \lambda_W^*$ and $f^{*n}(\omega(1)) \to f^*(\omega(1))$, plus the continuity of v.

This leaves convergence of expected utility; that is,

$$\lim_{n \to \infty} \mathbf{E}^n\big[u(\chi^{*n}(\lambda_W^{*n}, \omega)\big] = \mathbf{E}\big[u(\chi^*(\lambda_W^*, \omega)\big].$$

This may seem obvious: The integrands are converging and continuous, and the integrating measures are converging weakly. And, while the integrands are unbounded, we have bounds provided by inequalities (4.2) to fall back upon. But because both the integrands and the integrators are changing simultaneously, this does take a bit of work.

Note to begin that for $\{W_\ell; \ell = 1, 2, \ldots\}$, a sequence of wealth levels in the open interval for which we have solutions,

$$\lim_{\ell \to \infty} W_\ell = W \quad \text{implies} \quad \lim_{\ell \to \infty} \mathbf{E}\big[u(\chi^*(\lambda_{W_\ell}^*, \omega))\big] = \mathbf{E}\big[u(\chi^*(\lambda_W^*, \omega))\big].$$

The integrands are converging (monotonically on either side of W), and the integrating measure is P, so this is (take your pick) bounded or monotone convergence.

Fix W and $\delta > 0$. As before, choose $\underline{W}$ and $\overline{W}$ from the open interval such that $\underline{W} \leq W \leq \overline{W}$ and $\overline{W} - \underline{W} < \delta$. Since $\lambda_W^{*n} \to \lambda_W^*$, there is a nonincreasing sequence $\{\epsilon_m'\}$ such that $\epsilon_m' \to 0$ and $\big|\lambda_W^{*n} - \lambda_W^*\big| \leq \epsilon_m'$ for all $n \geq m$. Enlist the lemma and its sequence $\{\epsilon_n\}$, and find m

sufficiently large so that $\lambda_{\underline{W}}^* > \lambda_W^*(1 + \epsilon_m)(1 + \epsilon_m')$, and $\lambda_{\overline{W}}^* < \lambda_W^*(1 - \epsilon_m)(1 - \epsilon_m')$. Then, for all $n \geq m$,

$$\chi^{*n}(\lambda_{\overline{W}}^{*n}, \omega) = v(\lambda_{\overline{W}}^{*n} f^{*n}(\omega(1)))$$
$$\geq v(\lambda_W^*(1 - \epsilon_m') f^*(\omega(1))(1 - \epsilon_m)) \geq v(\lambda_{\underline{W}}^*, f^*(\omega(1))),$$

for all ω such that $|\omega(1)| \leq \sqrt{n}$. Hence, with P^n-probability 1,

$$u(\chi^{*n}(\lambda_{\overline{W}}^{*n}, \omega)) \geq u(\chi^*(\lambda_{\underline{W}}^*, \omega)),$$

which implies that

$$\mathbf{E}^n[u(\chi^{*n}(\lambda_{\overline{W}}^{*n}, \omega))] \geq \mathbf{E}^n[u(\chi^*(\lambda_{\underline{W}}^*, \omega))].$$

Applying (4.2) and the weak convergence of P^n to P, we get

$$\liminf_n \mathbf{E}^n[u(\chi^{*n}(\lambda_W^{*n}, \omega))] \geq \mathbf{E}[u(\chi^*(\lambda_{\underline{W}}^*, \omega))].$$

And, similarly,

$$\limsup_n \mathbf{E}^n[u(\chi^{*n}(\lambda_W^{*n}, \omega))] \leq \mathbf{E}[u(\chi^*(\lambda_{\overline{W}}^*, \omega))].$$

But since $\underline{W}$ and $\overline{W}$ were chosen to be (arbitrarily) close to W, and expected utilities in the BSM economy converge as wealth levels converge, we are done. ∎

Let me reiterate that, even with the lemma, the proof is not simple, because when it comes to comparing integrals for the nth discrete-time economies with the corresponding integrals for the limit economy, both the integrand and the integrating measure are changing. The lemma allows us to bound the integrands with a fixed (in n) integrand; then weak convergence of the measures, using the bounds of inequalities (4.2), allows us to pass to the limit in the integrating measure.

Concerning the Assumption in Proposition 4.4 that the Bounds (4.2) Hold

The following result is easily proved by integrating $-u''(x)/u'(x) > \alpha/x$ to bound u' and then integrating again to bound the form of u. So this is left for the reader.

Proposition 4.6. *If the consumer's coefficient of relative risk aversion,* $-xu''(x)/u'(x)$, *is everywhere above some* $\alpha > 0$, *then (4.2) holds for both the solution to the consumer's problem and her (random) utility at the solution.*

In particular, the condition holds for consumers with constant (positive) relative risk aversion, as can be easily verified by direct computation. It is perhaps worth pointing out that for this to be true, the domain of definition of u cannot extend into negative levels of wealth, although it is relatively straightforward to think of extensions of Proposition 4.6 that work for u whose domain is all of R. Also, it is generally thought that investors' coefficients of relative risk aversion are nondecreasing functions of their wealth; if you believe this, then the condition is quite mild.

On the other hand, suppose that $u'(x)$ goes to 0 very slowly. Suppose, for instance, that $u'(x) = (\ln(x+1))^{-2}$. Then $v(\ell) = e^{\ell^{-1/2}} - 1$. A solution, if one exists, would have to take the form $x^*(\omega) = Le^{S(1,\omega)^{1/2}} - 1$ for a constant L. This does not satisfy (4.2).

Other Binomial Random Walks

The developments in this chapter concern a very special random walk for the binomial-random-walk models: upticks and downticks are of equal size $(1/\sqrt{n})$, with equal probabilities. But the theory developed works nearly as well – with one problem – for a general class of binomial random walks.

By "a general class of binomial random walks," I mean: A mean 0 random variable ζ is given with two-point support: one point, call it A, greater than 0, and the other, B, less than 0. The probabilities of up- and down-ticks are determined by the values of A and B and the assumption that the mean of ζ is 0: Letting p^+ be the probability of an uptick, we must have $p^+A + (1 - p^+)B = 0$, or $p^+ = -B/(A - B)$ and so $1 - p^+ = A/(A - B)$. The variance of ζ is then $-B/(A - B) \cdot A^2 + A/(A - B) \cdot B^2 = -AB$. In the nth economy, the distribution (under P^n) of $\omega((k + 1)/n) - \omega(k/n)$ is the distribution of $\zeta/\sqrt{n}$, with the path of

ω between $(k+1)/n$ and k/n filled in by, say, linear interpolation, and with the increments $\{\omega((k+1)/n) - \omega(k/n); k = 0, 1, \ldots, n-1\}$ fully independent. By a simple application of Donsker's Theorem, $P^n \Rightarrow P$, where P is (now) Wiener measure adjusted so that $\{\omega(t)\}$ is a Brownian motion with zero drift and infinitessimal variance $-AB$.[20]

(I say "a general class of binomial random walks," and not "the entire class of binomial random walks" because with different methods of scaling the step sizes in the nth discrete-time economy, one can create binomial random walks (for each n) that converge to other sorts of limits. See, for instance, Chapter 7 and the introductory discussion of Cox and Ross (1976) and Cox, Ross, and Rubinstein (1979), where the limit in n is a Poisson jump process with compensating drift.)

From here: The unique equivalent martingale measure for P, P^*, adjusts the drift of the Brownian motion to $-AB/2$. The Radon–Nikodym derivative dP^*/dP is $e^{-\omega(1)/2 - AB/8}$. As for the nth economy, the unique equivalent martingale measure for P^n, denoted P^{*n}, is obtained from

$$\pi^{*n} e^{A/\sqrt{n}} + (1 - \pi^{*n}) e^{B/\sqrt{n}} = 1, \quad \text{which gives}$$

$$\pi^{*n} = \frac{1 - e^{B/\sqrt{n}}}{e^{A/\sqrt{n}} - e^{B/\sqrt{n}}} \quad \text{and} \quad 1 - \pi^{*n} = \frac{e^{A/\sqrt{n}} - 1}{e^{A/\sqrt{n}} - e^{B/\sqrt{n}}}.$$

To show that $P^{*n} \Rightarrow P^*$ is about as simple as before: In the appendix, I sketch the calculations required to show convergence of the finite-dimensional distributions. As for tightness, the trick used to show tightness for the case $A = 1$ and $B = -1$ requires that dP^{*n}/dP^n is a decreasing function of $\omega(1)$ only, which is true here.

Going further, much of the theory developed in this chapter can be extended to the general binomial random walk. In particular, let $f^{*n}(x)$ be the real-valued function that gives the Radon–Nikodym derivative

---

[20] To have P^n approach a Brownian motion with a nonzero drift, you cannot take ζ to have nonzero mean; if $E[\zeta] \neq 0$, the scaled increments will run away to either $+\infty$ or $-\infty$, depending on the sign of $E[\zeta]$. Instead, change the distribution of $\omega((k+1)/n) - \omega(k/n)$ under P^n to have the distribution of ζ shifted by the constant μ/n, where μ is the desired drift. If you do this, and if μ is large, the nth economy will not be viable for small n; the "mean correction" μ/n can be such that ω increases with probability 1. But since we scale ζ by $1/\sqrt{n}$ and add μ scaled by $1/n$, no matter what is μ, the nth economy is viable for sufficiently large n.

dP^{*n}/dP^n for x of the form $kA + (n - k)B$.[21]   And (temporarily) let $f^*(x) = e^{-x/2-AB/8}$, which gives dP^*/dP. Showing that f^{*n} converges to f^* pointwise is not difficult: A variation on the discussion of Esscher Transforms found in Chapter 5 is required, but the variation is straight-forward.

However, the proof of Proposition 4.5 cannot be extended if $A \neq -B$. The reason is that Lemma 4.2, which is crucial to the proof, is not true. It is true that $f^{*n} \to f^*$ pointwise, but the rate of convergence is inadequate to extend inequality (4.8). (The discussion in Chapter 5 of the Esscher Transform will show why this is.) This does *not* mean that the conclusions of Proposition 4.5 are false for general binomial random walks. I conjecture that they do hold. But I cannot provide a proof.

What can be shown – and much more generally – is that $\lim \sup_n U^{*n} \geq U^*$. In words, the consumer can do at least as well asymptotically in the discrete-time economies (for a general binomial random walk, and more) as she can in the BSM economy. This will be shown in the next chapter.

Finally, it is essential that we have a binomial *random walk*. In Chapters 6 and 7, I provide examples of sequences of discrete-time binomial processes that converge to "nice" continuous-time limits (in Chapter 7, to the BSM model), but for which the economics along the sequence give very different answers than the economics of the limit economy.

So Is BSM a Good Idealization of the Binomial-Random-Walk Economies?

I think the conclusion must be that the BSM economy is indeed a good economic idealization of binomial-random-walk economies with rapid opportunities to trade, but with two important caveats. Binomial random walks "converge" to BSM in terms of their "coarse" or "gross" features. As long as the objective is to synthesize contingent claims that are continuous functions of those features, or whose discontinuities are "few," we're fine. And in terms of consumer maximization problems, if the consumers only care about "coarse" features – which we've oper-ationalized by assuming that the consumer in question is an expected-utility maximizer with a utility function that is well behaved – then we're fine. But for claims that depend on the fine features of the path of relative

---

[21]   That is, $dP^{*n}/dP^n|_\omega = f^{*n}(\omega(1))$, which involves the observation that dP^{*n}/dP^n is a function of $\omega(1)$.

prices (such as, their squared variation, or whether or not the final stock price is or is not an algebraic number) – and for consumers who care about such things – the answer is no.

Bibliographic Remarks

As noted at the start of this chapter, the use of the binomial-random-walk model to illustrate the "logic" of BSM has become virtually universal in books and courses on option pricing. Sharpe (1978) is the earliest published account of which I know that takes this approach to explaining BSM. Sharpe also verified computationally that prices in the binomial model converged to the prices given by the BSM papers. The seminal paper Cox, Ross, and Rubinstein (1979) develops this idea and formally proves that the prices of the call option in the binomial models converge to its BSM price.

I have cited Billingsley (1999) as the wonderful reference on weak convergence of probability measures several places in the text, but wish to do so again here. (If you have a copy of the first edition of this book, which was published in 1968, it is adequate for everything in this chapter. But the first edition lacks the Skorohod Representation Theorem, which is used in Chapter 5.)

Merton (1969) is the seminal reference for solutions to the consumer's utility maximization problem in continuous-time models of financial markets, such as BSM. (His models have consumers who consume continuously, and so are significantly more general than what is done here.) Cox and Huang (1989) is, I believe, the first treatment of the problem that moved from Merton's dynamic programming approach to the simple one-budget-constraint approach, which is feasible because, in BSM, markets are complete. The seminal work on the question of convergence of binomial-random-walk models to BSM is He (1991).

5. General Random-Walk Models

Chapter 4 is fine as far as it goes, but it doesn't go very far. *If* it takes a binomial random walk (or even, more generally, an only-two-steps-at-a-time information structure) to have BSM as an idealization, then BSM doesn't idealize very much. Happily, it *does not* take two-steps-at-a-time, at least in some economically meaningful senses. In this chapter, we see how much of what happened in Chapter 4 can be extended to general random-walk models.

The setting is as in Chapter 4. The state space is $C[0, 1]$, endowed with the sup-norm topology and the Borel σ-algebra $F = F_1$. The natural filtration $\{F_t\}$ is employed. P denotes Wiener measure on $C[0, 1]$; that is $\{\omega(t); t \in [0, 1]\}$ is a standard Brownian motion under P. The BSM economy has a bond, which is the numeraire and whose price process is therefore the constant 1; a second financial security, the stock, is given by the function $S : C[0, 1] \to C[0, 1]$ defined by $S(\omega)(t) := e^{\omega(t)}$. P^* denotes the unique probability measure on $C[0, 1]$ that is equivalent to P and that makes $\{S(\omega)(t); t \in [0, 1]\}$ a martingale over $\{F_t\}$, $\mathbf{E}$ denotes expectation with respect to P, $\mathbf{E}^*$ denotes expectation with respect to P^*, and $p^* : C[0, 1] \to (0, \infty)$ denotes the Radon–Nikodym derivative dP^*/dP, which is $p^*(\omega) = (dP^*/dP)(\omega) = 1/e^{\omega(1)/2+1/8}$.

The discrete-time-process probability measures P^n are created from a fixed, mean 0, variance 1 random variable ζ. For each $n = 1, 2, \ldots$, a probability measure P^n is defined on $C[0, 1]$ so that, under P^n:

- $\omega(0) = 0$ with probability 1,

- $\omega((k+1)/n) - \omega(k/n)$ has the distribution of $\zeta/\sqrt{n}$, for $k = 0, 1, \ldots,$ $n - 1$,

- $\omega(t)$ for t between k/n and $(k + 1)/n$ is filled in by linear interpolation, and

- the increments $\{\omega((k+1)/n) - \omega(k/n); k = 0, 1, \ldots, n - 1\}$ are fully independent.

And then we imagine an economy in which there is a bond and a stock that trade at times k/n, where the bond is the numeraire and the stock's price relative to the bond is given by $S(\omega)(k/n) = e^{\omega(k/n)}$.

This formulation rates several remarks. First, back in Chapters 1 and 2, when I was introducing this sort of model, I worked with increments ζ_ℓ^n for the nth economy that came already scaled by $\sqrt{n}$. At this point, because we are (for now) putting everything on the state space $C[0,1]$, we can simply specify the unscaled distribution of "steps," given by the distribution of some fixed random variable ζ, and then build P^n as above. Second, the binomial-random-walk model of the last chapter had $\zeta = \pm 1$, each with probability $1/2$ (although at the end I asserted that much of the analysis extends to any mean 0, positive variance ζ with a two-point support). Because the support of ζ in Chapter 4 has two elements, P^n for that model has a support of 2^n paths. Here, for a general ζ, the support of P^n is finite if the support of ζ is finite, it is countable if the support of ζ is countable, and it is uncountable if the support of ζ is uncountable.

And, most importantly, because ζ is assumed to have mean 0 and variance 1, its law must assign positive probability to both $(0,\infty)$ and $(-\infty,0)$. Therefore, for each P^n, we can produce equivalent martingale measures, meaning probability measures on $C[0,1]$ that are equivalent to P^n and that, for each n, turn $\{S(\omega)(k/n); k = 0,\ldots,n\}$ into a martingale over $\{F_{k/n}; k = 0,\ldots,n\}$. The set of equivalent martingale measures for P^n is singleton if and only if ζ has a two-element support.

While the previous paragraph is true, it isn't "the whole truth." If the support of ζ is finite, then everything asserted is a consequence of the general theory developed in Chapter 2, and we can say moreover that the model is viable and admits no free lunches. But neither Chapter 2 nor Chapter 3 fits if the support of ζ is not finite. I'm *directly* asserting the existence of equivalent martingale measures, which isn't hard to prove: Define, for any (measurable) set A, $\eta^n(A)$ as the conditional probability that $\zeta/\sqrt{n}$ falls in A, conditional on η^n being nonnegative, or $\eta^n(A) = P(\zeta/\sqrt{n} \in A \cap [0,\infty))/P(\zeta/\sqrt{n} \in [0,\infty))$, and define $\nu^n(A)$ as the conditional probability that $\zeta/\sqrt{n}$ falls in A, conditional on $\zeta/\sqrt{n}$ being strictly negative. Then $\alpha\eta^n + (1-\alpha)\nu^n$ for $\alpha \in (0,1)$ is a probability measure (on R) that is equivalent to the given distribution of $\eta/\sqrt{n}$. The expectation of $e^{\zeta/\sqrt{n}}$ under $\alpha\eta^n + (1-\alpha)\nu^n$ is a continuous (and monotone) function of α that is strictly greater than 1 for α close to 1 and strictly less than 1 for α close to 0; the Intermediate Value Theorem tell us that for some α, the expectation is 1, which gives us one equivalent martingale measure (hereafter abbreviated emm).

But discussions of viability when ζ has infinite support require further development of the ideas in Chapter 2. It isn't hard to do, following the methods of Chapter 3 (or see Dalang, Morton, and Willinger, 1990). But it hasn't been done here.

As for convergence results: It is an immediate consequence of the classic Donsker's Theorem that $P^n \Rightarrow P$. But we can't write $P^{*n} \Rightarrow P^*$, because there is no single equivalent martingale measure P^{*n} for the nth economy. Or, to be precise, this is true if ζ has support larger than two elements.

The Esscher Transform and emm

For a variety of reasons (including the fact that this is the basis for the Lemma used in the proof of Proposition 4.5 in Chapter 4), it is useful to identify one particular (and very well behaved) equivalent martingale measure P^{*n} for each of the P^n. Three desirable properties for this selection of P^{*n} are: $P^{*n} \Rightarrow P^*$; dP^{*n}/dP^n, the Radon–Nikodym derivative of P^{*n} with respect to P^n, is a function of $\omega(1)$ only; and dP^{*n}/dP^n, viewed as a function of $\omega(1)$, is strictly decreasing. Going back to Chapter 4, where for each P^n there is a unique P^{*n}, we know – and have made extensive use of the fact that – all three of these desirable properties hold. We can have them for the "general" case where each P^n is generated by random walks built out of scaled copies of a fixed mean-0, variance-1 random variable ζ, if in addition ζ has bounded support: The *Esscher Transform*, which originated in the literature of actuarial science (Esscher, 1932) is just what we require.

Lemma 5.1. The Esscher Transform. *Suppose that ζ has mean 0, variance 1, and bounded support.*

a. *There exist unique constants a_n and b_n such that the measure P^{*n} given by the Radon–Nikodym derivative*

$$\frac{dP^{*n}}{dP^n} = e^{-a_n \omega(1) - b_n}$$

is an equivalent martingale measure for P^n.

b. *As $n \to \infty$, $a_n \to 1/2$ and $b_n \to 1/8$. Hence,*

$$\frac{dP^{*n}}{dP^n} \text{ "approaches" } \frac{dP^*}{dP} = e^{-\omega(1)/2 - 1/8},$$

where the scare quotes around "approaches" will be explained immediately following the statement of this lemma.

c. *In fact,* $a_n = 1/2 + \hat{\mathbf{E}}[\zeta^3]/(24\sqrt{n}) + o(1/\sqrt{n})$, *and* $\lim_n b_n = 1/8$, *where* $\hat{\mathbf{E}}[\cdot]$ *will be used to denote taking expectations over the variable* ζ.

Before launching into the proof, let me explain the scare quotes in part *b* of the lemma. (This is a story already told, but it bears retelling in this context.) Both dP^{*n}/dP and dP^*/dP are random variables, defined (respectively) for the probability measure P^n and P. As such, we can change dP^{*n}/dP^n on a set of P^n-probability 0, and we can change dP^*/dP on a set of P-probability 0, without "changing" them as random variables. Suppose ζ has support that consists only of rational numbers. Then, under P^n, the set of ω that end with $\omega(1)$ of the form $q/\sqrt{n}$ for rational q has probability 1. But under P, this set of ω has probability 0. So, *unless we fix versions of* dP^{*n}/dP^n *and* dP^*/dP, part *b* of the lemma makes no sense.

This – fixing specific versions of dP^{*n}/dP^n and dP^*/dP – is what we do. For $r \in R$, define

$$f^{*n}(r) := e^{-a_n r - b_n} \quad \text{and} \quad f^*(r) := e^{-r/2 - 1/8}.$$

Then: $f^{*n}(\omega(1))$ is a version of $(dP^{*n}/dP^n)(\omega)$; $f^*(\omega(1))$ is a version of $(dP^*/dP)(\omega)$; and part *c* gives an estimate of how far apart are the f^{*n} from f^* for every real number r.

Proof of Lemma 5.1. Think of how, mechanically, one creates an equivalent martingale measure in a finite-state, finite-time tree: The probabilities on the different branches are manipulated, without inventing new branches or assigning probability 0 to an existing branch, to turn the stock price process into one in which the expected rate of return over each time interval is the riskless rate, in this case, 1.

The Esscher Transform does this, in effect. Fix n and ζ, and think about the change in the stock price from time k/n to time $(k+1)/n$. Under P^n, the expected rate of return is $\hat{\mathbf{E}}\left[e^{\zeta/\sqrt{n}}\right]$. Because ζ has expectation 0 and variance 1 and the function e^r is convex, we know that $\hat{\mathbf{E}}\left[e^{\zeta/\sqrt{n}}\right] > 1$, so we need to move probability from larger values of ζ to smaller values of ζ. Consider, in this regard, a shift in probability where the previous probability of the outcome $\zeta = r$ is shifted multiplicatively by $e^{-a_n r - c_n}$.

(The role of the c_n will be explained momentarily.) For any two values r and r' in the support of $\zeta/\sqrt{n}$ such that $r > r'$, this is a *relative* shift in probability away from r and in favor of the outcome r'. If a_n is 0, there is no shift at all; as a_n increases from 0, the shift is more pronounced

For this multiplicative shift in probabilities to give us an emm (locally, for this one change in what happens from k/n to $(k+1)/n$), two constraints must be met. First, the total shift in probabilities must leave us with a probability distribution; some "normalization" will be needed. Second, the shift should be just enough to make the rate of return over the period equal to 1. These two constraints are, respectively,

$$
\begin{aligned}
&\hat{\mathbf{E}}\big[e^{-a_n\zeta/\sqrt{n}-c_n}\big] = 1 \text{ and} \\
&\hat{\mathbf{E}}\big[e^{\zeta/\sqrt{n}}e^{-a_n\zeta/\sqrt{n}-c_n}\big] = \hat{\mathbf{E}}\big[e^{(1-a_n)\zeta/\sqrt{n}-c_n}\big] = 1,
\end{aligned}
\tag{5.1}
$$

where the term e^{-c_n} is the normalizing constant, and the second equation is the "rate-of-return-equals-1" constraint.

Of course, if these two equations hold, then

$$
\hat{\mathbf{E}}\big[e^{-a_n\zeta/\sqrt{n}}\big] = \hat{\mathbf{E}}\big[e^{(1-a_n)\zeta/\sqrt{n}}\big],
\tag{5.2}
$$

which uniquely determines a_n: At $a_n = 0$, the term on the left-hand side of (5.2) is 1, while the term on the right-hand side is greater than 1. And when a_n reaches 1, the term on the right-hand side is 1. Both the term on the left and the term on the right move continuously in a_n, and they move monotonically in different directions: For the left-hand side, think of $-a_n\zeta/\sqrt{n}$ as $a_n(-\zeta/\sqrt{n})$. Since $\hat{\mathbf{E}}[\zeta] = 0$, the same is true of $-\zeta$, and so increasing a_n is a mean-preserving spread of $a_n(-\zeta/\sqrt{n})$. Since the exponential function is convex, this increases the expectation of $e^{\alpha(-\zeta/\sqrt{n})}$. And on the right-hand side, increasing a_n is a mean-preserving shrink of the random variable $(1 - a_n)\zeta/\sqrt{n}$; hence, by the convexity of the exponential function, the right-hand side is decreasing in a_n.

Once a_n is determined by equation (5.2), c_n is uniquely determined by either equation in (5.1).[1]

---

[1]   While I have restricted attention to ζ with bounded support, as long as the tails of the distribution of ζ are sufficiently "thin," everything so far can still work. But for what comes next, the bounded support assumption is needed.

Now consider Equation (5.2) for large n. Writing a Taylor series expansion in the exact form to the fourth degree term, this is

$$\hat{\mathbf{E}}\left[1 - \frac{a_n\zeta}{\sqrt{n}} + \frac{a_n^2\zeta^2}{2n} - \frac{a_n^3\zeta^3}{6n^{3/2}} - \frac{a_n^4\zeta^4}{24n^2}e^{(-a_n\zeta/\sqrt{n})\theta_\zeta}\right] =$$

$$\hat{\mathbf{E}}\left[1 + \frac{(1-a_n)\zeta}{\sqrt{n}} + \frac{(1-a_n)^2\zeta^2}{2n} + \frac{(1-a_n)^3\zeta^3}{6n^{3/2}} + \frac{(1-a_n)^4\zeta^4}{24n^2}e^{(-a_n\zeta/\sqrt{n})\theta'_\zeta}\right],$$

where θ_ζ and θ'_ζ are terms between 0 and 1. Passing the expectation into the sums, the second term on each side is 0, while the third term has $\hat{\mathbf{E}}[\zeta^2] = 1$. The leading term of 1 on both sides cancels, leaving terms with powers of n of 1 or greater in the denominators and so, multiplying both sides by n, we get

$$\frac{a_n^2}{2} - a_n^3\frac{\hat{\mathbf{E}}[\zeta^3]}{6n^{1/2}} + \hat{\mathbf{E}}\left[\frac{a_n^4\zeta^4}{24n}e^{(-a_n\zeta/\sqrt{n})\theta_\zeta}\right]$$

$$= \frac{(1-a_n)^2}{2} + (1-a_n)^3\frac{\hat{\mathbf{E}}[\zeta^3]}{6n^{1/2}} + \hat{\mathbf{E}}\left[\frac{(1-a_n)^4\zeta^4}{24n}e^{(-a_n\zeta/\sqrt{n})\theta'_\zeta}\right].$$

I assert in two steps that a_n is $1/2 + \hat{\mathbf{E}}[\zeta^3]/(24\sqrt{n}) + o(1/n^{1/2})$. The difference between the first terms on each side, $a_n^2/2 - (1-a_n)^2/2$, is $1/2 - a_n$, which is 0 at $a_n = 1/2$ and contributes a term linear in a_n as we move away from $a_n = 1/2$. The second and third terms on each side are uniformly bounded by $K/\sqrt{n}$ for some constant K, so the solution to the equation can't be different from $1/2$ by a term that is more than $O(1/\sqrt{n})$ from $1/2$. But then, for $a_n = 1/2 + O(\sqrt{n})$, and evaluating the second terms on each side of the equation give us $-\hat{\mathbf{E}}[\zeta^3]/(48n^{1/2}) + o(1/\sqrt{n})$ on the left-hand side and $\hat{\mathbf{E}}[\zeta^3]/(48n^{1/2}) + o(1/\sqrt{n})$ on the right. The third terms on each side are $o(1/\sqrt{n})$, so moving everything to the right, we get that the equation that determines a_n is

$$0 = \frac{1}{2} - a_n + \frac{\hat{\mathbf{E}}[\zeta^3]}{24n^{1/2}} + o(1/n^{1/2}) \quad \text{or} \quad a_n = \frac{1}{2} + \frac{\hat{\mathbf{E}}[\zeta^3]}{24n^{1/2}} + o(1/n^{1/2}).$$

The next step is to estimate the normalizing constant c_n from the equation

$$\hat{\mathbf{E}}\left[e^{-a_n\zeta/\sqrt{n}-c_n}\right] = 1 \quad \text{or} \quad e^{c_n} = \hat{\mathbf{E}}\left[e^{-a_n\zeta/\sqrt{n}}\right].$$

Take a Taylor series expansion of the expectation on the right to get

$$e^{c_n} = \hat{\mathbf{E}}\left[1 - \frac{a_n \zeta}{\sqrt{n}} + \frac{a_n^2 \zeta^2}{2n} - \frac{a_n^3 \zeta^3}{6n^{3/2}} + o(1/n^{3/2})\right].$$

Taking expectation term by term, this gives $e^{c_n} = 1 + a_n^2/2n + o(1/n)$, and since $a_n = 1/2 + o(1/n^{1/2})$, this is

$$c_n = \ln\left[1 + \frac{1}{8n} + o(1/n)\right] \quad \text{or} \quad c_n = \frac{1}{8n} + o(1/n).$$

Note that this shift in probabilities applies in precisely the same manner for each of the n time periods, from 0 to $1/n$, from $1/n$ to $2/n$, and so forth. Hence, the total shift in probability – the R-N derivative dP^{*n}/dP^n – is the product of each individual shift, or

$$\prod_{k=1}^{n} \exp\left[-a_n\big(\omega(k/n) - \omega(k-1)/n\big) - c_n\right]$$

$$= \exp\left[\sum_{k=1}^{n}\big(-a_n\big((\omega(k/n) - \omega(k-1)/n)\big) - c_n\big)\right] = e^{-a_n \omega(1) - n c_n}.$$

And since $c_n = 1/(8/n) + o(1/n)$, $b_n = n c_n = 1/8 + no(1/n)$, which is $\lim_n b_n = 1/8$. ∎

Corollary 5.1. *If $\hat{\mathbf{E}}[\zeta^3] = 0$, then $a_n = 1/2 + o(1/\sqrt{n})$.*

This corollary provides Lemma 4.2 (page 92) used in the proof of Proposition 4.5. In the simple binomial-random-walk model, $\zeta = \pm 1$, each with probability $1/2$, and so has third moment 0. Hence, for that model, dP^{*n}/dP^n – which of course is the R-N derivative of the emm based on the Esscher Transform because there is a unique emm – has $a_n = 1/2 + o(1/\sqrt{n})$. The ratio $f^{*n}(x)/f^*(x)$ is $e^{-a_n x - b_n}/e^{-x/2 - 1/8} = e^{-o(1/\sqrt{n})} \times e^{1/8 - b_n}$. Taking Taylor series approximations to the two pieces $e^{-o(1/\sqrt{n})}$ and $e^{1/8 - b_n}$, we get that the ratio is $(1 - o'(1/\sqrt{n}))(1 - (1/8 - b_n))$, which, since $b_n \to 1/8$, is $1 + o(1/\sqrt{n})$, as asserted in the lemma.

This explains why the proof of Proposition 4.5 can't be extended to asymmetric binomial random walks. If ζ is "binomial," meaning it has a two-element support, but it is not symmetric around 0, then $\hat{E}[\zeta^3] \neq 0$. We still have a nice estimate about how close is dP^{*n}/dP^n is to dP^*/dP. But the estimate $a_n = 1/2 + \hat{E}[\zeta^3]/(24n^{1/2}) + o(1/n^{1/2})$ isn't nice enough to generate the key lemma. I believe that the conclusions of Proposition 4.5 hold for asymmetric binomial random walks. But I am unable to provide a proof.

The Trinomial Random Walk and Near Synthesis of the Call Option

We return to the main plot: Suppose that ζ – I'll use the notation $\tilde{\zeta}$ to indicate this specific case – has the following distribution:

$$\tilde{\zeta} = \begin{cases} +1.5, & \text{with probability } 2/9, \\ 0, & \text{with probability } 5/9, \text{ and} \\ -1.5, & \text{with probability } 2/9. \end{cases}$$

This case was discussed in Chapter 2, where it was noted that, for any n, many emms $\tilde{P}^{*n}$ can be constructed. Begin with emms for which the transition probabilities for each step are time and position invariant: Let q for $0 < q < 1$ be the probability that $\omega((k+1)/n) - \omega(k/n) = 0$ (that $S((k+1)/n) = S(k/n)$), and then, given q, set the probability that $\omega((k+1)/n) - \omega(k/n) = 1.5/\sqrt{n}$ to be $(1-q)[1/(e^{1.5/\sqrt{n}} + 1)]$. As q varies, this gives a continuuum of emms. And there are many more, since the "adjustments" to the transition probabilities can be done on a time-dependent and state-up-to-now-dependent basis. [2]

Hence, markets are far from complete. Take, for instance, the canonical call option $x_C(\omega) = \max\{0, \omega(1) - 1\}$. With respect to the BSM model, the price for setting up a portfolio that synthesizes x_C is, to five decimal places, 0.38239. From the last chapter, we know that, for the binomial-random-walk economy, the price of synthesizing this contingent claim will approach this BSM value as $n \to \infty$.

In the trinomial world, this claim cannot be synthesized. If we take an emm $\tilde{P}^{*n}$ that chooses q very close to 1 at all transitions, under this emm, $E^{\tilde{P}^{*n}}[x_C]$ will be very close to 0, because for q close to 1, the P^{*n}-probability that $S(1) = 0$ approaches 1. If, on the other hand, we take

---

[2] Because the distribution of $\tilde{\zeta}$ is symmetric around 0, $\hat{E}[\tilde{\zeta}^3] = 0$, so for the specific emm derived from the Esscher Transform, we have the strong estimate and $a_n = 1/2 + o(1/\sqrt{n})$.

emms that have q approaching 0, the expectation of x_C under such emms approach ≈ 0.5954. Therefore, according to the general theory of Chapter 2, "arbitrage bounds" on the price of x_C – under both interpretations of "arbitrage bounds" given on pages 24 and 25 – are at least as wide as $(0, \approx 0.5954)$. Of course, the 0 lower bound is tight; holding a portfolio of no stock and no bond, at a cost of 0, is P^n-a.s. worth less than x_C. And one can show that this upper bound ≈ 0.5954 is tight as well.

But now recall the exercise described in Chapter 1. In the nth trinomial world for $n = 400$, start with a portfolio of 0.69145 shares of stock and -0.30906 bonds. At time $1/400$, adjust the stock holding to what would be held in the BSM world, if you were trying to synthesize x_C, as a function of $S(\omega)(1/400)$, and using the bond holding to finance any purchases (if $S(\omega)(1/400) > 1$) and to soak up sales (if $S(\omega)(1/400) < 1$). (If $S(\omega)(1/400) = 1$, which has probability 5/9, it turns out that you slightly decrease your stock holding, following the BSM rule for synthesizing x_C). Do the same at time $2/400$, and so on. At time 1, how does what you hold compare in value with $x_C(\omega)$?

See Figures 5.1 (which reproduces Figure 1.1), 5.2, and 5.3. These figures show the results of this strategy, based on 500 simulations of the process.

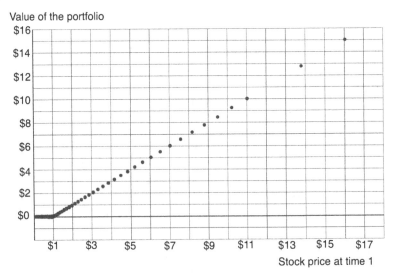

Figure 5.1. Scatter plot of stock price versus value of an imperfectly synthesized European call option with exercise price 1, using the trinomial (tilde) model for $n = 400$. This shows the results of 500 rounds of simulation.

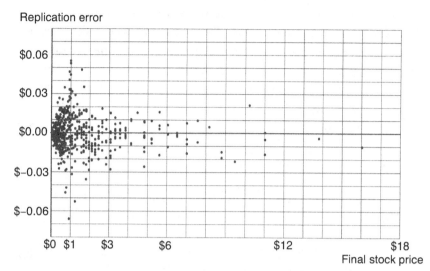

Figure 5.2. Scatter plot of replication errors. This figure shows a scatter plot of how far off the "imperfect relication" of a call option is from the value of the call option, in the trinomial world, with $n = 400$, for 500 iterations of a Monte-Carlo simulation. Positive values are where the final replicating portfolio is worth more than the call option; negative terms are where it is worth less.

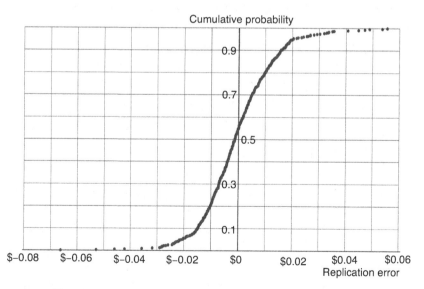

Figure 5.3. Cumulative distribution function of the replication errors.

Figure 5.1 plots the value of the investor's final portfolio (for each iteration of the simulation) against the final stock price in that iteration. Figure 5.2 plots the *replication error* – the value of the final portfolio less the correct price of the call option – against the final stock price. And Figure 5.3 plots the cumulative distribution function of the replication errors. The average replication error in 500 trials was -0.000504, with a standard deviation of 0.0139. The average absolute replication error was 0.0102.

The conclusion stares us in the face. Despite the wide arbitrage bounds on the price of the European call, an investor who wants to synthesize a claim that comes close is certainly able to do so. Based on this evidence, we might conjecture that, while markets in the trinomial world are incomplete, they are "nearly" complete, for large n.

Figures 5.2 and 5.3 tell us more. Figure 5.2 shows that the replication error is most likely to be "large" (on either side) when the final price of the stock is around the exercise price of 1. Presumably, this is because, in this region of the stock price and near time 1, the composition of the fully replicating portfolio changes most dramatically. And Figure 5.3 shows that, while the arbitrage bounds on the price of the call option for large n are from 0 to 0.5495, real-life arbitrageurs, placed in (say) the $n = 400$ trinomial economy, would probably be willing to undertake arbitrage operations if the price of the call option were more than $0.03 from the BSM price of $0.38239. Suppose, for instance, call options sold for $0.41239. An arbitrageur could sell call options and "buy" replicating portfolios, for an immediate profit of $0.03 per unit. The danger is that the replicating portfolios might wind up worth less than the final value of the call. But the chance that the replicating portfolios is more than $0.03 less is roughly 1.5% and, based on these simulations, gets no worse than $0.07 less. On the other side, if the options traded for less than $0.35239, an arbitrageur could buy options and short the replicating portfolio. Although, based on these simulations, the "worst case scenario" is that the arbitrageur would be out $0.055 or so per unit, that has very small probability; the odds that the replicating portfolio (which the arbitrageur must cover) is worth $0.03 or more than the call option is around 2.5%.

Moreover, this overstates the risk facing the arbitrageur. Because the distribution of replication errors is roughly symmetric around 0, the arbitrageur who, in our story, puts $0.03 in her pocket at the outset, has

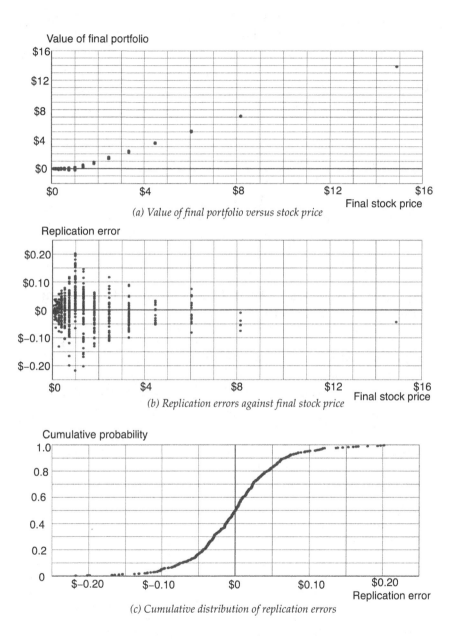

(a) *Value of final portfolio versus stock price*

(b) *Replication errors against final stock price*

(c) *Cumulative distribution of replication errors*

Figure 5.4. The case $n = 25$. This figure shows the results of simulating the strategy of approximating the synthesis of the call option with strike price 1 in the discrete-time economy with $n = 25$.

probability about 0.5 of making *more* money when she closes her position, whichever side she takes. So while the by-the-textbook arbitrage bounds on the price of the call option are from \$0 to \$0.5495, an arbitrageur willing to take a small chance of a (not very big) loss for a large chance of a gain would "enforce" prices in a much tighter band around the Black–Scholes price of \$0.35239. (Of course, in real life, there are transaction costs to consider, as well.)[3]

It should be clear that the ability to replicate the call option is worse the smaller is n. Figure 5.4 provides the same pictures as do Figures 5.1, 5.2, and 5.3 for $n = 25$ instead of $n = 400$ (again for 500 iterations of the simulation). For these 500 iterations, the average replication error was \$ − 0.00104, with a population standard deviation of \$0.0589, and the absolute replication error was \$0.04397, with a population standard deviation of \$0.03913.

Asymptotic Synthesis of Contingent Claims for General Random-Walk Economies

When shown Figures 5.1, 5.2, and 5.3, colleagues have expressed surprise (as did I upon seeing this); the wide arbitrage bounds on the price of the call option would seem to imply that one cannot get so close to synthesizing the option (in the trinomial world). But this should not have come as a surprise: Duffie and Protter (1991), based on work by Jakubowski, Mémin, and Pagès (1989) and Kurtz and Protter (1991a, 1991b), show (essentially) that this must happen. The following proposition adapts and extends this idea, in the specific context of discrete-time, random-walk economies that are driven by a general random variable ζ.

---

[3] For fun (this is not reality), imagine an arbitrageur with constant absolute risk aversion in the relevant range, and with coefficient of absolute risk aversion of 0.00001. (This coefficient of absolute risk aversion is reasonable for a well-to-do individual: A 50–50 gamble with prizes \$0 and \$100,000 has a certainty equivalent of approximately \$38,000.) Suppose this arbitrageur, on her own account, takes a covered position in 10,000 call options; that is, she follows the prescription of forming a portfolio in stock and bond to replicate 10,000 options, and she sells 10,000 options. Ignoring transaction costs entirely, based on the 500-iteration simulation, her certainty equivalent, not including the profit she makes due to the option being mispriced, is \$ − 60. So if, say, the option's price is \$0.02 more than the initial cost of the replicating portfolio, her certainty equivalent from this position is \$140, and her certainty equivalent increases by \$100 for every cent more the option is overpriced. If the option is underpriced, the numbers are slightly better. Of course, transaction costs at this scale of arbitrage could be quite substantial. On the other hand, a well-backed arbitrageur's effective coefficient of risk aversion is probably a good deal less than 0.00001.

Proposition 5.1. *Fix a bounded and continuous contingent claim x (on $C[0,1]$).*

a. *For every $\epsilon > 0$, there exists N such that, for all $n \geq N$, a claim x^n can be synthesized in the nth discrete-time economy with an initial investment of $\mathbf{E}^*[x]$ such that*

$$P^n\big(\{\omega : |x^n(\omega) - x(\omega)| < \epsilon\}\big) > 1 - \epsilon.$$

b. *Suppose that ζ has **bounded** support. Then x can be asymptotically as above where, in addition, if $V^n(t, \omega)$ is the value of the synthesizing portfolio in the nth economy at time t and in state ω, then, for the same ϵ,*

$$P^n\big(\{\omega : V^n(t, \omega) \in \big[\underline{x} - \epsilon, \overline{x} + \epsilon\big] \text{ for all } t \in [0,1]\}\big) = 1,$$

where $\underline{x} := \inf\{x(\omega); \omega \in \Omega\}$ and $\overline{x} := \sup\{x(\omega); \omega \in \Omega\}$.

Translating, Proposition 5.1a says that that a consumer in the nth discrete-time economy (whose probability assessment of things is therefore P^n) can, for a given bounded and continuous claim x, synthesize a claim that is arbitrarily close to x, with probability that is arbitrarily close to 1, for large enough n.[4]

This, by itself, indicates why we are able to get pictures like Figures 5.1 through 5.4. But it is not really satisfactory because, per this "convergence criterion," a consumer can asymptotically synthesize a free lunch: Consider, for example, the sequence of economies where $\zeta = \pm 1$, each with probability $1/2$; that is, the discrete-time economies of Chapter 4. In the nth of these, employ the classic doubling strategy: At time 0, buy $1/(e^{1/\sqrt{n}} - 1)$ shares of stock, financed by selling this many bonds. There is probability $1/2$ that, at time $1/n$, this portfolio is worth $e^{1/\sqrt{n}}/(e^{1/\sqrt{n}} - 1) - 1/(e^{1/\sqrt{n}} - 1) = 1$, and probability $1/2$ that it is in the red. In the first case, convert to bonds and hold until time 1; in the second, scale up your stock holding sufficiently so that, at time $2/n$, there is again probability $1/2$ (conditional on the first stock movement being a downtick) that your portfolio is worth 1. And so forth. In the nth discrete-time economy, this produces, for an initial investment of 0, a portfolio whose value at time 1 is 1 with probability $1 - 1/2^n$, but whose

---

[4] To be explicit, the order of quantifiers here is that the "large enough" n depends on how close to x and to probability 1 one wishes to come.

value is a very large negative number with probability $1/2^n$. Because part *a* of the proposition doesn't say what is the value of x^n on the small-probability event where it is more then ϵ away from x, this almost free lunch satisfies the convergence criterion of part *a*.

Proposition 5.1*b* fixes things. It says that, as long as the support of ζ is bounded, a bounded and continuous claim x can be asymptotically synthesized by a sequence of trading strategies that have *uniformly bounded risk*, in the sense that they involve with probability 1 a loss (or gain) that is uniformly bounded. Indeed, it says more: It puts upper and lower bounds on the value of the synthesizing portfolio that are arbitrarily close to the bounds on the claim x. This criterion, of course, is not satisfied by the doubling strategy, and, as we'll see both later in this chapter and in Chapter 7, insisting on asymptotic synthesis with bounded risk puts this theory on a much sounder footing from the perspective of its economic content.

The full proof of the proposition – that is, with part *b* – is complex, which hides its intuition. So, I provide here an "intuitive" proof of part *a* only. "Intuitive" is in scare quotes because the proof still requires a few bits of mathematical magic, but (I hope) it conveys some indication of why this works. The idea behind the proof of part *b* is briefly sketched after the proof of part *a*; the detailed proof, which is due in large measure to Walter Schachermayer, is provided in a more general setting in Kreps and Schachermayer (2019).

Proof Stage I: A Very Special Case

In the first stage of the proof, two assumptions make this a very special case.

A. Assume that the contingent claim x can be written as a bounded and continuous function of $\omega(1)$ (only).

B. Assume that ζ, the unscaled "step-size" random variable, is Normal with mean 0 and variance 1. Hence, the nth discrete-time economy, where trading takes place at times $t = 0, 1/n, 2/n, \ldots, (n-1)/n$, can be viewed as the BSM economy but where the consumer is allowed to trade *only* at times $0, 1/n$, etc.

To be clear about this, we can interpret this very special case in either of two ways. The first, which is in line with our general approach, is that, in the nth discrete-time economy, there are prices for the stock only at times $t = 0, 1/n, 2/n, \ldots, (n-1)/n$, and the probability distribution P^n on the space $C[0,1]$ attaches positive probability only to sets of paths that are continuous and whose logs are piece-wise linear between these times. The second interpretation is that there are prices for the stock at all times $t \in [0,1]$, governed by the probability law P (that is, $S(t)$ under P is geometric Brownian motion), but the investor is only allowed to trade at times $0, 1/n, \ldots, (n-1)/n$. In terms of what the investor can accomplish, if she is constrained only to trade at these times and if her trades depend only on the values of the stock price at these times, the distributions of her final portfolio for a given trading strategy under P and under P^n are the same. So as we prove Proposition 5.1 in this very special case, the conclusion could be stated in terms of P instead of P^n; they are *essentially* the same.[5]

With these assumptions in place, the proof involves the following six steps.

Step 1. Harrison and Pliska (1981) show that for any bounded claim $x \in X$, x can be constructed in the BSM world:

$$x = \mathbf{E}^*[x] + \int_0^1 \alpha(\omega, t) dS(t),$$

where α is an adapted Brownian functional and $\mathbf{E}^*$ denotes expectation with respect to the unique emm for the BSM model. (In fact, they show this for all square-integrable claims, but we only need their result for bounded claims.)

Step 2. By assumption, x is a continuous function of $\omega(1)$. Write this as $x(\omega) = f(S(1, \omega), 1)$ for a continuous function f.[6] (The second argument of f, 1, which at this point is superfluous, is explained momentarily.)

---

[5] In literal fact, they are, of course, not the same at all. For instance, the probability that ω has unit squared variation is 1 under P, while under P^n this probability is 0. But P and P^n coincide when it comes to the finite-dimensional distributions of ω and S^ω at times $0, 1/n, 2/n, \ldots, 1$, which is what matters when it comes to the result being proved.

[6] Since $S(1, \omega) = e^{\omega(1)}$, if $x(\omega) = \phi(\omega(1))$ for a continuous ϕ, then $x(\omega) = \phi(\ln(S(1, \omega)))$, which is continuous in $S(1)$. Note that the domain of $S(1)$ is $(0, \infty)$, so if at any point we invoke properties of f on a compact domain, we must be careful to bound $S(1)$ from above *and away from* 0. This issue will arise later.

Step 3. Define, for $s \in (0, \infty)$ and $t \in [0, 1)$,

$$f(s, t) = \frac{1}{\sqrt{2\pi(1-t)^2}} \int_0^\infty f(e^x, 1)e^{-(x-\ln(s)-(1-t)/2)^2/(2(1-t)^2)}dx.$$

This is a version of $E^*[f(S(1, \omega), 1)|F_t]$, obtained by integrating $f(S(1, \omega), 1)$ against the log-normal density of $S(1)$ if $S(t) = s$. Because of the averaging against the log-normal density, this is a very smooth (twice-continuously differentiable and more) function of s and t.[7] Of course, $E^*[x]$, the BSM price of x, is then $f(1, 0)$.

Step 4. Using the Itô calculus, we know that the number of shares of stock held at time t in state ω – that is, $\alpha(\omega, t)$ – is the partial derivative of the current value of the option, or

$$\alpha(\omega, t) = g(S(t), t) := \frac{\partial f(s, t)}{\partial s} = \frac{\partial E^*[f(S(1), 1)|S(t) = s]}{\partial s}.$$

To be very pedantic, the function $g : R_+ \times [0, 1]$ that is *defined* as the partial derivative in s of f, evaluated at S and t, is, by Itô calculus, the *value* of $\alpha(\omega, t)$ if $S(t)(\omega) = S$. So, going back to the first step, for this function g, we have

$$x = E^*[x] + \int_0^1 \alpha(\omega, t)dS(t) = f(1, 0) + \int_0^1 g(S(t)(\omega), t)dS(t),$$

where I've substituted $f(1, 0)$ for $E^*[x]$ and $g(S(t)(\omega), t)$ for $\alpha(\omega, t)$. Moreover, the smoothing accomplished in taking expectations makes this function g continuous (and more).

Step 5. Let $I_n(\omega)$ be the forward-looking Itô sum defined by

$$I_n(\omega) := \sum_{k=0}^{n-1} g\big(S(k/n, \omega), k/n\big)\big[S((k+1)/n, \omega) - S(k/n, \omega)\big].$$

Because g is jointly continuous,

$$\lim_{n\to\infty} I_n(\omega) = \left[\int_0^1 g(S(t), t)dS(t)\right]_\omega = x(\omega) - f(1, 0),$$

---

[7]   The continuity of f is not needed for this smoothness, although it certainly doesn't hurt.

where convergence is in probability. Hence, for given $\epsilon > 0$, we can find an M large enough such that, for all $n \geq M$,

$$P\left(\left\{\omega : \left|I_n(\omega) + \mathbf{E}^*[x] - x(\omega)\right| > \epsilon\right\}\right) < \epsilon. \tag{5.3}$$

Step 6. Now imagine a consumer in the nth discrete-time economy, who behaves as follows: At time 0, she purchases $g(1,0)$ shares of stock and $f(1,0) - g(1,0)$ bonds, a net investment of $f(1,0)$ (since $S(0) \equiv 1$). Then, at times k/n, she buys or sell stock so that she holds (after her time k/n trading) $g(S(k/n), k/n)$ shares of stock, where she finances her portfolio re-balancing by selling or buying bonds. For each ω, the sum $I_n(\omega)$ is the financial-gains from following this strategy, so her portfolio at time 1, in state ω, has value

$$f(1,0) + I_n(\omega) = \mathbf{E}^*[x] + I_n(\omega).$$

Inequality (5.1) then tells us that, for $n \geq M$, this trading strategy "approximately" synthesizes x, where "approximately" is defined by inequality (5.1). This concludes Stage I.

Commentary on Stage I: There are two pieces of "mathematical magic" here: The first of these comes in Step 1, the Harrison and Pliska result that "markets are complete" in BSM. This is, presumably, not magic to people who understand deeply the theory of stochastic integration, although I happily confess that, while I can read the proof of this and I understand every step, because it relies on the Martingale Representation Theorem, it still strikes me as something incredible. And then, in Step 5, what is being said is that the stochastic integral that synthesizes x can be thought of as the in-probability limit of the simple Itô forward-looking sums. This is a consequence of how the Itô integral is defined and depends on the continuity of the integrand and the fact that S has continuous sample paths. This is, more or less, a textbook result in the theory of stochastic integration; see, for instance, Le Gall (2016, Proposition 5.9). This is, perhaps, easier to comprehend than Step 1, but it still takes a solid understanding of the theory of stochastic integration.

Proof Stage II: A Less Special Case, Begun

In Stage II, assumption A is maintained – we are trying to synthesize approximately a claim whose value depends only on $S(1)$ – but assumption B concerning the distribution of $\log(S((k + 1)/n)) - \log(S(k/n))$ is dropped. The proof I offer involves a very powerful mathematical hammer, the Skorohod Representation Theorem, and before offering the proof (and completing Stage II), I provide a statement of the theorem and some limited intuition for it. But because I invoke the Skorohod Representation Theorem for measures on $C[0, 1]$, this comes off as a third bit of mathematical magic. So, before plunging into the formal details, here is an intuitive explanation of what is going on in the proof.

Fix some $\epsilon > 0$ and fix an M large enough so that (5.3) holds in the context of Stage I, where the distribution of $\log(S((j+1)/n)) - \log(S(j/n))$ is Normal with mean 0 and variance $1/n$. Next, fix some very large L, and consider the nth discrete-time economy for $n = LN$, where the distribution of $\log(S((j+1)/n)) - \log(S(j/n))$ is the distribution of $\zeta/\sqrt{n}$. In that economy, imagine that an investor employs the following trading strategy:

> At time 0, at a cost of $\mathbf{E}^*[x]$, purchase the portfolio with $g(1,0)$ shares of stock and $\mathbf{E}^*[x] - g(1,0)$ bonds. That is, make the initial investment that would be made in the BSM economy. Hold this portfolio until time $1/M$; *although the opportunity to trade exists at times $1/n, 2/n, \ldots, (L-1)/n$, make no trades until time $1/M$.* At time $1/M = L/n$, rebalance the portfolio in self-financing fashion so that the stock holding is $g(S(1/M), 1/M)$. Hold this portfolio until time $2/M$ (ignoring another $L-1$ opportunities to trade), and then "rebalance" again, so that from $t = 2/M$ to $t = 3/M$, hold $g(S(2/M), 2/M)$ shares of stock. And so forth.

The investor's financial gains through time 1 from this strategy (after her initial investment) are

$$I_M^n := \sum_{j=0}^{M-1} g(S(j/M), k/M)[S((j+1)/M) - S(j/M)],$$

where the superscript n on I_M^n is, at this stage, completely gratuitous, but reminds us that this is for the nth = LMth discrete-time economy (and so we are interested in the distribution of I_M^n under P^n). Then, for an initial investment of $\mathbf{E}^*[x]$, she is left with the contingent claim $I_M^n + \mathbf{E}^*[x]$. If L is very large, the Central Limit Theorem tells us that the distribution with respect to P^n of each change in stock price over the interval from j/M to $(j+1)/M$ under P^n is very close in distribution to the its distribution under P. That is, because L is large, there are a lot of little (properly scaled) steps between $t = j/M$ and $t = (j+1)/M$ under P^n, and so the (everyday, garden-variety) Central Limit Theorem can be employed (in terms of the logs of the stock prices, of course). But then – and here is where arms are waving wildly, necessitating the formal proof to come – for the fixed (but very large) $n = LM$ where L is sufficiently large, the distribution under P^n of I_M^n is close to that of I_M under P, which was chosen to be close to $x - \mathbf{E}^*[x]$ under P. Since $I_M + \mathbf{E}^*[x]$ is close to x under P by the first stage of our argument, so is $I_M^n + \mathbf{E}^*[x]$ under P^n.

It is worth observing at this point that the strategy sketched above is different from the strategy used to produce the pictures at the start of this chapter or in the proof of Stage I (or the investment strategies implicit in Duffie and Protter, 1992). In producing the pictures, in the proof of Stage I, and implicitly in Duffie and Protter, the trading strategy calls for rebalancing the portfolio at every opportunity. Here, in contrast, the trading strategy calls for many rebalances – M is large – but eschews the opportunity to trade far more often, since n is L times bigger than M, and L is large enough so we can invoke the CLT.

The Skorohod Representation Theorem

Of course, this "proof" is not at all a proof, since at the crucial juncture, arms are waving wildly. It is possible, but messy, to finish the proof rigorously without employing the Skorohod Representation Theorem. But it is easier to shift gears a bit and enlist this very useful result.

The Skorohod Representation Theorem. Consider a sequence of probability measures $\{Q^n; n = 1, 2, \ldots\}$ that converge weakly to the probability measure Q, all defined on a complete separable metric space $\mathcal{X}$. It is possible to produce a (generally, quite complex) probability space Ω with a single probability measure $\mathcal{Q}$ on which are defined random variables X^n and X with range $\mathcal{X}$ such that:

a. Each X^n has distribution Q^n on $\mathcal{X}$ under $\mathcal{Q}$, and X has distribution Q

under $\mathcal{Q}$.

b. $X^n \to X$ $\mathcal{Q}$-*almost surely.*

Many readers will know that this can be done in a quite straight-forward fashion if $\mathcal{X}$ is the real line R. For any cumulative distribution function F on the real line, and for U a random variable that is uniformly distributed on $[0, 1]$, define the random variable $X_F = F^{-1}(U)$ where, by convention,

$$F^{-1}(u) = \inf\{x \in R : F(x) \geq u\}.$$

Then X_F has the distribution F. And suppose $F_n \Rightarrow F$. Fix a single uniform random variable U, and define on the one probability space on which U is defined, $X_{F_n} = F_n^{-1}(U)$ and $X = F^{-1}(U)$. Then X_{F_n} converges to X_F almost surely. (Draw some pictures if this isn't obvious to you.)

The Skorohod Representation Theorem generalizes this result from R to a general complete and separable metric space $\mathcal{X}$ (such as, for our purposes, $\mathcal{X} = C[0, 1]$). For general $\mathcal{X}$, the underlying probability space Ω is a fairly complex animal, with an infinite number of independent random variables used to construct the random variables X^n and X bit by bit. I won't attempt to provide the proof or even give a sketch of how this result is proved; the interested reader should consult Billingsley (1999, p. 70).

Stage II Completed

We use this as follows:

Step 7. By Donsker's Theorem, $P^n \Rightarrow P$, on $C[0, 1]$. The Skorohod Representation Theorem says that we can find a single "grand" probability space $(\Omega, \mathcal{P})$ on which are defined random processes S and $\{S^n\}$ such that S has the distribution of S under P (that is, a geometric Brownian motion), each S^n has the distribution of S under P^n, and the S^n converge to S $\mathcal{P}$-almost surely.

Step 8. Fix $\epsilon > 0$. Fix M large enough so that (5.3) holds for this ϵ and $n = M$. Define the function $G^M : R_+^M \to R$ by

$$G^M(s_0, s_1, \ldots, s_M) := \sum_{j=0}^{N-1} g(s_j, j/M)[s_{j+1} - s_j].$$

Since g is continuous, G^M is a continuous function of $(s_0, \ldots, s_M)$. And $G^M(\mathcal{S}(0,\omega), \mathcal{S}(1/M,\omega), \ldots, \mathcal{S}(1,\omega))$ is the financial-gain integral (really, sum) for the portfolio strategy given by g, applied to the stock price process $\mathcal{S}$ at times $0, 1/M, 2/M, \ldots, (M-1)/M$: Define

$$\mathcal{I}(M,\omega) := G^M\big(\mathcal{S}(0,\omega), \mathcal{S}(1/M,\omega), \ldots, \mathcal{S}(1,\omega)\big).$$

Similarly, for $n = \ell N$, define

$$\mathcal{I}^n(M,\omega) := G^M\big(\mathcal{S}^n(0,\omega), \mathcal{S}^n(1/M,\omega), \ldots, \mathcal{S}^n(1,\omega)\big);$$

this is the financial-gains sum for the trading strategy given by g applied to $\mathcal{S}^n$ at times $t = 0, 1/M, \ldots, (M-1)/M$. Because we have fixed M, G^M is continuous, and since $\mathcal{S}^n \to \mathcal{S}$ almost surely, we know that, for the given ϵ, there is L large enough so that for all $\ell > L$ and $n = \ell M$,

$$P\left(\left\{\omega : \big|\mathcal{I}(M,\omega) - \mathcal{I}^n(M,\omega)\big| > \epsilon\right\}\right) < \epsilon. \tag{5.4}$$

Note carefully what is happening here: M has been fixed, and we are looking (only) at the values of $\mathcal{S}$ and $\mathcal{S}^n$ at times $0, 1/M, 2/M, \ldots, 1$, where $n = \ell M$ for very large ℓ. The values of $\mathcal{S}^n$ at times k/n, where k is not divisible by M, are only indirectly involved (in determining the values of $\mathcal{S}^n$ at times k/n for $k = 0, 1, \ldots, n$).

(Why fix M and then work in the nth $= \ell M$th economy? By fixing M, G^M involves a fixed number of terms, each of which is continuous, and so G^M is continuous *for fixed* M. If we tried instead to work with G^n, as n goes to infinity, we'd be looking at the sum of an increasing number of continuous functions, and showing "continuity" in the path of stock prices would be much more delicate. It can be done because we are working in the sup norm topology. But this way is easier, and this way provides the intuition offered back on pages 118–9.)

Step 9. On the grand probability space, define $\mathcal{F}(\omega) := f(\mathcal{S}(1,\omega), 1)$ and $\mathcal{F}^n(\omega) := f(\mathcal{S}^n(1,\omega), 1)$. Inequality (5.3), transferred to the grand probability space, is that, for the value of M fixed in Step 8,

$$P\left(\left\{\omega : \big|\mathcal{I}(M,\omega) - \mathcal{F}(\omega) + \mathbf{E}^*[x]\big| > \epsilon\right\}\right) < \epsilon. \tag{5.3'}$$

Step 10. And, since f is continuous, the almost-sure convergence of $\{\mathcal{S}^n\}$ to $\mathcal{S}$ implies that, for some N_1, for all $n > N_1$,

$$\mathcal{P}\left(\left\{\omega : \left|\mathcal{F}^n(\omega) - \mathcal{F}(\omega)\right| > \epsilon\right\}\right) < \epsilon. \tag{5.5}$$

As necessary, increase L in step 7 so that if $\ell > L$, then $\ell M \geq N_1$.

Step 11. Combine inequalities (5.3′), (5.4), and (5.5): For the M fixed in Step 8 and for all $\ell > L$, if $n = \ell M$, then

$$\mathcal{P}\left(\left\{\omega : \left|\mathbf{E}^*[x] - \mathcal{F}^M(\omega) + \mathcal{I}^n(M,\omega)\right| > 3\epsilon\right\}\right) < 3\epsilon.$$

Translated back to the original state space, this gives the result for multiples $n = \ell M$ of M for which $\ell > L$.

To complete this stage of the proof, it remains to fix things so that the result holds for all n greater than some N, not just for large-enough integer multiplies of the fixed M. But before doing so, it is worth observing that the continuity of f really only enters at step 10. Continuity of $f(s, 1)$ in s isn't needed at all for showing that $f(s, t)$ is continuously differentiable in s and t (for $t < 1$); that follows from the smoothing caused by taking expectations with respect to P^*. Suppose, in this regard, that we applied the machine in this proof to the contingent claim $x(\omega) = \mathbf{1}_{\{S(1) \text{ is transcendental}\}}$, for a ζ whose support consists (only) of rational numbers. In this case, $P^*\{x = 1\} = 1$, so $g \equiv 1$. All the steps in the proof are fine, up to step 10, and the trading strategy being considered, applied in the nth discrete-time economy, yields a contingent claim that is "close" to $\mathcal{F}$. (In fact, it is precisely $\mathcal{F}$ in this simple case, since the strategy involves buying and holding one bond.) But what is wanted is to get "close" to $\mathcal{F}^n$, which for this f is $\equiv 0$. To get from being close to $\mathcal{F}$ to being close to $\mathcal{F}^n$, we need that $\mathcal{F}$ and the $\mathcal{F}^n$ are "close" for large n. The proof achieves this because f is assumed to be continuous; the obvious extension to functions f that are discontinuous at a discrete set of continuity points of $S(1)$ is..., well, obvious.

Now to finish Stage II:

Step 12. Consider contingent claims x that are bounded and continuous functions of $S(t)$ for some fixed $t < 1$; following earlier notation, suppose

$x(\omega) = f(S(t)(\omega), t)$ for a bounded and continuous function $f(\cdot, t)$. At time t, the required value to be produced is known, so the problem of nearly synthesizing such an x comes down to whether one can nearly synthesize $f(S(t), t)$ (with an initial investment of $\mathbf{E}^*[f(S(t), t)]$ by time t; if this can be done, the portfolio at time t can be converted into bonds, thereby preserving its value. And there is nothing special in the proof given above about the time interval being $[0, 1]$; the proof works just as well for any time interval $[0, t]$, for $t \leq 1$.

Step 13. Next, we extend the result from $n = \ell M$ for $\ell > L$ (and the fixed M) to $n > N$ for sufficiently large N. Fix M and L from Step 8. For $n > LN$, let ℓ be such that $\ell M < n \leq \ell(M + 1)$. Of course, $\ell > L$. Suppose that the claim x that we are trying to nearly synthesize is $x = f(S(1), 1)$, for a continuous function $f(\cdot, 1)$. By step 11, one can nearly synthesize $f(S(\ell M/n), 1)$, and then convert the portfolio entirely to bonds. This will be adequate if, for any $\delta > 0$, we know that $|f(S(1), 1) - f(S(\ell M/n), 1)|$ is less than δ with P^n-probability at least $1 - \delta$.

But $\ell M < n \leq \ell(M + 1)$ implies

$$\frac{\ell M}{n} < 1 \leq \frac{\ell(M + 1)}{n}; \quad \text{hence}, \quad 1 - \frac{\ell M}{n} > 0 \geq 1 - \frac{\ell M}{n} - \frac{\ell}{n}$$

and so

$$\frac{1}{M} > \frac{\ell}{n} \geq 1 - \frac{\ell M}{n} > 0.$$

Since $f(\cdot, 1)$ is continuous, it is uniformly continuous on compact sets; and by tightness of the P^N, we know that the modulus of continuity of paths ω can be bounded with probability approaching 1. We can restrict attention to $\omega(t)$ lying inside some compact set of real numbers by Corollary 4.1 (page 68), since ω that go outside a large enough compact set can be placed into the exceptional set where the estimate does not necessarily hold; putting this together with the previous paragraph, using the continuity of f, and increasing M as needed, this gives us the displayed result, finishing Stage II.

Proof Stage III: General Contingent Claims in Three Steps

So far, we've proved Proposition 5.1*a* for bounded and continuous contingent claims that depend only on the value of the stock at time 1. To finish, I sketch how the argument given so far can be extended to general bounded and continuous contingent claims.

This sketch (and a rigorous proof) repeatedly uses the fact that the family of probability distributions $\{P^n\}$ is tight, which in turn is a consequence of Donsker's Theorem. In particular, the necessary and sufficient conditions for tightness in $C[0,1]$, conditions c and d of Theorem 4.1 (page 67), and Corollary 4.1 (page 68) are extensively used. Of course, condition c holds trivially in this application, since $\omega(0) = 0$ with P^n-probability 1 for all n. And note that, since $S(t, \omega) = e^{\omega(t)}$, we can rewrite Corollary 4.1 as: *For every $\eta > 0$, there exist $A > 0$ and N such that*

$$P^n\left(\{\omega : \sup_{t\in[0,1]} S(t,\omega) > A \ \ or \ \ \inf_{t\in[0,1]} S(t,\omega) < 1/A\}\right) < \eta, \quad for \ all \ n \geq N.$$

Step 14. Consider claims x that are bounded and continuous functions of S at two (fixed) times, $t_1 < t_2$. Write the claim as $f\big(S(t_1), S(t_2)\big)$. For the moment, suppose that $t_1 = k_1/n$ and $t_2 = k_2/n$ for large n. Suppose that at time t_1, in the nth economy, a consumer is provided with $\mathbf{E}^*\big[f(S(t_1), S(t_2))\big|F_{t_1}\big]$ funds. I assert that the argument developed so far says that she can nearly synthesize $f(S(t_1), S(t_2))$ by time t_2. The complication here is that we are now starting from a random position, whereas in the original proof we started at time 0; perhaps the N that is produced in the proof depends on the starting position? But this can be finessed using continuity of f and Corollary 4.1: We can ignore any paths that take us outside a compact set (at the cost of some amount of probability), and within the compact set, we can use uniform continuity of f (and the independent increments properties of paths ω) to reduce the problem to one with finitely many starting points. And, by the sort of construction given in step 13, we can "fix" things if t_1 and t_2 are not of the form k/n, as long as n is sufficiently large.

Step 15. From here, an induction argument extends the proof to claims x that are bounded and continuous functions of S at a finite number of fixed times $t_1 < t_2 < \ldots < t_i$, $x = f(S(t_1), S(t_2), \ldots, S(t_i))$. Suppose we have the result for $i-1$ times. Use the proposition to prove that one can nearly synthesize the claim that pays $\mathbf{E}^*[f(S(t_1), \ldots, S(t_i)|F_{t_1}]$, which proves a portfolio at time t_1 with enough value (and a function of S_{t_1}) to synthesize (for paths that live inside a compact domain) the claim x, using the induction hypothesis. Again, the argument is complicated by the fact that the starting point is random, but the same argument as in the previous paragraph works.

Step 16. Finally, we need to extend the result to general bounded and continuous claims x. Fix a bounded and continuous claim $x : C[0,1] \to R$ and devise claims x^k as follows: For any path ω, let $\omega^k(t) = \omega(t)$ if t is of the form j/k, and let $\omega^k(t)$ be the obvious linear interpolate of $\omega(j/k)$ and $\omega((j+1)/k)$ for $j/k \le t \le (j+1)/k$. Then let $x^k(\omega) = x(\omega^k)$ for each ω. Clearly, x^k is a bounded and continuous claim that depends (only) on the value of ω at times $0, 1/k, 2/k, \ldots, 1$. So, we know from the previous step that we can "synthesize in probability" each x^k.

I assert that, for every $\delta > 0$, there are K and N sufficiently large so that

$$P^n \left(\left\{ |x^k(\omega) - x(\omega)| > \delta \right\} \right) < \delta,$$

for all $k \ge K$ and $n \ge N$. This is (one more time) a consequence of $P^n \Rightarrow P$ by Donsker's Theorem, implying that the family of distributions $\{P^n\}$ is tight. For this step, I'll spell things out a bit more than before: Tightness implies there is a compact set $Z \subseteq C[0,1]$ such that $P^n(Z) \ge 1 - \delta/2$ for all n. Of course, $P(Z) \ge 1 - \delta/2$ as well. Since x is continuous, it is uniformly continuous on Z; let ρ be such that, if $\|\omega - \omega'\| \le \rho$, then $|x(\omega) - x(\omega')| \le \delta$ for ω and ω' in Z. Because $\{P^n\}$ is tight, there exists $\eta > 0$ and an integer N such that, for all $n > N$, $P^n\{\omega : w_\omega(\eta) \ge \rho\} < \delta/2$, where $w_\omega(\eta)$ is the modulus of continuity function of ω; that is, $w_\omega(\eta) = \sup|\omega(t) - \omega(t')| : |t - t'| \le \eta\}$. But now if K is such that $1/K < \eta$, and ω comes from the intersection of Z and $\{\omega : w_\omega(\eta) \le \rho\}$ (which has probability $1 - \delta$ or more, then $\|\omega - \omega^k\| \le \rho$ for all kK: On each interval $[j/k, (j+1)/k]$, $t \in [j/k, (j+1)/k]$ can be no futher than η from both j/k and $(j+1)/k$; hence, $\omega(t)$ can be no further than ρ from both $\omega(j/k)$ and $\omega((j+1)/k$, and so it can be no further than ρ from any convex combination of the two. Hence, for ω in this intersection and for $n \ge N$ $\|\omega - \omega^n\| \le \rho$. And so, for $n \ge N$, $k \ge K$, and ω in this intersection, $|x(\omega) - x^n(\omega)| \le \delta$.

But then, putting all the estimates together (and choosing the ϵs and δs sufficiently small), we (finally) have the full result. ∎

Concerning the Proof of Proposition 5.1*b* and the Boundedness of the Support of ζ

This proves Proposition 5.1*a*. Significantly more work is required to prove Proposition 5.1*b*. A detailed proof is provided in a more general setting in Kreps and Schachermayer (2019). Below is a rough sketch of how it goes.

The investor interested in approximately synthesizing x in the nth discrete-time economy proceeds roughly in the manner sketched above. For a fixed ϵ, there are large M and L such that, in the nth $= \ell M$th discrete-time economy, where $\ell > L$, rebalancing her portfolio at times j/M gives x to the desired degree of approximation with high probability, for much the same reasons as above. What is added is that the investor keeps a close watch on the value of her portfolio as well as on the price of the stock: If and when the value of the portfolio gets "too far" from the value it should have "in theory," or if and when the stock price goes outside some pre-set bounds, she stops at the first opportunity k/n, puts all her money into the bond, and waits until time 1. Three things must be shown: First, we must show that, for initially given ϵ, by setting precisely what is "too far" and the bounds on the stock price that determine the convert-to-bonds stopping time, then for large enough n, the probability that she stops the process can be made less than $1 - \epsilon$. Second, if she doesn't stop the process, then her final portfolio is within ϵ of x. Finally, if she does stop, the value of her portfolio is within the interval $[\underline{x} - \epsilon, \overline{x} + \epsilon]$ with P^n probability 1.[8]

This is where the bound on the support of ζ enters the picture. In continuous time, the investor can react instantaneously if things get out of hand. In discrete time, she must wait for the "next" time k/n. But *if* we can put a uniform bound on the number of shares of stock she holds, and if she stops when and if the price of the stock becomes large, then her portfolio cannot move in a single step more than the number of shares of stock times the stock price times $e^{\zeta/\sqrt{n}} - 1$. Given the bounds on the number of shares of stock in her portfolio and on the stock price, for

---

[8] In fact, the proof shows more: The value of the portfolio, stopped or not, lies within this interval for *every* ω such that $\omega(0) = 0$.

large enough n, the product of these three terms can be made as small as desired. Putting the pieces together, including her stopping rule, gives the result.

What makes the proof difficult is that we need to put a bound on the number of shares of stock she will ever hold. In general, this cannot be done. But, a bound of this sort is possible if x is bounded and *Lipschitz* continuous. So, the result is first proved for bounded and Lipschitz-continuous claims; then it is extended to claims that are bounded and (merely) continuous, by approximating such claims with sequences of Lipschitz-continuous claims.

The assumption that ζ has bounded support is key: If ζ has unbounded support, say, above, then a probability-1 bound on the value of any portfolio that is long in the stock fails in each discrete-time economy, let alone uniformly across the sequence of discrete-time economies.

That said, I believe that a bound on the support of ζ is, from the perspective of the economics of BSM, a natural requirement. In the BSM economy, investors can react instantaneously to movements in the stock price, movements that are always continuous. In contrast, in a discrete-time world, big and sudden moves – moves that happen within a single time period – are unhedgeable. For BSM to be a reasonable idealization of discrete-time worlds, the discrete-time worlds that BSM idealizes must offer investors the ability to intervene before things get too far out of hand.

Unbounded Claims

From an economic perspective, the limitation in Proposition 5.1a or b to bounded claims is probably sufficient; we can probably ignore claims that promise to pay 10^{100} (dollars?) or that require a payment of that size. However, it would be nice on theoretical grounds to extend the result to unbounded claims.

In fact, an easy corollary to Proposition 5.1b does "extend" the result to unbounded (and continuous) claims, but in a manner that has (at least) two significant flaws. Begin with the corollary:

Corollary 5.1. *Suppose contingent claim x is continuous on $C[0, 1]$. Then for every $\epsilon > 0$, there exists N such that, for all $n \geq N$, a claim x^n can be* *synthesized in the n th discrete-time economy such that*

$$P^n \left(\left\{ \omega : |x^n(\omega) - x(\omega)| > \epsilon \right\} \right) < \epsilon.$$

If x is integrable with respect to P^*, then this can be done with an initial investment of $\mathbf{E}^*[x^n]$. And if ζ has bounded support, it can be done with bounded risk in the sense that, for each ϵ, there exists D_ϵ, such that if $V^n(t, \omega)$ is the value of synthesizing portfolio in the nth economy, then $P^n \left(\left\{ \omega : |V^n(t, \omega)| > D_\epsilon \right\} \right) = 0$ for all n.

Proof sketch. Since $P^n \Rightarrow P$, the set of measures $\{P^n; n = 1, \ldots\} \cup P$ is tight. Hence, for each fixed ϵ, there is a compact set $Z_\epsilon \subseteq C[0, 1]$ such that $P^n(Z_\epsilon) > 1 - \epsilon/2$ and $P(Z_\epsilon) > 1 - \epsilon/2$. Since x is continuous, it is bounded on Z_ϵ by, say, B_ϵ. Apply Proposition 5.1b to x_{B_ϵ}, where x_{B_ϵ} is is x truncated at $\pm B_\epsilon$, but with $\epsilon/2$ replacing ϵ in the statement of the proposition. The rest of the proof should be clear, when you note that if x is P^*-integrable, then $\lim_{B \to \infty} \mathbf{E}^*[x_{B_\epsilon}] = \mathbf{E}^*[x]$.

At least one of the two flaws is obvious. The compact set K_ϵ – hence, the bound B_ϵ – depend on ϵ and, in particular, as $\epsilon \to 0$, $B_\epsilon \to \infty$ (as long as x is truly unbounded). Hence, the "bounded risk" portion of this corollary is not a uniform bound in ϵ, unlike what Proposition 5.1b provides for bounded x.

The second flaw takes us back to the case where $\zeta = \pm 1$, each with probability $1/2$, and the example from pages 63–4 that shows why (in that setting) continuity of x is not sufficient in general to show that $\lim_{n \to \infty} \mathbf{E}^{*n}[x] = \mathbf{E}^*[x]$. For that example, it is true that $\mathbf{E}^*[x]$ is finite and that, as the corollary promises, for each $\epsilon > 0$, we can find a sequence of trading strategies that get within ϵ of x with probability at least $1 - \epsilon$, for an initial investment of $\mathbf{E}^*[x]$. But, once ϵ is fixed, the bound B_ϵ is fixed, and for fixed B_ϵ, $\mathbf{E}^{*n}[x_{B_\epsilon}] \to \mathbf{E}^*[x]$, while (as the discussion of that example shows) $\lim_n \mathbf{E}^{*n}[x] \to \infty$. If x satisfies something like the bound (4.2) from page 75, this doesn't become an issue. But, in general, this surely counts as a (theoretical, if not practical) problem.

What's Going on Here? "Arbitrage," as Defined in the Literature, Asks Too Much

Time for a short editorial: If, in the trinomial world, an investor – let me call her an arbitraguer – can get close to synthesizing the call option for an initial investment of 0.38239 (the BSM price), what do we make of the theory that establishes "arbitrage bounds" that, for large n, settle down to the the interval (roughly) $(0, 0.5495)$? Any respectable arbitrageur in the $n = 400$ economy, seeing this claim trade for less than 0.35 or for more than 0.42, in the trinomial economy for large n, would lick her chops at the "arbitrage" opportunity presented. How is this to be understood?

The simple answer is that the arbitrage bounds 0 to 0.5495 are bounds established with an economically much-too-severe criterion: The arbitrageur must have *probability 1* of ending up without a loss of *any* size. If $n = 400$, there is a $(5/9)^{400}$ (roughly, 7.8×10^{-103}) chance that each of the 400 increments to the stock price is 0, and to accomplish an arbitrage as defined in this part of the finance literature, the arbitrageur must be hedged against this possibility. The textbook definition of arbitrage makes for some elegant theory, but as an economic criterion, it is ridiculous.[9] To quote Ayman Hindy, a friend and colleague who works in the financial industry, "Most of [real-life] arbitrageurs' activities involve eliminating 'near arbitrages.' They are willing to take a small chance of a negative outcome, in exchange for the arbitrage profit. And this narrows the arbitrage bounds on the prices."

Based on this sort of near-arbitrage or almost-arbitrage consideration, a reasonable price of the call option in the trinomial world for large n is a lot tighter band around the BSM price of 0.38239.

Please observe that, to get the Fundamental Theorem of Asset Pricing of Chapter 3 – that viability implies the existence of an equivalent martingale measure – for infinite-state models, "almost arbitrage" in the form of fattening up the positive orthant to make it solid is employed.[10] The difference is that, in proving FTAP, almost arbitrage in a single, infinite-state economy is employed. Here, we are using a notion of asymptotic arbitrage across a sequence of different economies. This is, of course, a formal difference. But if we accept one as

---

[9] Indeed, in the literature of financial mathematics, the "bounds" $(0, 0.5495)$ are referred to as "super-hedging" bounds.

[10] The alternate approach, invoking free lunches with bounded risk, adopts essentially the same perspective.

economically sensible, it is hard to see why we wouldn't accept the other. See Chapter 8 for further discussion of this point.

Arbitrageurs versus Consumers

For the remainder of this chapter, we move from the question, *Which contingent claims can be approximately synthesized, and at what cost?*, to the question, *Relative to living in the BSM economy, how well does an expected-utility maximizing consumer, living in nth discrete-time economy, do?* These different questions take us back to the two interpretations of what is meant by arbitrage bounds on the price of, say, a call option, provided back on pages 24 and 25.

The first interpretation supposes that the price processes of the stock and bond are given and then asks: If a third security – in this case the call option – is added, and if its addition does not change the given prices of the stock and bond, what (reasonable) bounds can be put on its equilibrium price? Or, alternatively, if this third security is already being marketed, but we do not see its price, what bounds can we put on its equilibrium price, consistent with the prices that we see, namely the prices of the stock and bond?

It is this interpretation of arbitrage bounds that, I contend, is behind the discussion around Proposition 5.1. Informally, the question is whether a community of arbitrageurs in the nth discrete-time economy for large n, upon seeing the price for the call option greater than, say, 0.41, would take covered short positions in the call (covered by offsetting positions in stock and bond) sufficient to push the price of the call closer to its BSM price of 0.38239. If so, we conclude that, in an equilibrium where the call option is among the list of securities, its price will lie "close" to its BSM price. This, of course, depends on the risks arbitrageurs face relative to the potential arbitrage profits they can reasonably expect to make by engaging in this near-arbitrage activity. Given the balance of potential gains and losses demonstrated through simulation, my guess is that, for $n \geq 400$, they would do so. What Proposition 5.1b tells us is that, with uniformly bounded risk of loss (uniform in n), they are pretty nearly sure (increasingly so, as $n \to \infty$) to make money doing so. [11]

---

[11] Since a call option is continuous but not bounded, Proposition 5.1 doesn't quite tell us this, directly. But put–call parity together with Proposition 5.1 does: A fixed position that is long one European call and one bond and short one share of stock is equivalent to being

Put it this way. The first interpretation of arbitrage bounds is after a *negative* result: Given the prices of the stock and bond, which prices for securities (other than the stock and bond) can be *ruled out*, because arbitrageurs would not permit those prices to persist?

The second interpretation of arbitrage bounds, on the other hand, asks a *positive* question: In a world in which only the stock and bond are traded, which contingent claims can be synthesized, either exactly or approximately? If someone wanted to *create*, say, a call option, can we put bounds on what this would cost and how close they might be able to come? This question takes on economic significance if we have some reason to suppose that some individual wishes to create a call option. And while creation of, say, the call option may be hard to motivate, it is easy to contemplate reasons why individuals might want to trade through time to create specific final portfolios: This is the obvious aim of utility-maximizing consumers who inhabit the two-security-only economy.

So it is natural to ask: Would consumers, placed in the nth discrete-time economy for large n *and taking prices of the two securities as given*, choose a trading strategy and (hence) final consumption bundle that is idealized by what they would do if placed in the BSM economy? From the perspective of the Arrow (1964), *this* is the interesting economic question, at least if you are interested in the efficiency of markets with frequent trading opportunities.[12] For discrete-time economies based on a binomial random walk, markets are complete – hence, equilibrium allocations are efficient.[13] And, more than that, as shown in Proposition 4.5, the efficient allocation in the nth binomial discrete-time economy converges to the (efficient) allocation in the BSM model, at least for a population of expected-utility maximizers with sufficiently well-behaved utility functions.

However, for the more general random walks of this chapter, markets are incomplete. Presumably, this means that a fully Pareto-optimal allocation cannot be reached. But suppose we could show that the optimal

---

short one put (with the same exercise price as the call), and Proposition 5.1 does apply to the put.

[12] Although, from the perspective of General Equilibrium Theory, taking equilibrium prices as exogenous is not altogether satisfactory.

[13] And, following up on the previous footnote, one can show that with two securities and a "binomial" event tree, for generic final payoffs of the two securities, the efficient allocation can be supported by a Radner equilibrium of plans, prices, and price expectations, in which prices are endogous; see Kreps (2013, Problem 16.8).

expected utility a well-behaved consumer can achieve in the nth-discrete time economy (for a general random walk driving stock prices) converges to her expected utility in the BSM economy. (This, presumably, is for consumers who are expected-utility maximizers with well-behaved utility functions.) Since the BSM equilibrium allocation is efficient (because markets there are complete), then, even though markets are incomplete in the discrete-time economies, these incomplete markets provide allocations that are approximately efficient. The incompleteness is there, but it only compromises the efficiency of the final allocation by a small amount.

Convergence of Optimal Consumption, 1: Bounded Support

The ideal result that we seek is: For an expected-utility-maximizing consumer with well-behaved utility function u, if her utility-maximization problem has a solution in the BSM world – let x^* denote her optimal consumption bundle and U^* denote the expected utility it provides – then in the nth (general) discrete-time world, her problem has a solution x^{*n} that provides her with expected utility U^{*n}, and:

- Her portfolio strategy in the nth discrete-time economy approaches her optimal strategy in the BSM world, in some meaningful sense.

- Her optimal consumption bundle x^{*n} approaches x^*, also in some meaningful sense.[14]

- $\lim_{n \to \infty} U^{*n} = U^*$.

None of this is true for general ζ and u. A simple counter-example, originally due to Merton (1975), involves CRRA utility functions with coefficients of relative risk aversion less than $1/2$. Take, for instance, the function $u(x) = x^{3/4}$ (so the coefficient of relative risk aversion, the parameter a on page 87, is $1/4$). We know that, in the BSM world, the optimal strategy is always to hold 200% of current wealth in the stock; that is, if $V(t)$ is the value of the consumer's portfolio at time t, she should hold $2V(t)/S(t)$ shares of stock and be short $-V(t)$ bonds.

But now suppose that ζ has unbounded support. (Suppose, for instance, that it is Normal, so that the discrete-time problem is just the

---

[14] See the discussion on page 89 and discussion point 3 on pages 91–2 for why I'm prevaricating here.

problem of trading in the BSM world, but where the consumer can only trade at times k/n.) The consumer can never short bonds to lever her position in the stock, as doing so runs the risk of having her wealth become negative before she can unwind this position.[15] And once her net wealth becomes negative, it must (by a martingale argument, and then using the equivalence of the original probability measure with any emm) end negative with positive probability. With the utility function $u(x) = x^{3/4}$, this means an expected utility of $-\infty$ in any reasonable interpretation of what negative consumption means for her expected utility.[16] The best she can do is to be 100% in the stock (and, for large n, that is what she will do), which gives her expected utility that is uniformly bounded away from her expected utility in the BSM world.

Several paths for fixing this problem are naturally suggested.

1. Restrict attention to utility functions u for which the optimal strategy never involves shorting either security (e.g., CRRA utility functions with coefficient $1/2$ or more).

2. Look at utility functions u whose domain of definition is all of R – e.g., CARA utility functions – and do not impose nonnegativity constraints.

3. Following Proposition 5.1b, assume that ζ has bounded support: With bounded support, when we scale by $1/\sqrt{n}$ in the nth discrete-time economy, stock prices cannot move "far" in any one step, so the consumer can short one or the other securities most of the time, at least.

Over the next three sections, I follow the third path, assuming that ζ has bounded support and providing results that *to some extent* meet the desired "ideal."

Convergence of Optimal Consumption, 2: Discrete Time Is Asymptotically at Least as Good as Continuous Time

Proposition 5.2. *Assume that ζ has bounded support and that u is continuous*

---

[15] This is true if the support of ζ is unbounded below, so that the stock portion of the portfolio can, in a single step, have nearly 0 value. If the support of ζ is unbounded above, a similar issue arises for any portfolio strategy that calls for shorting the stock, although such strategies are unusual in solutions to the consumer's problem.

[16] Adding the notion of bankruptcy might save the interpretation. But if consumers are allowed to go bankrupt, the entire theory must be rethought.

and nondecreasing on its domain. Suppose that, in the BSM economy, the consumer with initial wealth W and no time-1 consumption endowment can attain expected utility $\hat{U}$ from a continuous contingent claim $\hat{x}$. Then for every $\epsilon > 0$ there exists N such that, for all $n > N$, the same consumer in the nth discrete-time economy can achieve expected utility at least $\hat{U} - \epsilon$.

Three remarks are in order:

1. The phrase "u is continuous and nondecreasing on its domain" has the following meaning. I have not specified whether, in the consumer's problem, the nonnegativity constraint $x \geq 0$ is imposed. If it is not, assume that u has domain all of R. (An example is constant absolute risk averse utility). In what follows, this is called Case 1. On the other hand, if $x \geq 0$ is imposed, the domain of definition of u is $[0, \infty)$. This is Case 2. A careful examination of the proof shows that it works in Case 2 whether $u(0)$ is finite or $u(0) = -\infty$ (in which [sub]case it might be more proper to say that the domain of u is $(0, \infty)$).

2. The proposition imposes the condition that, in the BSM economy, the consumption claim $\hat{x}$ that gives expected utility $\hat{U}$ is continuous. To justify the title of this subsection, one would like to know that if $\check{U}$ can be attained as expected utility by the consumer in the BSM economy, then she can attain at least $\check{U} - \epsilon$ with a continuous consumption claim, for every $\epsilon > 0$. When this is true, we can conclude that if U^* is the supremum of all expected utilities she can attain in the BSM economy and U^{*n} is the supremum of what she can attain in the nth discrete-time economy, then $\liminf_n U^{*n} \geq U^*$. Standard conditions on u (for instance, strictly increasing and concave) give this result, but the proposition, stated as it is, is true without any further conditions on u.

3. This result is, essentially, an extended corollary to Proposition 5.1*b*. The proof starts with the following lemma.

Lemma 5.2. *Suppose that ζ has bounded support.*

a. *(Case 1.) Fix a continuous and nondecreasing utility function u whose domain is all of R. Fix a contingent claim x that is bounded and continuous. For every $\epsilon > 0$, there exists N such that, for all $n > N$, there is a contingent claim x^n that can be synthesized in the nth discrete-time economy for an* *initial investment* $\mathbf{E}^*[x]$, *such that* $\left|\mathbf{E}^n[u(x^n)] - \mathbf{E}[u(x)]\right| < \epsilon.$

b. *(Case 2.) Fix a utility function* u *that is continuous and nondecreasing on* $[0, \infty)$, *including the case where* $u(0) = -\infty$, *as long as* u *is "continuous" at 0 in the sense that* $\lim_n u(1/n) = -\infty$. *Fix a contingent claim* x *such that* $\underline{x} > 0$ *and* $\overline{x} < \infty$. *(That is,* x *is bounded away from zero below and is bounded above.) Then for every* $\epsilon > 0$, *there exists an* N *such that, for all* $n > N$, *there is a contingent claim* x^n *that can be synthesized in the* n*th discrete-time economy for an initial investment* $\mathbf{E}^*[x]$, *such that* $\left|\mathbf{E}^n[u(x^n)] - \mathbf{E}[u(x)]\right| < \epsilon.$

Proof of Lemma 5.2. Fix $\epsilon > 0$. In the case of part b, reduce ϵ as needed so that $\underline{x} - \epsilon > 0$.

Since u is continuous on the compact domain $[\underline{x} - \epsilon, \overline{x} + \epsilon]$, it is uniformly continuous and bounded on this domain. Let δ' be such that, if $c, c' \in [\underline{x} - \epsilon, \overline{x} + \epsilon]$ are such that $|c - c'| < \delta'$, then $|u(c) - u(c')| < \epsilon/3$. Let B be such that, if $c, c' \in [\underline{x} - \epsilon, \overline{x} + \epsilon]$, then $|u(c) - u(c')| \leq B$, and let $\delta'' = \epsilon/(3B)$. And let $\delta = \min\{\delta', \delta'', \epsilon\}$.

The continuity of u (on its domain) and of x (on $C[0, 1]$) implies that $u \circ x : C[0, 1] \to R$ is a continuous function on $C[0, 1]$ (in the sup norm, of course). It is bounded because x is bounded (below by something strictly greater than 0 in Case 2), so $u \circ x$ is bounded. So, since $P^n \Rightarrow P$, $\mathbf{E}^n[u(x)] \to \mathbf{E}[u(x)]$. Hence, there exists N' such that for all $n > N'$, $\left|\mathbf{E}^n[u(x)] - \mathbf{E}[u(x)]\right| < \epsilon/3$.

Apply Proposition 5.1b to x and δ: For some N'' and for all $n > N''$, a claim x^n can be synthesized in the nth discrete-time economy with initial investment $\mathbf{E}^*[x]$ such that $x^n(\omega) \in [\underline{x} - \delta, \overline{x} + \delta]$ with P^n probability 1, and $P^n\left(\{\omega : |x^n(\omega) - x(\omega)| > \delta\}\right) < \delta$. Fix the sequence $\{x^n\}$.

Let $N = \max\{N', N''\}$. For any $n > N$, write Λ_n for the event $\{\omega : |x^n(\omega) - x(\omega)| < \delta\}$. Then, for $n > N$,

$$
\begin{aligned}
\left|\mathbf{E}[u(x)] - \mathbf{E}^n[u(x^n)]\right| &\leq \left|\mathbf{E}[u(x)] - \mathbf{E}^n[u(x)]\right| + \left|\mathbf{E}^n[u(x)] - \mathbf{E}^n[u(x)]\right| \\
&\leq \epsilon/3 + \left|\mathbf{E}^n[u(x)] - \mathbf{E}^n[u(x)]\right| \\
&= \epsilon/3 + \left|\mathbf{E}^n[u(x); \Lambda_n] + \mathbf{E}^n[u(x); \Lambda_n^C] - \mathbf{E}^n[u(x^n); \Lambda_n] - \mathbf{E}^n[u(x^n); \Lambda_n^C]\right| \\
&\leq \epsilon/3 + \left|\mathbf{E}^n[u(x); \Lambda_n] - \mathbf{E}^n[u(x^n); \Lambda_n]\right| + \left|\mathbf{E}^n[u(x); \Lambda_n^C] - \mathbf{E}^n[u(x^n); \Lambda_n^C]\right| \\
&\leq \epsilon/3 + \mathbf{E}^n\left[|u(x) - u(x^n)|; \Lambda_n\right] + \mathbf{E}^n\left[|u(x) - u(x^n)|; \Lambda_n^C\right].
\end{aligned}
$$

On Λ_n, x^n is within δ of x, so $|u(x) - u(x^n)| < \epsilon/3$, and so $E^n\big[|u(x) - u(x^n)|; \Lambda_n\big] < \epsilon/3$. And both x and $x^n \in [\underline{x} - \delta, \overline{x} + \delta]$ P^n-a.s.; hence, $|u(x) - u(x^n)| < B$ P^n-a.s. Since $P^n(\Lambda_n^C) < \delta < \epsilon/(3B)$, $E^n\big[|u(x) - u(x^n)|; \Lambda_n^C\big] \leq \epsilon/3$. Putting all these two estimates together, we have $\big|E[u(x)] - E^n[u(x^n)]\big| < \epsilon$ for all $n > N$.   ∎

Proof of Proposition 5.2. If the target expected-utility level $\hat{U}$ is less than or equal to $u(W)$, then the result follows immediately: In any discrete-time economy, the consumer can purchase and sit on W bonds, for utility level $u(W)$. So, for the rest of the proof, assume that $\hat{U} > u(W)$.

The method of proof from this point is probably obvious. In either Case 1 or Case 2, suppose that x is a continuous contingent claim satisfying $\hat{U} = E[u(x)]$, the budget constraint $E^*[x] \leq W$, and any other constraints that are applied. For fixed ϵ, construct a continuous contingent claim x' that is bounded above and below in Case 1 and bounded away from 0 and bounded above in Case 2, such that $E^*[x'] \leq W$ and $E[u(x')]$ is within $\epsilon/2$ of $E[u(x)]$. Apply the lemma (for $\epsilon/2$ in place of ϵ), and the result is immediate.

The only task we face is to produce x'. The two cases are handled separately.

In Case 1, u is defined on all of R. Begin to produce x' by looking at $x^B(\omega) = \min\{x(\omega), B\}$ for large B. Since $x^B(\omega) \nearrow x(\omega)$ as $B \nearrow \infty$ (and recalling that u is assumed to be nondecreasing), we have that $E[u(x^B(\omega)] \nearrow E[u(x(\omega)]$ by monotone convergence. Moreover, since $\hat{U} \geq W$, $x(\omega) \geq W/2$ on a set of positive measure. So by parametrically varying B, we can find a B^* such that $E^*[x^{B^*}] < E^*[x] \leq W$ and, at the same time, $E[u(x^{B^*})]$ is no more than $\epsilon/2$ below $\hat{U}$.

Now bound x^{B^*} below, by looking at $x^{B^*,C}(\omega) = \max\{x^{B^*}(\omega), -C\}$, for large C. For any C, $E^*[x^{B^*,C}] \geq E^*[x^{B^*}]$ but, again invoking monotone convergence, we can find C large enough so that the added cost of $E^*[x^{B^*,C}]$ is less than the slack in the budget constraint we obtained by replacing x with x^{B^*}. And going from x^{B^*} to $x^{B^*,C}$ for any $C < \infty$ only raises the consumer's expected utility from $E[u(x^{B^*})]$, which is already within $\epsilon/2$ of $\hat{U}$, finishing Case 1.

In Case 2, u is defined on $[0, \infty)$. Begin by replacing x with x^α given by $x^\alpha(\omega) = \alpha x(\omega) + (1 - \alpha)W$, for $\alpha \in (0, 1)$. For all α, x^α is budget feasible, since $E^*[x] \leq W$ implies that $E^*[x^\alpha] = \alpha E^*[x] + (1 - \alpha)W \leq W$. And, since $x(\omega) \geq 0$, $x^\alpha(\omega) \geq (1 - \alpha)W$, so for $\alpha < 1$, $x^\alpha(\omega)$ is bounded away from zero by $(1 - \alpha)W$. Moreover, by a double application of monotone convergence, $\lim_{\alpha \to 1} \mathbf{E}[u(x^\alpha)] = \mathbf{E}[u(x)]$. (The integrand x^α for ω such that $x(\omega) \geq W$ is bounded below by $u(W)$ and above by $u(x)$; and for ω such $x(\omega) \leq W$, it is bounded above by $u(W)$ and below by $u(x)$.) So one can find α^* so that $\mathbf{E}[u(x^{\alpha^*})]$ is no less than $\mathbf{E}[u(x)] - \epsilon/4$. Now cut off x^{α^*} for very large values in the fashion of the first step in Case 1, and one produces a claim x^{α^*,B^*} that is budget feasible, bounded above, and bounded below away from 0, and such that $\mathbf{E}[u(x^{\alpha^*,B^*})]$ is within $\epsilon/2$ of $E[u(x)]$, finishing Case 2. ∎

Convergence of Optimal Consumption, 3: Is Discrete Time Asymptotically No Better than Continuous Time?

Proposition 5.2 doesn't preclude the possibility that, asymptotically, the consumer can do strictly better in the discrete-time world for arbitrarily large n than she can do in the continuous-time BSM world. This possibility may seem incredible, but if it seems so to you, Chapters 6 and (especially) 7 may surprise you.

However, I stongly conjecture that, at least with more assumptions of the sort in Proposition 4.5, this cannot happen in the current setting, where P^n is constructed from scaled random walks, based on a random variable ζ that has mean 0, variance 1, and bounded support.

Indeed, we know from Proposition 4.5 that if ζ is the ± 1 random variable of Chapter 4, if u is continuously differentiable, strictly concave, and strictly increasing, and if the consumer's problem in the BSM economy has solutions for all initial wealth levels W in an open subinterval of $(0, \infty)$, then this does not happen: For any wealth level W_0 in that interval, the consumer's optimal level of expected utility in the nth discrete-time economy converges to her optimal level of expected utility in the BSM economy. Moreover, we get convergence (pointwise in $\omega(1)$) of specific versions of her optimal consumption claims.

So it is natural to ask: Why not impose similar restrictions – u is strictly concave, strictly increasing, and continuously differentiable, and the consumer's problem has solutions for an open interval of strictly positive initial wealth levels – and prove the same result?

A quick but insufficient reason why we can't do this is that for general ζ there is not one but many emms for each P^n. In Proposition 4.5, P^n

had a single emm; hence, markets are complete and, therefore, we can pose the consumer's problem both in the discrete-time economies and in the limit economy as choosing an optimal consumption claim among all consumption claims (that are square-integrable for BSM and) that satisfy a single budget constraint. With general ζ, the consumer in the discrete-time economies is limited to claims she is able to synthesize.

But her *limitations* in the discrete-time economies should only help to establish that she can't do better asymptotically in the discrete-time economies. And the problem of multiple emms can be finessed by specifying a particular and well-behaved emm P^{*n} for each P^n, the emm provided by the Esscher Transform.

Let P^{*n} denote this specific emm for P^n. Since every synthesizable contingent claim x^n in the nth discrete-time economy "costs" $\mathbf{E}^{*n}[x^n]$ for every emm, it does so for this specific choice of emm, and we can formulate the consumer's problem in the nth discrete-time economy as

> *Maximize* $\mathbf{E}^n[u(x)]$ *subject to* $\mathbf{E}^{*n}[x] \leq W$, $x \geq 0$ *perhaps,*
> *and* x *is synthesizable.*

The final constraint x *is synthesizable* is not easy to deal with, but consider instead the problem where this constraint is dropped,

> *Maximize* $\mathbf{E}^n[u(x)]$ *subject to* $\mathbf{E}^{*n}[x] \leq W$, *and* $x \geq 0$ *perhaps.*

This is a relaxed version of the consumer's real problem (a problem with a constraint removed), so the optimal level of utility she can attain in this relaxed problem, which I denote U^{**n} is at least as great as her optimal level of utility U^{*n} in her real problem.

Suppose we can employ the proof of Proposition 4.5 to show that $\lim_n U^{**n} = U^*$. We know from Proposition 5.2 that, with all the extra assumptions we've made, $\liminf_n U^{*n} \geq U^*$. And, so, since $U^{*n} \leq U^{**n}$ on first principles, we'd know (at least, and with the extra assumptions about u and the existence of solutions in the BSM economy) that $\lim_n U^{*n} = U^*$.

A careful examination of the proof of Proposition 4.5 shows that it in no way depends on ζ being the symmetric binomial random variable, *except in one place*: The proof Lemma 4.2, concerning how quickly

dP^{*n}/dP^n converges to dP^*/dP. And, as we saw in the discussion of the Esscher Transform for general (bounded-support) ζ, while we get (in general) convergence of dP^{*n}/dP^n (for the Esscher Transform emm) to dP^*/dP, what the lemma requires – and so what the proof of Proposition 4.5 requires – is that $\hat{E}[\zeta^3] = 0$, so that, writing

$$dP^{*n}/dP^n$$

as $e^{-a_n\omega(1)-b_n}$, we have $a_n = 1/2 + o(1/\sqrt{n})$.

That's the bottom line for this section: For a general (bounded support) ζ, the distribution of which is symmetric around 0 (such as the trinomial random walk) or which otherwise has $\hat{E}[\zeta^3] = 0$, this plan of attack, combined with Proposition 5.2, shows that $\lim_n U^{*n} = U^*$. And it provides a sense in which (specific versions of) the optimal consumption bundles converge. But, just as with binomial random walks with asymmetric ζ, unless $\hat{E}[\zeta^3] = 0$, the proof can't be applied.

This doesn't mean that the result is false. To reiterate, I strongly conjecture that it is true. But I cannot offer you a proof.

Convergence of Optimal Consumption, 4: CRRA (and CARA) Utility

Finally: Rather than making assumptions about the distribution of ζ (beyond bounded support), one can make very strong, parametric assumptions about u and get everything: convergence of portfolio strategies, consumption bundles, and maximal utilities. All these nice results hold for utility functions that have constant relative risk aversion or constant absolute risk aversion. This is so because, as has been well known since early papers by Merton (1969) and Hakkanson (1970), the utility-maximizing portfolio strategies *both* in continuous and discrete time are very simple. I state and prove the result for CRRA utility here; the case of CARA utility is provided in the Appendix.

Proposition 5.3. *Assume that ζ has bounded support. Fix an expected-utility maximizer whose utility function is of the constant relative risk aversion class, $u(x) = x^{1-a}/(1-a)$ for $a > 0$ (and, for the case $a = 1$, $u(x) = ln(x)$) and whose endowment consists (only) of a portfolio of stock and bond, with time-0* *value* W.[17] *The optimal consumption/investment strategy for this consumer (for any level of wealth W), at all times and in all contingencies, is to invest a constant fraction of her current wealth in the stock, a fraction that depends on n and on a. Letting $\alpha_n(a)$ be that constant fraction for the nth discrete-time economy when the consumer's coefficient of relative risk aversion is a, then $\lim_{n \to \infty} \alpha_n(a) = 1/(2a)$, which is the optimal investment strategy in the BSM world. The consumer's optimal expected utility (for given a, n, and initial wealth W) converges to her optimal expected utility in the BSM world. And the distribution of her (optimal) final consumption bundle converges in distribution to the distribution of her final consumption bundle in the BSM world.*

Proof. Fix $a > 0$ throughout this proof. I will give the proof for $a \neq 1$; the special case of $a = 1$, so that $u(x) = \ln(x)$, is done by a very similar argument.

We know (from Merton, 1969) that an expected-utility-maximizing consumer with CRRA utility function (having parameter a), placed in the Black–Scholes economy, continuously rebalances her portfolio so that $1/(2a)$ of her wealth is in the bond. We know (from Merton or from the analysis on pages 87–8) that her optimal consumption bundle is

$$x^*(\omega) = W_0 \times \exp\left(\frac{1}{4a} - \frac{1}{8a^2} \right) S(1, \omega)^{1/(2a)}.$$

And we know that the consumer's expected utility from this optimal strategy is

$$U_a^*(W_0) = \frac{W_0^{1-a}}{1-a} \times \exp\left(\frac{1-a}{8a} \right).$$

These – the portfolio weights, the distribution of her final consumption bundle, and her expected utility – are our targets for the consumer's optimal strategy in the nth economy, as $n \to \infty$.

In several places, we will require the Taylor series expansion of the function

$$g_\alpha(x) = \frac{[\alpha e^x + 1 - \alpha]^{1-a}}{1-a},$$

---

[17] Allowing the consumer to have endowment in the form of a general time-1 contingent claim is not consistent with the approach taken in this proposition.

for x near 0. (The dependence of g on α is indicated because, later, we will want to consider α as a parameter to be optimized; $a > 0$ and $\neq 1$ is fixed, so it is not indicated.) By direct evaluation:

$g_\alpha(x)$ is as above, and $g_\alpha(0) = 1/(1 - a)$

$g_\alpha'(x) = \alpha e^x [\alpha e^x + 1 - \alpha]^{-a}$, and $g_\alpha'(0) = \alpha$

$g_\alpha''(x) = \alpha e^x [\alpha e^x + 1 - \alpha]^{-a} - a\alpha^2 e^{2x} [\alpha e^x + 1 - \alpha]^{-a-1}$,
and $g_\alpha''(0) = \alpha - a\alpha^2 = \alpha(1 - a\alpha)$

$g_\alpha'''(x) = \alpha e^x [\alpha e^x + 1 - \alpha]^{-a} - 2a\alpha^2 e^{2x} [\alpha e^x + 1 - \alpha]^{-a-1}$
$+ (1 + a)a\alpha^3 e^{3x} [\alpha e^x + 1 - \alpha]^{-a-2}$, and so $g_\alpha'''(0) = \alpha - 2a\alpha^2 + (1 + a)a\alpha^3$

To the third-order term, and in exact form, we therefore have

$$g_\alpha(x) = \frac{1}{1 - a} + \alpha x + \frac{\alpha(1 - a\alpha)x^2}{2} + \frac{x^3}{6} g_\alpha'''(\theta x),$$

for some θ between 0 and 1.

The next step is to show that, for fixed n, the consumer's optimal strategy is to rebalance her portfolio at each time and in each contingency so that she holds a constant α_n of her wealth in the stock and $1 - \alpha_n$ in the bond. (I suppress the dependence of α_n on a.) This is standard, so a sketch follows:

Suppose that, in the nth discrete-time economy, the consumer has a portfolio with current value V at time $(n - 1)/n$ and invests αV in the stock and $(1 - \alpha)V$ in the bond. Then, at time 1, the value of her portfolio will have the distribution of

$$W(n) = \frac{\alpha V}{S\big((n - 1)/n\big)} S(1) + (1 - \alpha)V$$

$$= V \times \left(\alpha \frac{S(1)}{S\big((n - 1)/n\big)} + 1 - \alpha \right) = V \times \left(\alpha e^{\zeta_{n-1}/\sqrt{n}} + 1 - \alpha \right),$$

where ζ_{n-1} has the distribution of ζ. Hence, her expected utility from consumption will be

$$\frac{1}{1 - a} \left[V \times \left(\alpha e^{\zeta_{n-1}/\sqrt{n}} + 1 - \alpha \right) \right]^{1-a} = V^{1-a} \frac{\left(\alpha e^{\zeta_{n-1}/\sqrt{n}} + 1 - \alpha \right)^{1-a}}{1 - a}.$$

Regardless of the value of V, then, at time $(n-1)/n$ she should choose α to maximize

$$\hat{\mathsf{E}}\left[\frac{\left(\alpha e^{\zeta_{n-1}/\sqrt{n}}+1-\alpha\right)^{1-a}}{1-a}\right], \qquad (5.6)$$

where $\hat{\mathsf{E}}[\cdot]$ means to take expectation over the variable ζ_{n-1} (and, in some places, just ζ). Let α_n be the maximizing value of α, and let $\gamma_n = \hat{\mathsf{E}}\big[\big(\alpha_n e^{\zeta_{n-1}/\sqrt{n}}+1-\alpha_n\big)^{1-a}\big]$ then the continuation value at time $(n-1)/n$ to the consumer who, at that time, has wealth V, is

$$\frac{\gamma_n}{1-a}V^{1-a}.$$

But then going back one step to time $(n-2)/n$ and applying Bellman's Principle (technically, that for this finite horizon problem, any conserving strategy is optimal), the consumer faces a problem with the same solution: The consumer should invest α_n of her wealth in the stock. This result continues back to time 0, which proves the assertion that her optimal strategy is, at all stages, to invest $\alpha_n(a)$ of her wealth in the stock, where α_n is the value of α that maximizes the expression (5.6) (where now I've indicated the dependence on a). A similar argument applies for the case of $u(x) = \ln(x)$.

(In places in the remainder of the text, I employ variations on this basic result; when I do, I refer to it as "the standard argument for CRRA utility functions." A similar argument works for constant absolute risk aversion utility functions, except that the conclusion for CARA utility is that the consumer wishes to maintain a constant (dollar) amount of her wealth invested in the stock; that similar argument is provided in the Appendix.)

Note that the expression in (5.6), viewed as a function of α, is strictly concave and continuous (strict concavity as long as ζ is not identically 0, which we do not allow since the variance of ζ must be 1), and so any local maximum is *the* global maximum. Write out the integrand using the exact Taylor series expansion out to the third term:

$$\hat{\mathsf{E}}\left[\frac{\left(\alpha e^{\zeta/\sqrt{n}}+1-\alpha\right)^{1-a}}{1-a}\right] =$$

$$\hat{\mathbf{E}}\left[\frac{1}{1-a} + \alpha\frac{\zeta}{\sqrt{n}} + \frac{\alpha(1-a\alpha)}{2}\left(\frac{\zeta}{\sqrt{n}}\right)^2 + \frac{g_\alpha'''(\theta\zeta/\sqrt{n}))}{6}\left(\frac{\zeta}{\sqrt{n}}\right)^3\right],$$

where I should indicate that the value of θ inside the expectation depends on the value of $\zeta/\sqrt{n}$ (but is, in any case, bounded by 0 and 1). Since $\hat{\mathbf{E}}[\zeta] = 0$ and $\hat{\mathbf{E}}[\zeta^2] = 1/n$, this is

$$\hat{\mathbf{E}}\left[\frac{\left(\alpha e^{\zeta_k^n} + (1-\alpha)\right)^{1-a}}{1-a}\right] = \frac{1}{1-a} + \frac{\alpha(1-a\alpha)}{2n} + \frac{1}{6n^{3/2}}\hat{\mathbf{E}}\left[(\zeta)^3 g_\alpha'''(\theta\zeta/\sqrt{n})\right].$$

The first term on the right-hand side is constant, so can be ignored, and so the maximizing value α^n is the maximizer of

$$\alpha(1-a\alpha) + \frac{1}{6n^{1/2}}\hat{\mathbf{E}}\left[(\zeta)^3 g_\alpha'''(\theta\zeta/\sqrt{n})\right].$$

But this function, which is strictly concave in α (removing a constant and multiplying by n doesn't change that), approaches the function $\alpha \to \alpha(1 - a\alpha)$ pointwise in n and, *because ζ has bounded support*, does so uniformly on compact sets of α. Employ the following simple lemma.

Lemma 5.3. *For a sequence of continuous and strictly concave functions $\{f_n\}$ (with, for simplicity, domain a convex subset of R^ℓ and range R), if $f_n \to f$ pointwise and does so uniformly on compact sets, where f is continuous and strictly concave and is maximized at x^*, then for all large n, f_n has a (unique) maximizer x_n, and $x_n \to x^*$.*

Proof. Since $f_n(x^*) \to f(x^*)$, the only way this could fail is if, for some $\epsilon > 0$ and for all sufficiently large n, there exists x_n such that x_n is more than ϵ away from x^* and $f_n(x_n) \geq f_n(x^*)$. Take the convex combination of x_n and x^* that is precisely ϵ away from x^*; call it x_n'. By concavity of f_n, $f_n(x_n') \geq f_n(x^*)$. The set of points precisely ϵ away from x^* is compact, and so we can find a subsequence m_n along which x_n' converges to, say, x', which is ϵ away from x^*. But then $f(x') = \lim_n f_{m_n}(x_{m_n}') \geq \lim_n f_{m_n}(x^*) = f(x^*)$, where the first step uses the uniform convergence of f_n to f on compact sets. But, by assumption, x^* maximizes f and f is strictly concave, so x^* uniquely maximizes f, a contradiction.   ∎

Apply this lemma to conclude that $\alpha_n \to$ the unique maximizer of $\alpha(1 - a\alpha)$, which is $\alpha = 1/2a$; investment strategies converge.

Recall the formulas for the distribution of the investor's final wealth (denoted $x_n^*(\omega)$) and expected utility in the nth discrete-time economy, if she puts α_n of her wealth into the stock in each period. Her terminal wealth has the distribution of

$$W \times \prod_{k=0}^{n-1} \left[\alpha_n e^{\zeta_k/\sqrt{n}} + 1 - \alpha_n \right],$$

where $\{\zeta_k\}$ is an i.i.d. sequence of random variables having the distribution ζ, and her expected utility is

$$\frac{1}{1-a}\hat{\mathbf{E}}\left[\left\{ W \times \prod_{k=0}^{n-1} \left[\alpha_n e^{\zeta_k/\sqrt{n}} + 1 - \alpha_n \right] \right\}^{1-a} \right],$$

which is equal to

$$\frac{W^{1-a}}{1-a} \times \left[\hat{\mathbf{E}}\left[\left(\alpha_n e^{\zeta/\sqrt{n}} + 1 - \alpha_n \right)^{1-a} \right] \right]^n.$$

Now that we know that $\alpha_n = 1/2a + o(1)$, we have (from the Taylor series expansion from before) that

$$\hat{\mathbf{E}}\left[\left(\alpha_n e^{\xi/\sqrt{n}} + 1 - \alpha_n \right)^{1-a} \right] = 1 + \frac{(1-a)\alpha_n(1 - a\alpha_n)}{2n} + o(1/n)$$

$$= 1 + \frac{(1/2a)(1-a)(1/2)}{2n} + o_1(1/n).$$

Hence, we know that

$$\left[\hat{\mathbf{E}}\left[\left(\alpha_n e^{\xi/\sqrt{n}} + 1 - \alpha_n \right)^{1-a} \right] \right]^n \to \exp\left[\frac{1-a}{8a} \right]$$

as $n \to \infty$. Optimized expected utilities converge.

Turning to the distribution of her final wealth $x_n^*(\omega)$, from the formula above, the log of her terminal wealth has the distribution of

$$\ln(W_0) + \sum_{k=1}^{n} \ln\left(\alpha_n e^{\zeta_k/\sqrt{n}} + 1 - \alpha_n\right).$$

Let $g_1(x)$ be the function (in x) $g_1(x) := \ln\left(\alpha_n e^x + 1 - \alpha_n\right)$. An exact Taylor series expansion of g_1 for x near 0 gives

$$\ln\left(\alpha_n e^{\zeta_k/\sqrt{n}} + 1 - \alpha_n\right) = \alpha_n \frac{\zeta_k}{\sqrt{n}} - \frac{\alpha_n - \alpha_n^2}{2}\left(\frac{\zeta_k}{\sqrt{n}}\right)^2 + \frac{1}{6}\left(\frac{\zeta_k}{\sqrt{n}}\right)^3 g_1'''\left(\theta \frac{\zeta_k}{\sqrt{n}}\right).$$

By the same argument as before, the third term is $o(1/n)$, Hence, the expected value of $\ln\left(\alpha_n e^{\zeta_k/\sqrt{n}} + 1 - \alpha_n\right)$ is $(-\alpha_n + \alpha_n^2)/(2n) + o(1/n)$, and its variance is $\alpha_n/n + o(1/n)$. As $n \to \infty$, the Central Limit Theorem for triangular arrays tells us that the sum term is converging to a Normal distribution with mean $(-1/(2a) + 1/(4a^2))/2 = (1 - 2a)/(8a^2)$ and a variance of $1/(2a)$, which implies convergence to the distribution of x^* in the BSM world. ∎

It is worth noting that while $x^*(\omega)$ is a function of $S(1, \omega)$ in the BSM world, in the nth discrete-time world, even for n large, it is not true that x^{*n} is a function of $S^n(1, \omega)$. Take, as example the trinomial world, and take the case of $u(x) = \ln(x)$, so the optimal strategy is to put (asymptotically) $1/2$ of the consumer's wealth into the stock. Two paths that result in $S(1, \omega) = 1$ are $\zeta_k^n = 0$ every time, and $\zeta_k^n = 1.5/\sqrt{n}$ half the time and $= -1.5/\sqrt{n}$ half the time. Any strategy will, along the first sample path, give you $x^*(\omega) = 1$. For the second sample path, as n grows, the (optimal) final consumption bundle is assymptotically 1.32478 or so. This doesn't mean that, if we ran things on a grand probability space in which the discrete processes converged to Brownian motion almost surely, we wouldn't get a.s. convergence of the final consumption bundle. I conjecture that this *would* happen. But no proof is offered here.

As already noted, the analogous result for CARA utility functions is presented in the Appendix.

Chapter 4 versus Chapter 5

Although it is probably clear, let me be pedantic as to why the methods of Chapters 4 are 5 are so different.

Of course, the subject of Chapter 4, where ζ has a two-point support – and, in particular, the very specific ± 1 support that takes up all but the very end of the chapter – is a special case of the subject of this chapter. So the methods employed in proving Propositions 5.1, 5.2, and 5.3 apply to the special case of Chapter 4.

But, when ζ has a two-point support, entirely different and significantly better methods are available. The reason is that, when ζ has two-point support, markets in the discrete-time economy are complete. The prices of all contingent claims are fixed by arbitrage in the strict sense. And solutions to the consumer's utility-maximization problem can be obtained by maximizing (expected) utility subject to a single, once-and-for-all, budget constraint. None of that is available, of course, for ζ with support of size three or more.

This does raise an interesting issue: In Chapter 4, for a general (say, continuous and bounded) contingent claim x, we showed that the strict-arbitrage price in the nth discrete-time economy converges to the BSM price. Chapter 5 logic shows how to synthesize x approximately, for an initial investment equal to the BSM price of x. If the (asymptotic) price derived for x in Chapter 4 were different from the price for (approximate) x that is derived in this chapter, it would be (at least) a conundrum. But since in both cases, by the different methods, we get the same "answer" concerning what it costs to synthesize (exactly in Chapter 4, approximately in Chapter 5) x, we can breath a sigh of relief and move on.

On this point, wait for Chapter 7!

The Bottom Line?

So, *can the BSM model be regarded as an idealization of not only the binomial-random-walk models, but more general discrete-time, random-walk models?*

When ζ has unbounded support, we have some partial results (Proposition 5.1a), but we know that for at least some purposes (CRRA utility functions whose coefficient of relative risk aversion is less than $1/2$), things don't work. So the assumption that ζ has bounded support is, at some level, necessary. And, there is good economic intuition for imposing this assumption: In the BSM model, price paths are continuous, and consumer-investors can react (in continuous-time) when things change quickly, *as long as they change continuously*, which they do in BSM. This is an important feature of the BSM model and while, by definition, consumer-investors cannot react continuously in a discrete-time economy, if things can get out of hand before they have the opportunity to react, the continuous-time BSM model *with continuous changes in prices* is a poor idealization.

But, with this stipulated, I contend that the three propositions of this chapter strongly (although not entirely conclusively) suggest that for the general discrete-time, random-walk sequence of models, for ζ with bounded support, BSM is a good idealization in terms of desirable economic properties.

Bibliographic Notes

References for the mathematical tools used in this chapter have been given and so are not repeated here.

As for the economic ideas, Proposition 5.1*a* or, rather, something in the spirit of this proposition, is given (first, I believe) by Duffie and Protter (1992), based on work by Jakubowski, Ménin, and Pàges (1989) and Kurtz and Protter (1991a, b). Of course, the problem of unbounded support (when a consumer cannot trade continuously, even if stock prices move continuously) is due to the very early and seminal work of Merton (1969, 1975).

I mention again my debt to Walter Schachermayer for providing a proof of Proposition 5.1*b*. I believe this is a new result.

The proof of Proposition 5.2 depends on Proposition 5.1*b*, so if Proposition 5.1*b* is a new result, I think that Proposition 5.2 must be new, as well. On the other hand, the method of proof of Proposition 5.3 is independent of earlier analysis in the chapter. The result is so natural that I am reluctant to claim it as new. But I know of no prior reference for it.

6. Barlow's Example

In Chapters 4 and 5, the discrete-time economies were based on scaled (geometric) random walks: In the nth economy, the ratio of the stock price at time $(k+1)/n$ to its price at time k/n had distribution $e^{\zeta/\sqrt{n}}$, independent of whatever came before, and with the same distribution over each interval. To generalize this, suppose we keep independent (multiplicative) increments but not the identical (scaled) distribution part. This leads to some interesting phenomena.

In this chapter and the next, we present two examples of such phenomena. Both examples follow the basic scheme so far: For $n = 2, 4, 6, \ldots$, there are discrete-time economies with trading between a stock and a bond, at times $0, 1/n, \ldots, (n-1)/n$. The bond is the numeraire and pays a constant dividend of 1 at time 1. The price of the stock (in units of the bond) at times k/n and the dividend it pays at time 1 are random; the stock-price-and-dividend processes are driven by an underlying not-quite-random-walk, independent increments process. Instead of a random walk, the two underlying processes have an *even–odd* character. In each case, we look only at even n, letting m denote $n/2$. Each interval $k/m = 2k/n$ to $(k+1)/m = (2k+2)/n$ is divided in half, from $2k/n$ to $(2k+1)/n$, and from $(2k+1)/n$ to $(2k+2)/n$. In odd sub-intervals (the first half), ω changes according to one scaled distribution ζ^n; in the even sub-intervals, the distribution of the increment in ω is given by the scaled random variable ζ'^n. To reiterate, increments are independent. In both examples, ζ^n and ζ'^n have two-element support, with one element strictly positive and the other strictly negative. We assume consumers can trade at all times j/n; hence, according to Chapter 2, markets are complete, and for each n there is a unique equivalent martingale measure P^{*n}. Hence, for each n, the economies are very well behaved. The questions are, What happens asymptotically as $n \to \infty$? And is what happens asymptotically the same (in economic terms) as what happens *at* the continuous-time limit?

Background: The Cox–Ross–Rubinstein Models

The first example combines the BSM model with the Poisson-jump-process models studied in Cox and Ross (1976) and Cox, Ross, and Rubinstein (1979),[1] so before providing the example, a very fast sketch of these models (hereafer, the CRR models), put in the terms of this monograph, is helpful.

The nth discrete-time model of an economy is built from a process $\{\omega(k/n) : k = 0, \ldots, n\}$ that is a random walk, but a random walk that converges to a Poisson jump process rather than to Brownian motion. Specifically, consider a model (for n) in which $\{\zeta_k^n ; k = 1, \ldots, n\}$ is an i.i.d. sequence of random variations, each of which has the distribution

$$\zeta_k^n = \begin{cases} -\gamma/n, & \text{with probability } (n - \rho)/n, \\ \beta, & \text{with probability } \rho/n, \end{cases}$$

and, in the usual fashion, define

$$\omega\left(\frac{k}{n}\right) = \sum_{j=0}^{k} \zeta_j^n, \quad \text{and} \quad S\left(\frac{k}{n}\right) = e^{\omega(k/n)},$$

for parameters β, γ, and ρ, all strictly positive and such that $\rho(e^\beta - 1) > \gamma$. Concerning this sequence of models:

- For this to make sense, n must exceed ρ.

- One could have the γ and β both < 0, and, indeed, if one is trying to model the idea that sharp movements in stock prices tend to be movements downward, as in a panic, $\beta < 0$ seems more appropriate. This changes none of the results to follow.

- This constraint $\rho(e^\beta - 1) > \gamma$ captures the economically reasonable requirement that the risky asset provides expected returns strictly greater than the riskless rate (of 0), for all large enough n: The appreciation of \$1 invested in the stock over one of these periods is $[\rho/n][e^\beta - 1] + [(n - \rho)/n][e^{-\gamma/n} - 1]$, which should exceed 0. Take

---

[1] Cox and Ross (1976) propose and analyze the "limiting" continuous-time model; Cox, Ross, and Rubinstein (1979) analyze the sequence of discrete-time models that approach this limiting model.

a Taylor series approximation to $e^{-\gamma/n}$ for large n, and you find $\rho(e^{\beta} - 1) > \gamma$.

- In such models, one might like some (small) random movement in stock price in the absence of a jump, for which see the Barlow model later in this chapter.

Because this process, in the limit, will have discrete jumps, we can no longer work in $C[0, 1]$. Instead, we work in $D[0, 1]$, the space of real-valued functions on $[0, 1]$ that are continuous to the right and with limits to the left (what probabilists term *càdlàg*), endowed with the Skorohod topology. I will not go into details here,[2] except to say the following: For each n, we "fill out" ω defined as above by having it be constant over intervals $[k/n, (k + 1)/n)$, taking on, on each such interval, the value $\omega(k/n)$.[3] This construction then creates a measure Q^N on $D[0, 1]$, which converges weakly to the measure Q induced by a (compensated) Poisson jump process that drifts downward at rate γ and jumps upward at Poisson arrival times, with arrival rate ρ, where each jump is of size β. Denote by Q the probability distribution on $D[0, 1]$ induced by this process.

Each of the n-discrete-time processes and corresponding measures Q^n has a unique equivalent martingale measure, that is, a measure Q^{*n} under which $\{S(k/n); k = 0, \ldots, n\}$ is a martingale. This is just Chapter 2 stuff, since the support of the stock price at time $(k + 1)/n$, given the stock price at time k/n, has only two possible values. Specifically, under the unique emm, Q^{*n}, $\zeta_k^n = \beta$ with probability q^n and $-\gamma/n$ with probability $1 - q^n$, such that $(1 - q^n)e^{-\gamma/n} + q^n e^{\beta} = 1$. By taking a Taylor series approximation, we find that

$$q_n = \left(\frac{1}{n}\right) \times \left(\frac{\gamma}{e^{\beta} - 1}\right) + o\left(\frac{1}{n}\right).$$

And so $Q^{*n} \Rightarrow Q^*$, where Q^* is the unique measure on $D[0, 1]$ that is equivalent to Q and that makes $\{S(t) = e^{\omega(t)}; t \in [0, 1]\}$ into a martingale; namely a Poisson process with drift $-\gamma$ and jumps of size β, with jump rate $\gamma/(e^{\beta} - 1)$. Please note: Since we assumed that

---

[2] My go-to reference for details about $D[0, 1]$ endowed with the Skorohod topology is Billingsley (1999).

[3] This is as opposed to the linear interpolations we used earlier. Since we are working in D, this sort of piece-wise constant but discontinuous extension is okay.

$\rho(e^\beta - 1) > \gamma$, we have that the new asymptotic jump rate $\gamma/(e^\beta - 1)$ is $< \rho$. This is not surprising: The condition $\rho(e^\beta - 1) > \gamma$ was made to ensure that, at least for large n, the stock's rate of return exceeded 1. Since jumps are upwards, to form a martingale, we must slow down the jump rate. (If we took β and γ to be less than 0, converting to the unique emm would require speeding up the jumps.)

Why unique? The structure of the paths is fixed: When there is a jump, the stock appreciates by the multiplicative factor e^β. Otherwise, the price of the stock declines (geometrically) at rate γ. The free parameter is the jump rate, and to make a martingale, the jump rate must be set so that the expected price of the stock tomorrow, given its price today, is its price today. Since the jump size is fixed (by equivalence) and the drift downward is fixed (also be equivalence), we have one equation in the only remaining unknown, the jump rate, which is therefore determined to be $\gamma/(e^\beta - 1)$.

So, each of the discrete-time processes have a unique emm, hence markets are complete in each of those economies. The continuous limit of those discrete-time processes, a continuous-time Poisson jump process with upward jumps and compensating downward drift, has a unique equivalent martingale measure. And the (weak) limit of the emms of the discrete-time processes is the (unique) emm of the continuous-time process. Everything fits in the fashion of Chapter 4, except that instead of having geometric Brownian motion (the BSM model) as the idealization of the discrete-time processes, we get a "geometric Poisson jump process with compensating drift."

From this point, the theory developed in Chapter 4 can be adapted pretty much entirely to this setting. Because you must work in $D[0,1]$ instead of $C[0,1]$, the higher mathematics involved is a bit more complex. But, there are substantial compensations, because the "stochastic integrals" for the CRR model involve a path-by-path integrator that is a garden-variety integrator from Calculus 1.

Before proceeding to the main point of this chapter, there is one more change to be rung on the CRR models. Suppose we have an consumer whose initial wealth is W and who wishes to trade dynamically in the stock and bond to maximize her expected utility. Suppose her utility function is $u(x) = \ln(x)$. By a simple variation on the standard argument (pages 141–2), when we place this consumer in the nth discrete-time economy, her optimal strategy is to always hold a fraction α_n of her current wealth in the stock. By a slightly more complex but still standard argument, the same is true in the continuous-time CRR economy; she wishes to keep a constant fraction α of her wealth in the stock. Optimizing over α_N for the N th discrete-time economy comes down to maximizing

$$\frac{\rho}{n} \ln \left(\alpha_n e^{\beta} - \alpha_n + 1 \right) + \frac{n - \rho}{n} \ln \left(\alpha_n e^{-\gamma/n} - \alpha_n + 1 \right).$$

Without subjecting you to the detailed calculations,

$$\lim_{n \to \infty} \alpha_n = \alpha = \frac{\rho}{\gamma} - \frac{1}{e^{\beta} - 1} .$$

(The diligent reader with lots of time can verify this as well as verifying similar results for the whole family of CRRA utility functions.)

Barlow's Example

With this background, we come to the first even–odd example, due to Martin Barlow.[4] The model is driven by the two scaled random variables

$$\zeta^n = \begin{cases} \sqrt{2}/\sqrt{n}, & \text{with probability } 0.5, \\ -\sqrt{2}/\sqrt{n}, & \text{with probability } 0.5, \end{cases}$$

and

$$\zeta'^n = \begin{cases} -2\gamma/n, & \text{with probability } (n-2)/n, \\ \beta, & \text{with probability } 2/n, \end{cases}$$

where α and β are strictly positive and satisfy $2(e^{\beta} - 1) > 2\gamma$. One might be tempted to say that the limit process "alternates" between the Black–Scholes–Merton model and the Cox–Ross–Rubinstein model, except that, in the limit, this sort of alternation doesn't make sense. Instead, the limiting process does both things at once: In the limit, as $n \to \infty$, we get a Brownian motion with drift 0 and infinitessimal variance 1 plus an independent Poisson process that drifts down at rate γ and jumps up by β with arrival rate 1. (This describes the underlying process. The stock price process is e to this process.)

---

[4]   This example was an off-hand comment made orally circa 1982 and, in fact, when asked, Barlow could not recall having contributed this insight.

Hence, we have a striking phenomenon. The discrete-time processes are all binomial processes. They have complete markets. But the limit process does not give complete markets. The two "free parameters" in the limit process – free in the sense that you can change them without changing the null sets of the probability law – are the jump rate for the Poisson arrivals and the drift in the Brownian motion. When constructing emms for the limit process, this gives us one equation and two unknowns; a faster jump rate can be compensated for with a more negative drift, and vice versa. Indeed, while the squared variation along paths must be maintained, the jump rate can be any positive value, because it can be compensated for by a properly selected negative drift rate.[5] But it is evident that, while the call option has a specific price in the nth discrete-time world, in the limit world there is a range of prices consistent with the "classic" definition of arbitrage.

How can this be? Consider an expected-utility-maximizing consumer with the utility function $\ln(x)$. In this case, the standard argument from pages 141–2 tells you that, in these discrete-time economies, she wishes to invest fixed fractions of her wealth in the stock, where the fraction depends on n *and also on whether the period is even or odd*. It is straightforward to show that, in odd periods, as n goes to infinity and with this log utility function, she wishes to invest half her wealth in the stock.[6] And, in even periods, she chooses α_n according to the optimal rule for the CRR world. So, for instance, if $\gamma = \beta = 1$ and n is very large, she holds approximately $1 - 1/(e - 1) \approx 0.418023$ of her wealth in the stock in the even subperiods. But in the continuous-time "limit" economy, she can't do both: She still holds a constant fraction of her wealth in the stock, but this fraction is a compromise between the optimal fractions of 0.5 and ≈ 0.418023 that are "available" in each of the discrete-time models. And, of course, this compromise means that her optimal expected utility in the discrete-time models converge to a value that is strictly greater than what she attains in the continuous-time limit economy.

---

[5] The reason this is possible is that the Brownian component can "cover" for any drift rate you might choose. Indeed, at its most general, the jump-rate intensity can be any strictly positive, predictable, and locally integrable process.

[6] Merton's $(\mu - r)/\sigma^2$ rule applies. In the odd subperiods, when the increments look "Brownian," the infinitesimal variance has increased to 2, but the drift of the stock price process has also increased, from $1/2$ to 1. In fact, for the logarithmic utility function, the optimal fraction of wealth for the investor to hold in the stock is precisely $1/2$ *for all* n.

As for synthesizing contingent claims, the same story applies. Consider the standard European put option with exercise price 1, x_P. If it could be synthesized in the continuous-time limit, its expectation would have to be constant. But consider $E^{P^*}[x_P]$ for an emm P^* with a very, very slow jump rate: The corresponding drift approaches the drift in the BSM model, and so $E^{P^*}[x_P]$ will approach the BSM price for x_P, namely 0.38239.[7] On the other hand, suppose P^* has a very fast jump rate and a correspondingly fast downward drift. One can show that, as the jump rate goes to infinity, $\mathbf{E}^*[x_P] \to 1$. I'll sketch the argument: For fixed $B > 0$, the probability that $-B < \omega(1) < B$ goes to 0: While the downward drift is certain, the probability of having a number of jumps that just balances this downward drift becomes small. (The number of jumps is Poisson, and as the mean of a Poisson increases, so does its variance.) Now for any emm P^*,

$$1 = \mathbf{E}^{P^*}[S(1)] = \mathbf{E}^{P^*}[S(1); \omega(1) \leq -B]$$
$$+ \mathbf{E}^{P^*}[S(1); -B \leq \omega(1) \leq B] + \mathbf{E}^*[S(1); \omega(1) > B].$$

Since the probability of the middle term of the three on the right-hand side vanishes, the entire term vanishes. (Fix large B and then take the limit as the rate of jumps goes to infinity.) And the third term has $S(t) > e^B$, so its probability must be small, if the sum of the three is to be 1. Hence, with probability close to 1, $S(t) < e^{-B}$, in which circumstances, the put has value $1 - e^{-B}$ or more. This argument can be made rigorous to show that, in the limit (as the jump rate goes to infinity), the corresponding value of the put approaches 1.

Nonetheless, an investor who wishes to synthesize the put in the discrete-time economies can do so; markets are complete. But doing so requires rapidly switching the synthesizing portfolio depending on whether the period is even or odd, a rapid-switching strategy that has no analogue in continuous time.

---

[7] For this specification, if x_C is the European call with exercise price 1, then $x_C - x_P = S - 1$. Hence, for any emm, $\mathbf{E}^{P^*}[x_C] - \mathbf{E}^{P^*}[x_P] = \mathbf{E}^{P^*}[S] - 1 = 0$; the put and the call have the same price in any viable extension of prices to an economy where they are both present.

Variations on Barlow's Example

Many variations can be played on Barlow's example. For instance, suppose that, in the nth economy, we alternate between ζ^n and ζ'_n whose distributions are given by

$$\zeta^n = \begin{cases} -3\gamma/n, & \text{with probability } (n-2)/n, \\ 2\beta, & \text{with probability } 2/n, \end{cases}$$

and

$$\zeta'^n = \begin{cases} -\gamma/n, & \text{with probability } (n-1)/n, \\ \beta, & \text{with probability } 1/n. \end{cases}$$

In the usual fashion, this defines an underlying stochastic process $\{\omega^n(k/n)\}$; the stock price is then defined by $S(k/n) = e^{\omega(k/n)}$. Each discrete-time economy has complete markets, but, in the limit, the log of the stock price is a Poisson jump process with downward drift at rate 2γ and with jumps at rate 1.5 per unit time, where conditional on a jump occurring, the jump is of size 2β with probability $2/3$ and size β with probability $1/3$. Hence, markets are not complete at the limit.

Barlow with Consecutive Steps Combined

Suppose we take a sequence of discrete-time random-walk economies where, in the mth of these economies, the underlying random walk has step-size distribution equal to the distribution of $\zeta^n + \zeta'^n$; that is, if we write ξ^m for the step-size distribution

$$\xi^m = \begin{cases} \sqrt{2}/\sqrt{n} - 2\gamma/n = 1/\sqrt{m} - \gamma/m, & \text{with prob. } (m-4)/(2m), \\[2mm] \sqrt{2}/\sqrt{n} + \beta = 1/\sqrt{m} + \beta, & \text{with prob. } 2/m, \\[2mm] -\sqrt{2}/\sqrt{n} - 2\gamma/n = -1/\sqrt{m} - \gamma/m, & \text{with prob. } (m-4)/(2m), \\[2mm] -\sqrt{2}/\sqrt{n} + \beta = -1/\sqrt{m} + \beta, & \text{with prob. } 2/m. \end{cases}$$

In the (weak) limit, this looks just like the Barlow example, namely a Poisson jump process with compensating downward drift plus and independent Brownian motion. So, markets are incomplete in the continuous-time limit. And they are incomplete in the discrete-time economies. But, it would take only one more security in the continuous-time limit to have dynamically complete markets. For instance, if we had a security that removed the Brownian part of the stock price, drifting down at a deterministic rate while jumping up whenever the stock price jumps up, that would do. Meanwhile, in each of the discrete-time economies, to get complete markets takes not one but *two* more (independent) securities.

Still, one wonders: Is the continuous-time limit economy (with only the stock and the bond) a good economic idealization of the discrete-time economies, for large m? Can (say, bounded and continuous) contingent claims that can be synthesized in the continuous-time limit be asymptotically synthesized in the discrete-time economies? Do the solutions to a consumer's expected-utility maximization problem in the discrete-time economies give, in the limit, the same expected utility as the consumer can achieve in the continuous-time economy?

And, if we add to the discrete-time economies a third security that picks up the jumps (only), while that discrete-time economy is incomplete, is it asymptotically complete in the sense of Chapter 5? Do the solutions to a consumer's expected-utility maximization problem in the discrete-time economies give, in the limit, the same expected utility as the consumer can achieve in the continuous-time economy, in this setting?

I conjecture that the answers to both questions are yes, but these are only conjectures: The hard work of showing these things (or showing that they are wrong) remains.

A Two-by-Two Summary Table

Markets in the continuous-time limit economy may be complete or incomplete. Markets in the discrete-time economies approaching the limit economy may be complete or incomplete. We now have examples for each of the four joint possibilities, as shown in Table 6.1.

| | In the continuous-time limit economy | |
	markets are complete	not complete
In the discrete-time economies in the sequence — markets are complete	Chapter 4: Binomial random walks converging to Brownian motion. Also, the Cox–Ross–Rubinstein binomial random walks (scaled differently) converging to Poisson jump with compensating drift	Barlow's example and variants, in which consumers can do better asymtotically along the sequence than in the limit economy, because discrete time allows for strategies that cannot be replicated in continuous time
In the discrete-time economies in the sequence — markets are not complete	Chapter 5: General random walks converging to Brownian motion Along the sequence, markets are "asymptotically complete" (Proposition 5.1), and some EU-maximizing consumers can do as well, asymptotically (Propositions 5.2 and 5.3)	Barlow's example, with the consecutive steps combined (Many questions remain)

Table 6.1. The two-by-two table of possibilities

7. The Pötzelberger–Schlumprecht Example and Asymptotic Arbitrage

The Example

The second (and even more striking) even–odd example is attributed to K. Pötzelberger and Th. Schlumprecht, independently, by Hubalek and Schachermayer (1998).[8] Let

$$\zeta^n = \begin{cases} 1/\sqrt{n}, & \text{with probability 0.2,} \\ -1.5/\sqrt{n}, & \text{with probability 0.8,} \end{cases}$$

and

$$\zeta'^n = \begin{cases} 1.5/\sqrt{n}, & \text{with probability 0.8,} \\ -1/\sqrt{n}, & \text{with probability 0.2.} \end{cases}$$

Note that this gives us

$$\zeta^n + \zeta'^n = \begin{cases} 2.5/\sqrt{n}, & \text{with probability 0.16,} \\ 0, & \text{with probability 0.68, and} \\ -2.5/\sqrt{n}, & \text{with probability 0.16.} \end{cases}$$

That is, viewed "from afar," the nth of these economies is similar to the mth trinomial economy (for $m = n/2$); each of the m pair of steps of ω having mean 0 and variance $2/n = 1/m$. Hence, as $n \to \infty$ and viewed from afar, the discrete-time models approach the BSM world.

Suppose, then, that we wish to sythesize the European put option with exercise price 1, or $x_P(\omega) = \max\{1 - e^{\omega(1)}, 0\}$.[9] In the BSM world, this has price 0.38239. Per Proposition 5.1, for an initial investment of 0.38239, we can create in the nth discrete-time economy (for large n) a portfolio and, trading in self-financing manner, wind up with a portfolio value very close to x_P, with bounded risk.

---

[8] Hubalek and Schachermayer (1998) develops in detail the theory of this example. Here, I skim their results.

[9] I use the put instead of the call because x_P is bounded, so Proposition 4.5 applies directly.

Let P be Wiener measure on $C[0, 1]$, and let P^n be the measure on $C[0, 1]$ induced by this process for n. Let P^* be the equivalent martingale measure to P (turning $\{e^\omega(t)\}$ into a martingale). It is easy to see that $P^n \Rightarrow P$; the fact that, under P^n, the paths are more "jagged" (have a lot of very local negative correlation) doesn't matter. (You can prove $P^n \Rightarrow P$ by showing that the finite-dimensional distributions converge and that the measures are tight: Compare the modulus of continuity of paths under P^n to the modulus of continuity under Q^n, where Q^n is the measure on $C[0, 1]$ with steps only at $1/m$, $2/m$, etc., and with steps driven by $\zeta^n + \zeta'^n$.)

However, viewed "up close," the nth economy is driven by a binomial process, albeit not a binomial *random walk*. Hence, per Chapter 2, markets in each of the discrete-time economies are complete, and all contingent claims are priced by arbitrage at their expectation with respect to the unique emm, which I denote P^{*n}. Under P^{*n}, the increment at "odd" times (the first half an interval of length $1/m$) have upticks with probability π_1 given by

$$\pi_1 e^{1/\sqrt{n}} + (1 - \pi^1) e^{-1.5/\sqrt{n}} = 1, \quad \text{or} \quad \pi^1 = \frac{1 - e^{-1.5/\sqrt{n}}}{e^{1/\sqrt{n}} - e^{-1.5/\sqrt{n}}}.$$

And, similarly, the uptick probability π^2 under P^{*n} in the second half of each interval is

$$\pi^2 = \frac{1 - e^{-1/\sqrt{n}}}{e^{1.5/\sqrt{n}} - e^{-1/\sqrt{n}}}.$$

Therefore, in the nth such economy, under P^{*n}, the distribution of $\omega((k+1)/m) - \omega(k/m)$ is

$$\begin{cases} 2.5/\sqrt{n}, & \text{with probability } \dfrac{\left(1 - e^{-1.5/\sqrt{n}}\right)\left(1 - e^{-1/\sqrt{n}}\right)}{e^{2.5/\sqrt{n}} + e^{-2.5/\sqrt{n}} - 2}, \\[2ex] 0, & \text{with probability 1 minus the other two probabilities, and} \\[2ex] -2.5/\sqrt{n}, & \text{with probability } \dfrac{\left(e^{1/\sqrt{n}} - 1\right)\left(e^{1.5/\sqrt{n}} - 1\right)}{e^{2.5/\sqrt{n}} + e^{-2.5/\sqrt{n}} - 2}. \end{cases}$$

The asymptotic mean and variance of $\omega((k+1)/m) - \omega(k/m)$ is most easily computed by finding the mean and variance of the two "pieces" separately and then using the fact that $\omega((k+1)/m) - \omega(k/m)$ is the independent sum of the two halves: It turns out that the means and variances of both "half steps" are asymptotically the same: The mean of each is $-0.75/n + o(1/n)$, while the variances are $1.5/n + o(1/n)$.[10] Hence, enlisting the Lindeberg Central Limit Theorem for Triangular Arrays as in Chapter 4, the sum of these n increments approaches (as $n \to \infty$) a Normal with mean -0.75 and variance 1.5.[11] Although the methods developed here don't show that $P^{*n} \Rightarrow Q^*$, where ω under Q^* is Brownian motion with drift -0.75 and infinitesimal variance 1.5, this extension of Donsker's Theorem is well known; see, for instance, Billingsley (1999, Problem 8.4).

Note that while Q^* is a martingale measure, it is not equivalent to P: Squared variation under P is 1 almost surely; under Q^* it is 1.5. But we know that the price of option x in the nth economy is precisely $\mathbf{E}^{*n}[x]$. And since $P^{*n} \Rightarrow Q^*$, we know that these prices converge (as $n \to \infty$) to $\mathbf{E}^{Q^*}[x]$, at least for x sufficiently well behaved; certainly for x that are continuous and bounded. Quite clearly, for many claims x, $\mathbf{E}^{Q^*}[x] \neq \mathbf{E}^*[x]$. In particular, $\mathbf{E}^{Q^*}[x_C] = \lim_n \mathbf{E}^{*n}[x_C] = 0.4594$, approximately.

This is quite the economic conundrum: The exact price of x_P in the nth economy is, for large n, approximately 0.4594. But a consumer can buy a portfolio of stock and bond for 0.38239, trade in self-financing fashion, and end up with a portfolio whose value is very close to x_P. Are there (approximate) arbitrage profits to be made?

In fact, it is easy to see directly that there are approximate arbitrage profits to be made. Consider the following trading strategy: At time $1/n$, sell 10 bonds and buy as many shares of stock as these funds permit. At time $2/n$, convert to bonds. At time $3/n$, convert back to stock, and so forth: In intervals of the form from $2k/n$ to $(2k+1)/n$, hold only bonds. In intervals of the form $(2k+1)/n$ to $(2k+2)/n$, hold only stock. For an initial investment of 10, the value of this portfolio at time 1 (in the nth discrete-time economy) will have the distribution of

$$10 \times \exp\left[\sum_{k=1}^{n/2} \zeta_k'^n\right],$$

---

[10] Use Taylor's Theorem yet again. Or see Hubalek and Schachermayer (1998, Equation (3.11)).

[11] I am grateful to F. Hubalek who caught and corrected an error in this computation in an early draft.

where $\{\zeta_k'^n; k = 1, \ldots, m\}$ is a i.i.d. sequence of random variables, each with distribution ζ'^n. Hence, the distribution of the log of the portfolio value will be the distribution of $\ln(10) + \sum_{k=1}^{n/2} \zeta_k'^n$. But:

The distribution of $\displaystyle\sum_{k=1}^{n/2} \zeta_k'^n$ is the distribution of $\displaystyle\frac{1}{\sqrt{n}} \sum_{k=1}^{n/2} \xi_k,$

where $\{\xi_k\}$ is an i.i.d. sequence of random variables which equal 1.5 with probability 0.8 and -1 with probability 0.2. This is a random walk in which each step size has mean 1. By the strong law of large numbers, $\left[\sum_{k=1}^{n/2} \xi_k\right]/n \to 1$ a.s., so $\left[\sum_{k=1}^{n/2} \xi_k\right]/\sqrt{n} \to \infty$ a.s. Hence, the log of the value of the portfolio, as $n \to \infty$, approaches ∞ "almost surely." Which of course means that the value of the portfolio, as $n \to \infty$, approaches ∞ "almost surely." (I'll explain the scare quotes in the next paragraph.) *And the down-side risk from this trading strategy is bounded below by the initial investment of 10:* because the stock price is never negative, the value of the portfolio, which alternates between being fully invested in the stock and fully invested in the bond (except for the initial sale of 10 bonds) is nonnegative. As $n \to \infty$, arbitrage profits – extraordinary approximate arbitrage profits, derived from an initial investment of fixed size – are feasible *in the limit*.[12]

Why are there scare quotes around "almost surely" in the previous paragraph? Because, as n increases, the relevant probability measure P^n shifts. Almost-sure convergence requires a single probability measure. But what we can say, precisely, is that for every large constant M and $\epsilon > 0$, there exists an N such that for all $n > N$,

$$P^n\left(\left\{\omega : 10 \times \exp\left[\sum_{k=1}^{n/2} \zeta_k'^n\right] > M\right\}\right) > 1 - \epsilon.$$

Indeed, suppose, for $n > N$, the investor, instead of beginning by selling 10 bonds and buying stock with the proceeds of this sale, sell $10/\sqrt{M}$ bonds and buys stock with the proceeds; and then goes back and

---

[12] A greedy arbitrageur might try to speed things up by investing entirely in stock in even-numbered periods and selling the stock short in odd numbered periods. Indeed, a greedy arbitrageur might leverage her bets. But doing so exposes the arbitrageur to downside risk; the simple trading strategy described in the text runs no such risk.

forth between holding stock and bond. She then earns, with probability $1 - \epsilon$ or more at least $\sqrt{M}$, where her risk (what can happen in the complementary event with probability ϵ or less) is her initial sale of $10/\sqrt{M}$ bonds: Her risk is not only bounded, *but vanishes.*

Although it may not be necessary to demonstrate further, consider an expected-utility-maximizing consumer in the nth of these economies, seeking to maximize her expected utility, starting with some given level of wealth. Suppose, in particular, that her utility function is $u(x) = \ln(x)$. (Any utility function out of the CRRA family exhibits the same phenomena.)

Once again, we enlist the standard result that, for any CRRA utility function, her optimal strategy is to hold a constant fraction of her wealth in the stock, where (in this case) the fraction depends on n and on whether it is an even or odd subperiod. If she is at an odd-numbered time – that is, today is k/n for odd k – her optimal fraction of wealth to invest in the stock is the value α that maximizes

$$\left(0.2\ln(\alpha e^{1/\sqrt{n}} - \alpha + 1) + 0.8\ln\left(\alpha e^{-1.5/\sqrt{n}} - \alpha + 1\right)\right).$$

For $n = 100$, the optimal value of α is approximately -3.52; for $n = 400$, the optimal value of α is approximately -7.50.[13] In words, for $n = 400$, she optimally puts 850% of wealth in the bond, going short in the stock an amount equal to 750% of her current wealth. Meanwhile in even periods, she puts fraction α' of her wealth into the stock, where α' maximizes

$$0.8\ln(\alpha' e^{1.5/\sqrt{n}} - \alpha' + 1) + 0.2\ln(\alpha' e^{-1/\sqrt{n}} - \alpha' + 1).$$

For $n = 100$, the optimal value of α' is approximately 7.17; for $n = 400$, it is approximately 13.81, which means that (for $n = 400$) she leverages her wealth by shorting the bond so that 1381% of her current wealth is invested in the stock.

If you compute the consumer's optimal expected utility, you'll find that it rockets off to $+\infty$ as $n \to \infty$. This simply echoes what we saw with the simple trading strategy described previously: In odd periods, the expected returns to the stock are $0.2e^{1/\sqrt{n}} + .8e^{-1.5/\sqrt{n}} - 1 \approx -1/\sqrt{n}$, while the variance is of the order $O(1/n)$. By shorting the stock in amounts that

---

[13]   These optimizing values of α were found numerically.

go to ∞ in n, in these periods, the consumer makes huge financial gains with relatively low risk. And in the even periods, by going very long in the stock, she makes huge financial gains, also with relatively low risk.

Of course, the optimal strategy will generate a huge volume of trade. For $n = 400$, the consumer with log utility alternates between being short in stock at 750% of her wealth and being long in stock at 1381% of her wealth. Equally of course, this strategy has no analogue in continuous time; in the continuous-time limit, the optimal strategy for this consumer (with utility function $\ln(x)$) is to have half her wealth in the stock and half in the bond at all times.

And in similar fashion, to sythesize x_P exactly in the discrete-time economy for large n calls for back-and-forth swings in portfolio contents at every trading time. In the limit economy, to exactly synthesize x_P calls for a much smoother portfolio strategy, a strategy that, adapted to discrete time in the manner of the example constructed at the start of Chapter 5 or (alternatively) in the fashion of the proof of Proposition 5.1, will "converge" in final value to x_P, where convergence is in the fashion of Proposition 5.1.[14]

Asymptotic Arbitrage – the Philosophy

The Pötzelberger–Schlumprecht example inherits some of the characteristics of the Barlow example from last chapter. But it adds three new features:

1. In both the Barlow and this example, the consumer's optimal portfolio strategy involves alternation between even and odd periods, a strategy with no continuous-time analogue. Hence, in both models, the consumer does better asymptotically (as $n \to \infty$) in the discrete-time economies than she can do at the continuous-time limit. But in the Barlow example, as $n \to \infty$, the utility-maximizing consumer's optimal expected utility in the discrete-time economies converges to a finite limit. In this example, as $n \to \infty$, the consumer's optimal expected utility diverges to $+\infty$. (This is for the log utility function; more generally, it converges to $\lim_{x \to \infty} u(x)$.)

---

[14] Both in the limit economy and in the limit of the sequence of economies, the trading volume is infinite; that is, the portfolios have infinite variation. But in the limit economy the portfolios have bounded squared variation; in the limit of the discrete-time economies, the squared variation is infinite, as well.

2. In both examples, for every n, markets are complete, and so a consumer can synthesize precisely any contingent claim. But, at the continuous-time limit, markets are complete in this example and incomplete in the Barlow example; for instance, in the Barlow example, at the continuous-time limit, an investor *cannot* synthesize x_P. In the Pötzelberger–Schlumprecht example, an investor can synthesize any bounded and continuous contingent claim at the continuous-time limit, but at an initial cost different from the limit of what it costs to do so in the discrete-time economies.

3. Most strikingly, as $n \to \infty$, in this example, an investor is "capable" of attaining asymptotic arbitrage with bounded and even vanishing risk. She can't do that in the Barlow sequence of discrete-time economies, or in the discrete-time economies of Chapters 4 and 5. . .

. . . although we have yet to show that this is so; that is, that investors are incapable of constructing an asymptotic arbitrage in the sequences of economies of Chapters 4 and 5, or in the CRR sequence of economies, or in the Barlow example. And, I contend, to show this is something of an obligation, if we are to "trust" the sequences of economies in those cases.

The basic philosophy of this monograph is that continuous-time models are idealizations of models in which the opportunities to act are frequent but discrete. And, so, the central question has been: *Which discrete-time models does the BSM model idealize?* This question has been attacked by looking at sequences of discrete-time models in which the opportunities to act approach "continually," and asking whether economic phenomena in models far out in the sequence asymptotically give the economic phenomena in the continuous-time idealization. So, for instance, in the Barlow example, the answer is No, because discrete time provides investors and consumers with valuable opportunities that have no counterpart in the continuous-time limit. [15]

In this case, while I believe that there is something "wrong" with the Pötzelberger–Schlumprecht sequence of economies and its continuous-time limit, *the flaw lies not in the continuous-time limit but instead in how the*

---

[15]   In the models of Chapters 4 and 5, discrete time provides consumers and investors with opportunities that they don't have in the continuous-time limit – namely, the ability to do this type of rapid switching – but in those models, these extra opportunities *are not valuable*, at least, not for expected-utility maximizers. See the concluding chapter for an explanation of this cryptic remark.

sequence of discrete-time economies has been constructed. It is unreasonable to think that the return process of a financial asset flips back and forth between two distinctly different modes, ever more rapidly, and a model – perhaps I should say a "meta-model," because I mean the sequence of discrete-time models – that posits that this happens is silly. This is not to say that dramatic changes in the return processes of financial assets don't occur. They do, but dramatic changes, when they happen, probably endure for some length of time.

So, while the basic question has been: *Are economic phenomena along the sequence of models asymptotically the same as those phenomena in the continuous-time limit?*, another important question is: *Is the constructed sequence of discrete-time models a reasonable **sequence** of models on economic grounds?* For the Pötzelberger–Schlumprecht sequence of discrete-time models, I contend that the answer is, No. Is it true that each model in the sequence is viable as a model of economic equilibrium; this takes us back to Proposition 2.1 on pages 13–4. But viability is, in the terms of Proposition 2.1, about the existence of some set of consumers (and, in fact, in the proof, the existence of a single consumer) who would support the given prices as a Radner equilibrium of plans, prices, and price expectations. *If, as $n \to \infty$, it takes an increasingly strange (set of) consumer(s) to justify the price process in the nth economy, we ought to conclude that, while each economy in the sequence is formally reasonable, the sequence as a sequence is not.*

How can this be formalized? Here is one test:

Definition. *For a sequence of models of the sort explored in this monograph, say that the sequence admits an **asymptotic arbitrage** if, for a each economy in a subsequence $\{m_n\}$ of the sequence of models, an investor, for zero net investment, can produce in the m_nth economy a contingent claim x^{m_n} with a self-financing trading strategy, such that for every $\epsilon > 0$, there exists N such that for all $n \geq N$,*

$$P^{m_n}\left(\left\{\omega : x^{m_n}(\omega) > 1\right\}\right) > 1 - \epsilon,$$

and, if $V^{m_n}(t)$ is the value process of the m_nth trading strategy, there is a *positive constant B such that*

$$P^{m_n}\left(\left\{\omega : V^{m_n}(\omega, t) > -B\right\}\right) = 1, \quad \text{uniformly in } t \text{ and } n.$$

In words, the sequence admits asymptotic arbitrage if, looking along the subsequence of the models, an investor can create an asymptotic free lunch (which, moreover, is strictly positive with probability approaching 1 as $n \to \infty$) with uniformly bounded risk.

My subjective punchline is: If a sequence of models of discrete-time economies of the sort that populate this monograph admits asymptotic arbitrage, then there is something fishy about this sequence of models. No asymptotic arbitrage in this sense is a *necessary* condition for the sequence of models to be reasonable.

Let me stress that imposing the *no-asymptotic-arbitrage* requirement is a subjective judgment. An asymptotic arbitrage typically requires a vanishingly small but still positive probability of taking a discrete (that is, non-vanishing) loss. The maximum size of the loss is uniformly bounded, but for some consumers – consumers whose utility functions are not defined for negative values, such as utility functions in the CRRA class – any loss that exhausts their resources is too great. If consumers in an economy are all of this variety, and if they have limited resources, it is possible that they could live with the existence of an asymptotic arbitrage: they can each take advantage of the opportunity to a limited degree, but those limits may be consistent with overall equilibrium. A weaker requirement, based on a stronger notion of what it takes to have asymptotic arbitrage – for instance, requiring that a strictly positive return can be (asymptotically) attained with probability approaching 1 with vanishing risk, which is feasible in the Pötzelberger–Schlumprecht example – might be judged more appropriate.

However, I will proceed with no-asymptotic-arbitrage requirement, for asymptotic arbitrage as defined here on four grounds:

1. This requirement is satisfied by the sequences of discrete-time models in Chapters 4, 5, and 6. So, should you decide that a weaker requirement is subjectively better, we know that those sequences will satisfy your weaker requirement as well.

2. This requirement is tailor-made to provide a very nice complement to Proposition 5.1, given as the Corollary to Proposition 7.1 to follow.

3. Criteria for verifying this requirement have been developed in the literature; see the next section.

4. I contend that the philosophy here is in the spirit of the philosophy of viability for continuous-time models that is the basis for the Fundamental Theorem of Asset Pricing, albeit this adaptation introduces some subtle differences.

Asymptotic Arbitrage – the Theory

The formal theory of asymptotic arbitrage is developed in Kabanov and Kramkov (1994) and Klein and Schachermayer (1997). These papers deal (in much more generality than is done here) with sequences of viable financial-market economies and the question of whether the sequence admits asymptotic arbitrage. Kabanov and Kramkov develop the theory for the case in which each model in the sequence has complete markets (that is, a unique emm); Klein and Schachermayer extend this to sequences of economies in which markets may not be complete. Hence, to accommodate the models of Chapter 5 in which there are infinitely many emms, I will follow Klein and Schachermayer here.

The setting (for this simplified rendering of their results) is a sequence of discrete-time economies, with the nth economy characterized by the probability measure P^n on $C[0, 1]$ or, to accommodate the Cox–Ross–Rubinstein economy and the Barlow example, $D[0, 1]$, where there is a bond that serves as numeraire and a stock that trades at times $0, 1/n, \ldots, (n - 1)/n$ whose price at time n, in state ω, is $e^{\omega(t)}$. Each model is viable, and we write $\mathcal{M}(P^n)$ for the set of equivalent martingale measures P^{*n} for P^n; that is, the set of probability measures equivalent to P^n that make $\{S(k/n); k = 0, 1, \ldots\}$ into a martingale.

Theorem of Klein and Schachermayer (1997, Theorem 2.2). *The sequence of economies does not admit asymptotic arbitrage if and only if, for each $\epsilon > 0$, there exist a sequence of measures $\{P^{*n}\}$, with $P^{*n} \in \mathcal{M}(P^n)$, and a $\delta > 0$ such that for any event A^n for the nth economy (measurable with respect to the natural sigma-field) such that $P^n(A^n) \le \delta$, we have that $P^{*n}(A^n) \le \epsilon$.*

I will not attempt to indicate how this remarkable result is proved; the reader should consult the source papers. And, if you do consult the source, please note that what I am calling an asymptotic arbitrage here is called an asymptotic arbitrage of the second kind in the original papers.

We can use this theorem to answer the question: Do the sequences of models in Chapters 4, 5, and 6 admit asymptotic arbitrage?

Proposition 7.1. *The sequences of models of economies in Chapters 4, 5, and 6 – the binomial-random-walk models of Chapter 4; the general-random-walk models of Chapter 5, for ζ with bounded support; and the Cox–Ross–Rubinstein models; and the Barlow example from Chapter 6 – do not admit asymptotic arbitrage.*

At least two methods of proof are available. The first is to show directly that these sequences of economies satisfy the no-asymptotic-arbitrage condition provided by Klein and Schachermayer. I'll sketch this method for the general ζ-with-bounded-support models from Chapter 5.

The criterion in Klein and Schachermayer allows the choice of P^{*n} to depend on ϵ. But for the general ζ-with-bounded-support models, one choice of P^{*n} works for all ϵ, namely the emms provided by the Esscher Transform, for which $(dP^{*n}/dP^n)(\omega) = e^{-a_n\omega(1)-b_n}$. We know that the sequences of coefficients $\{a_n\}$ and $\{b_n\}$ converge, the former to $1/2$ and the latter to $1/8$. Now, what we must show is that for every $\epsilon > 0$, there is a $\delta > 0$ such that for any sequence of events $\{A_n\}$ with $P^n(A_n) < \delta$, we have $P^{*n}(A_n) < \epsilon$. But recall that $P^{*n}(A_n) = \int_{A_n}[dP^{*n}/dP^n]\,P^n(d\omega)$. Note that dP^{*n}/dP^n is largest for paths ω with the smallest values of $\omega(1)$. So the most stringent test of the Klein and Schachermayer criterion – that is, the set A^n with $P^n(A) \leq \delta$ that gives the largest value of $P^{*n}(A_n)$ – is the "set" of paths $\{\omega : \omega(1) \leq r_n(\delta)\}$, where $r_n(\delta)$ is chosen as large as possible while keeping the probability of this set less or equal to δ. I put "set" in scare-quotes here because, if ζ has finite support, say, there will typically be ties for the set that meets this condition: there can be many paths leading to $\omega(1) = r_n(\delta)$, and a selection of some number of them will be needed to keep the probability less or equal to δ. However, it is easy to go from this point – knowing the structure of the sets A_n that are the most severe test of Klein and Schachermayer, and knowing that the Radon–Nikodym derivatives dP^{*n}/dP^n converge to dP^*/dP – to show that the Klein and Schachermayer criterion is met.

The less direct method of proof is, given what we've done already, even easier to provide. Suppose an asymptotic arbitrage were available. Then the optimal expected utility that a consumer with, say, a CRRA or CARA utility function, could achieve in the nth discrete-time economy would have to explode to $\lim_{x \to \infty} u(x)$, which, to give one example, is $+\infty$ if $u(x) = \ln(x)$. But we've shown that there are solutions to the log-utility-consumer's maximize-expected-utility problem that converge to a finite limit in all the cases of Proposition 7.1 (for Barlow, without giving all the details). So there cannot be, in any of those examples, asymptotic arbitrage.

No Asymptotic Arbitrage – the Consequences

Proposition 5.1*b*, paraphrased, says: For any bounded and continuous contingent claim x, in the sequence of discrete-time economies built from random walks based on a ζ with bounded support, an investor can asymptotically synthesize x with bounded risk, employing (self-financing) trading strategies that require an initial investment of $\mathbf{E}^*[x]$, the BSM price of x.

But Proposition 5.1*b* *doesn't say* that one *cannot* asymptotically synthesize x in the same sense for an initial investments less than $\mathbf{E}^*[x]$ in the limit. Happily, Proposition 7.1 tells us that this is not possible.

Corollary 7.1. *In the context of Chapter 5, where ζ has bounded support: For a fixed bounded and continuous contingent claim x, suppose a sequence of contingent claims $\{x^n\}$ can be produced from self-financing strategies with the following characteristics:*

a. The claim x^n is produced in the nth discrete-time economy.

b. The initial investment required for x^n is v^n.

c. For some constant B, $P^n(\{\omega : |V^n(t,\omega)| \le B\}) = 1$, uniformly in t and n, where $V^n(t,\omega)$ is the value at time t and in state ω of the trading strategy that produces x^n.

d. For every $\epsilon > 0$, there exists n^0 such that for all $n > n^0$,
$$P^n(\{\omega : |x^n(\omega) - x(\omega)| > \epsilon\}) < \epsilon.$$

Then $\lim_{n \to \infty} v^n = \mathbf{E}^*[x]$.

Or, in words, asymptotically synthesizing x with bounded risk *must* cost $\mathbf{E}^*[x]$ in the limit.

The proof is straightforward.[16] Suppose one could asymptotically

---

[16] That is, it is straightforward based on a careful reading of Klein and Schachermayer's Theorem 2.2: Their sequence of model economies can have the nth model in the sequence

synthesize x with bounded risk where, along a subsequence $\{m_n\}$, $\lim_{n\to\infty} V^{m_n}(0) < \mathbf{E}^*[x]$. Then by implementing these trading rules and simultaneously "shorting" the sequence of trading rules guaranteed by Proposition 5.1b, buying and holding bonds with the cash in hand from this "covered" position, the investor has a portfolio whose value at the end is asymptotically the number of bonds she purchased for the initial difference in prices, with risk bounded by the bound B plus the bound provided by Proposition 5.1b. This would be an asymptotic arbitrage along the subsequence $\{m_n\}$. But we know that asymptotic arbitrage is impossible by Proposition 7.1. A similar argument works if $\liminf_n V^n(0) > \mathbf{E}^*[x]$, where the investor "goes short" in these portfolio strategies and "long" in the strategies given by Proposition 5.1b. ∎

---

by the m_n th model in a fixed subsequence of one of the full sequence of economies we have considered. And, since Proposition 7.1 shows that their condition for no asymptotic arbitrage holds for the full sequence of economies in one of our cases, that condition holds for every fixed subsequence of one of our cases.

8. Concluding Remarks, Part 1: How Robust an Idealization is BSM?

I draw two sets of conclusions on two different levels from this work. The first concerns BSM as an idealization of discrete-time economies and, a bit more generally, the concept of arbitrage in financial market theory.

While not all the loose ends have been tied down, the case that the BSM model idealizes more than binomial-random-walk models is surely compelling and, for most mainstream financial market scholars, probably somewhat surprising. The surprise, in turn, probably derives from the textbook definition of arbitrage employed in the theory of financial markets. With that definition, the "arbitrage bounds" on the price of the call option x_C in the trinomial economy from Chapter 1 are from 0 to 0.5954; if BSM idealized the trinomial economies for large n, the price of x_C in the trinomial models for large n "ought" to be in a narrow band around 0.38239. "Surely," then, the conclusion goes, "the trinomial economy for large n is 'far' from BSM." And, indeed it is, if we operationalize "far" based on the classic definition of arbitrage.

However, operationalizing "distance" in this fashion is, from the perspective of what is important in economics, much too strong. Arrow's original insight was that many opportunities to trade in a relatively small number of assets gives consumers, investors, and arbitrageurs the ability to synthesize many contingent claims. Arrow's point was that, insofar as this is true, markets may be much closer to complete, and so equilibria may be closer to efficient, than may (at first) seem. His basic insight is also important to asset-pricing theory, insofar as the equilibrium prices of contingent claims that can be synthesized are determined by the "law of one price." The BSM model provides the ultimate expression of both economic conclusions: Markets are fully complete, with the obvious implications for efficiency; and the prices of all derivative securities are fully determined.

Taking the position that BSM is a theoretical ideal, the question becomes: How close to this theoretical ideal is "close enough" so that equilibrium allocations in "close-by" models are nearly efficient? How close is "close enough" so that the prices of derivative securities are, if not nailed down precisely, at least approximately fixed though arbitrage considerations? I contend that the right "distance metric" to use is not the metric of classic arbitrage but instead the metric implicit in Proposition 5.1b; that is, being close with probability close to 1 and with a bound on how far off one can be in the small-probability event that the synthesized portfolio is not close to the target contingent claim. And if this is the proper distance metric, then the results of Chapter 5 provide a compelling argument that general random-walk-based models, with bounded support for the unscaled driving random variable, are asymptotically close to the BSM model in economically important ways.

That said, economies driven by random-walk processes are quite special. The mainstream financial-markets literature has gone well beyond the simple model I've labeled BSM; there are models with stochastic infinitessimal variance terms and stochastic interest rates, along with models in which, superimposed on stock prices that move "like" Brownian motion, sometimes make large and discontinuous jumps. It probably takes more than two securities to achieve something approximating complete markets; Arrow's classic paper prompts the obvious question: How many more?

This suggests that we go back to the Barlow example in Chapter 6, or, rather, to the example in which we combine into a single period the two steps in the Barlow model. As noted there, the continuous-time limit economy – Brownian motion plus Poisson jumps of a fixed size – requires two "independent" securities plus the bond to get complete markets. But for each n, the nth discrete-time economies require three independent securities plus the bond. One wishes for a general theory of asymptotic synthesis of contingent claims in "large n" economies, for contingent claims that can be synthesized in the appropriate limit economy. And note that there are two issues to addess here: If there are enough securities around so that, in the continuous-time limit, markets are complete, are the discrete-time economies for large n "approximately" complete? And if there are insufficiently many securities, so that the continuous-time limit economy is incomplete, is it at least true that anything that can be synthesized in the continuous-time limit can be approximately synthesized in the discrete-time economies for large n? Chapter 5 hints at such a general theory but only scratches the surface.

That said, as someone who isn't invested in the practical implications of BSM and its descendants, I record two objections to this entire stream of work:

1. The problem of discrete-time, random-walk processes for which the (pre-scaled) increment has unbounded support has been noted: In extraordinary times, consumers don't have the ability to "react" quickly enough to events. By assuming bounded support before scaling, we give the consumers in our models sufficient time to react adequately, as the time between markets being open goes to 0. In the real world, however, it is precisely when extraordinary events are afoot that markets have a tendency to suspend trading. This may be good for avoiding panics. But consumers' ability to react rationally to extraordinary events is severely compromised as a consequence. Or, to put a more positive spin on this, the further investigation of economies which combine securities prices that vary "locally" most of the time but that occasionally have large and discontinuous jumps (and jumps of varying size) should be a focus of attention.

2. More fundamentally, the level of rational foresight required of consumers in these models probably outbids what real consumers can do. We need a theory of the "middle ground" between the sort of rationality and rational foresight assumed of consumers in the Radner–Merton world of prices, plans, and price expectations on the one hand and the starkly behavioral consumers predicated in the literature of temporary equilibrium on the other.

9. Concluding Remarks, Part 2: Continuous-Time Models as Idealizations of Discrete Time

Continuous-time models in economics have been very popular recently, largely because of the tractibility of such models when compared with messier discrete-time analogues. But one must be careful when it comes to trusting in the conclusions of those continuous-time models, especially models that invoke Brownian motion or some other diffusion process. Brownian motion is a very special stochastic process, so circumspection is required in interpreting the range of validity of the results obtained. The philosophy pushed here is that one should invest faith in conclusions from continuous-time models only insofar as they are limits of discrete-time models, as the time between actions (in discrete time) goes to 0. And the faith one invests in these conclusions should be proportional to the range of discrete-time models that exhibit this convergence.

As a tool for deciding how much faith to invest (and when to invest any at all), it would be nice to have general theories about convergence of discrete-time optimization and equilibrium models to continuous analogues. To reiterate from the Preface, my original intention was to develop such general theories; when I found it difficult, I retreated to the "case study" of discrete- and continuous-time models of financial markets. This monograph essentially relays – in relative accessible terms, I hope – that case study at its simplest but still nontrivial level.

What is learned from this case study about the prospects for a general theory? My instincts are that Berge's Theorem, also known as the Theorem of the Maximum, presents a model for how to construct a general theory. Essentially, one needs to show that whatever the one agent (in an optimization problem) or agents (in an equilibrium setting) *wishes* to do at the limit, in continuous time, can be approximately done in discrete time, as the time interval in the discrete-time models goes to 0, *and vice versa*.

Readers familiar with Berge's Theorem will know that this *vice versa* is formalized by a pair of assumptions on feasible and desirable strategies, a lower semi-continuity assumption and an upper semi-continuity assumption.

1. If a strategy (or a strategy profile, one strategy for each agent) is optimal for the limit model, it must be that, along the sequence, the agent has available strategies that converge in terms of their impact (or agents have available strategies that, together, converge) to the limit outcome. This, essentially, requires lower semi-continuity of the "available strategy" correspondence, in a topology that ensures the outcomes engendered by a sequence of converging strategies themselves converge.

    In these terms, Propositions 11 and 12 are "lower semi-continuous" results: With BSM as the limit model, the financial-gain stochastic integral for a particular stock-holding process can be approximated by a discretized version of the stock-holding process and the corresponding financial-gains sums (Proposition 11). And so, consumers can do at least as well along the sequence (in the limit) as they can at the limit model (Proposition 12, more or less).

2. But Berge's Theorem also requires a converse condition: It can't be that the limit of what can be achieved along the sequence is better than what can be achieved at the limit. This leads to the requirement in plain-vanilla versions of Berge's Theorem that the feasible-strategy correspondence is upper semi-continuous and compact. But, in many applications, this is too much to reasonably require. So, in fancier versions of Berge's Theorem (e.g., the version in Kreps, 2013, p. 476), the requirement is that there is a subcorrespondence of the available strategies that is upper semi-continuous and locally bounded, such that, *restricted to this subcorrespondence*, the consumer can do just as well for herself as she can without being so restricted.

    In these terms, Proposition 13 is an upper semi-continuous piece of the puzzle: In the limited context of Proposition 13, one can show that optimal investment strategies for the consumer for finite n are found in a very small subset of all possible investment strategies, a subset that has the required upper semi-continuity and local boundedness.

    On the other hand, Barlow's example shows a breakdown of the upper semi-continuity half. In discrete time, one can, and in Barlow's example, *it is optimal to,* alternate quickly between two different modes of operation, something that has no feasible analogue in the limit model of continuous time.

So how can a general theory be constructed? The easier half, it seems to me, is the first half; finding conditions under which what is optimal in the continuous-time idealization can be approximated in "close by" discrete-time models. The more difficult half will be the second part: Finding conditions under which what is optimal in discrete time converges to something meaningful in the continuous-time limit model. For one thing, strategies that move back and forth ever more rapidly in discrete-time models should not be optimal; perhaps including some sort of nonzero switching cost, proportional or even convex in the distance moved, will work.

One other, associated problem in moving from discrete to continuous time is information flow. Information flow issues don't arise in the context of this monograph because, by assumption, all relevant information is available at no cost. But in the game-theoretic applications of continuous-time models and "near-by" discrete-time models, this is a substantial problem. In the introduction, I referenced Fudenberg and Levine (2009) and Sadzik and Stacchetti (2015): This is the issue that gives non-convergence in their models. Essentially, small changes in observables can convey huge amounts of information – this is an issue in economics that goes back to the early literature on rational expectations equilibrium, at least – and, in discrete time, it is possible for information to be conveyed that "washes out" in the continuous-time limit. So, in discrete time, agents have tools – the ability to condition their actions on observed small changes in observables that convey a lot of information – that they lack in continuous time.

If switching costs are used to eliminate rapidly changing actions, some sort of small, but nonzero noise in all observables might play a similar role. I conjecture that, if there is some "big theorem" out there about convergence as one moves from discrete to continuous time, this will be an important part of the story.

At this point, this is only speculation. I'm better informed by what has been done here, but the hard work of formulating and proving results remains to be done.

Appendix

Two Equivalent Ways to Represent a Field of Events for a Finite State Space

On page 6, it is claimed that the following two ways of depicting a field of events for a finite state space are equivalent:

1. A field of events is a collection of subsets of the state space Ω that is closed under taking of unions, intersections, and complements, and that contains Ω itself.

2. A field of events is constructed from a partition of Ω, as the collection of all unions of cells in the partition, plus the empty set.

Here is proof that these are equivalent:

If G is a partition of Ω and F consists of the empty set and all unions of elements (cells) of G, then F is clearly closed under the taking of complements (the complement of the union of a set of cells is the union of those cells not in the original union), unions (the union of all cells in the events in the union), and intersections (the union of all cells that are in every union in the intersection), so is a field.

Going in the other direction, suppose F is a field (for a finite set Ω) per the first definition above. For each $\omega \in \Omega$, write $G(\omega)$ for the intersection of all sets in F that contain ω. Since ω is contained in every such set, $\omega \in G(\omega)$. If $\omega' \in G(\omega)$, then ω' is contained in every set $A \in F$ that contains ω. But then ω is in every set $A \in F$ that contains ω'; were this not so, there would be some $A \in F$ that contains ω' but not ω, and then the complement of A would contain ω but not ω', contradicting the hypothesis that ω' is in every set $A \in F$ that contains ω.

Suppose that $\omega'' \in G(\omega)$ and $\omega' \in G(\omega)$. We have just shown that if $\omega' \in G(\omega)$, then $\omega \in G(\omega')$, so $\omega \in A$ for all $A \in F$ that contain ω'. But since $\omega'' \in G(\omega)$, ω'' is in every $A \in F$ that includes ω, which implies that $\omega'' \in A$ for all $A \in F$ that contain ω', and $\omega'' \in G(\omega')$. This immediately implies that, for every pair ω and ω', either $G(\omega) = G(\omega')$ or $G(\omega) \cap G(\omega') = \emptyset$.

Since each $\omega \in G(\omega)$, this implies that the sets $G(\omega)$ for $\omega \in \Omega$ partition Ω. All that is left to do is to show that every $A \in F$ is the (finite) union of sets $G(\omega)$. But that is trivial: If we take the union

$$\bigcup_{\omega \in A} G(\omega)$$

this is surely A, since it contains every $\omega \in A$, and if $\omega \in A$, $G(\omega) \subseteq A$, since the intersection that defines $G(\omega)$ includes A.

Proof of Proposition 4.2*a*

The condition on x given in Proposition 4.2*a* is sufficient. We begin with a lemma that provides *necessary and* sufficient conditions.

Lemma A.1. *For an unbounded, continuous, nonnegative contingent claim* $x \in L^2(\Omega, F, P)$, *define* $x^M(\omega) := min\{M, x(\omega)\}$; *that is,* x^M *is* x *truncated at* M. *Then a necessary and sufficient condition for* $lim_{n \to \infty} \mathbf{E}^{*n}[x] = \mathbf{E}^*[x]$ *is*

$$\lim_{M \to \infty} sup\left\{\mathbf{E}^{*n}[x - x^M]; n = 1, 2, 3, \dots\right\} = 0. \qquad (A.1)$$

Note: Condition $(A.1)$ is similar to uniform integrability, but it is different: Uniform integrability as usually defined deals with a sequence of random variables – in this context, contingent claims – and a single probability measure. Here the contingent claim is fixed, and we are examining whether that one claim is "uniformly integrable" over a sequence of probability measures.

Proof. Temporarily write $\hat{x}^M$ for $x - x^M$, so that $x = x^M + \hat{x}^M$. Then, for fixed M,

$$\lim_{n \to \infty} \mathbf{E}^{*n}[x], \text{ if it exists,} = \lim_{n \to \infty}\left\{\mathbf{E}^{*n}[x^M] + \mathbf{E}^{*n}[\hat{x}^M]\right\}. \qquad (A.2a)$$

Since, for each fixed M, x^M is bounded, we know from Proposition 5 that $lim_{n \to \infty} \mathbf{E}^{*n}[x^M] = \mathbf{E}^*[x^M]$; hence, we can rewrite $(A.2a)$ as

$$\lim_{n \to \infty} \mathbf{E}^{*n}[x], \text{ if it exists,} = \mathbf{E}^*[x^M] + \lim_{n \to \infty} \mathbf{E}^{*n}[\hat{x}^M]. \qquad (A.2b)$$

The left-hand side of $(A.2b)$ doesn't depend on M, and $\mathbf{E}^*\left[x^M\right] = \mathbf{E}^*\left[x\right] - \mathbf{E}^*\left[\hat{x}^M\right]$, so we can rewrite $(A.2b)$ as

$$\lim_{n\to\infty} \mathbf{E}^{*n}[x], \text{ if it exists,} = \lim_{M\to\infty} \left\{\mathbf{E}^*\left[x\right] - \mathbf{E}^*\left[\hat{x}^M\right] + \lim_{n\to\infty} \mathbf{E}^{*n}\left[\hat{x}^M\right]\right\}.$$

$$(A.2c)$$

By dominated convergence, $\lim_M \mathbf{E}^*\left[\hat{x}^M\right] = 0$, so if we pull the $\mathbf{E}^*\left[x\right]$ out of limit in M on the right-hand side of $(A.2c)$, we get

$$\lim_{n\to\infty} \mathbf{E}^{*n}[x], \text{ if it exists,}$$

$$= \mathbf{E}^*\left[x\right] - \lim_{M\to\infty} \mathbf{E}^*\left[\hat{x}^M\right] + \lim_{M\to\infty} \left\{\lim_{n\to\infty} \mathbf{E}^{*n}\left[\hat{x}^M\right]\right\}.$$

$$= \mathbf{E}^*\left[x\right] + \lim_{M\to\infty} \left\{\lim_{n\to\infty} \mathbf{E}^{*n}\left[\hat{x}^M\right]\right\}$$

$$(A.2d)$$

So $\lim_n \mathbf{E}^{*n}[x] = \mathbf{E}^*[x]$ if and only if $\lim_M \lim_n \mathbf{E}^{*n}\left[\hat{x}^M\right] = 0$. And this is clearly necessary and sufficient for $(A.1)$. This finishes the proof of the Lemma A.1.

Now to prove Proposition 4.2a. This proof contains almost no intuition; it is just a matter of grinding through various estimates of things. The proof proceeds in a series of steps.

Step 1. It suffices to prove the result for nonnegative claims.

Take a general continuous claim x. Write x^+ and x^- for the positive and negative parts of x, respectively. Then both x^+ and x^- are continuous and both satisfy the hypothesized bounds (4.2). If we prove the result for nonnegative claims, then we have certainly proved the result for x^+ and, by considering $-x^-$, we have proved the result for x^-. But since $x = x^+ + x^-$, if we have the result for each of x^+ and x^-, we have it for their sum.

Therefore, for the remainder of the proof, we assume that x is nonnegative.

Step 2. The second step is the following lemma:

Lemma A2. *For any scalar a, $\lim_{n\to\infty}\left(1 + a/n + o(1/n)\right)^n = e^a$.*

I am certain that this is a standard exercise in (advanced?) calculus textbooks, but as I can't find a reference, I'll give the proof. Instead of looking at $\lim_{n\to\infty}\left(1+a/n+o(1/n)\right)^n$, look at $\lim_{n\to\infty}\left(n\cdot\ln(1+a/n+o(1/n))\right)$. A Taylor series expansion of the log part is

$$\ln\left(1+\frac{a}{n}+o\left(\frac{1}{n}\right)\right) = \ln(1) + \left(\frac{a}{n}+o\left(\frac{1}{n}\right)\right) + o_1\left(\frac{1}{n}\right) = \frac{a}{n}+o_2\left(\frac{1}{n}\right).$$

Hence

$$n\ln\left(1+\frac{a}{n}+o\left(\frac{1}{n}\right)\right) = n\frac{a}{n} + n\,o_2\left(\frac{1}{n}\right) = a + o(1).$$

Take e to both sides, pass to the limit, and we're done.

Step 3. For any positive integer N, each of the following limits exists and is finite:

$$\lim_n \mathbf{E}^n\left[e^{N\omega(1)}\right], \quad \lim_n \mathbf{E}^n\left[e^{-N\omega(1)}\right], \quad \lim_n \mathbf{E}^{*n}\left[e^{N\omega(1)}\right], \quad \lim_n \mathbf{E}^{*n}\left[e^{-N\omega(1)}\right].$$

Because, under P^{*n}, $\omega(1)$ has a "smaller" distribution function than its symmetric distribution under P^n, the last of these four expectations is the "biggest." So I'll prove the result for the fourth, only; the others have very similar proofs (and, as you will discern, easier proofs in the case of the first two).

First, note that $\omega(1)$ under P^{*n} is $\sum_{k=1}^n \zeta_k^n$, so

$$\mathbf{E}^{*n}\left[e^{-N\omega(1)}\right] = \mathbf{E}^{*n}\left[\exp\left(-N\sum_{k=1}^n \zeta_k^n\right)\right] = \mathbf{E}^{*n}\left[\prod_{k=1}^n \exp\left(-N\zeta_k^n\right)\right].$$

Since the ζ_i^n are i.i.d., the expectation of the product is the product of the expectations, and so

$$\mathbf{E}^{*n}\left[e^{-N\omega(1)}\right] = \left(\mathbf{E}^{*n}\left[e^{-N\zeta_1^n}\right]\right)^n.$$

We can directly compute $\mathbf{E}^{*n}\left[e^{-N\zeta_1^n}\right]$; it is

$$\mathbf{E}^{*n}\left[e^{-N\zeta_1^n}\right] = \left(\frac{1}{1+e^{1/\sqrt{n}}}\right)e^{-N/\sqrt{n}} + \left(\frac{1}{1+e^{-1/\sqrt{n}}}\right)e^{N/\sqrt{n}}.$$

Create a common denominor of $(1 + e^{1/\sqrt{n}})(1 + e^{-1/\sqrt{n}})$, and we get

$$\mathbf{E}^{*n}\left[e^{-N\zeta_1^n}\right] = \frac{e^{-N/\sqrt{n}} + e^{(-N-1)/\sqrt{n}} + e^{(N+1)/\sqrt{n}} + e^{N/\sqrt{n}}}{2 + e^{1/\sqrt{n}} + e^{-1/\sqrt{n}}}.$$

Take a Taylor series expansion of each term in $1/\sqrt{n}$ out to the second term: In the numerator, this gives

$$\{1 - N/\sqrt{n} + N^2/(2n)\} + \{1 - (N+1)/\sqrt{n} + (N+1)^2/(2n)\}+$$
$$\{1 + N/\sqrt{n} + N^2/(2n)\} + \{1 + (N+1)/\sqrt{n} + (N+1)^2/(2n)\} + o(1/n),$$

where I've collected all the little o terms. The terms of order $1/\sqrt{n}$ cancel out, leaving a numerator of $4 + N^2/n + (N+1)^2/n + o(1/n)$. And, similarly, the denominator reduces to $4 + 1/n + o_1(1/n)$. Multiply numerator and denominator by $1/4$, and we have

$$\mathbf{E}^{*n}\left[e^{-N\omega(1)}\right] = \frac{\left[(1 + (N^2 + (N+1)^2)/4)(1/n) + o_2(1/n)\right]^n}{\left[1 + (1/4)(1/n) + o_3(1/n)\right]^n}.$$

As $n \to \infty$, Lemma A.1 tells us that the numerator approaches $e^{(N^2+(N+1)^2)/4}$, while the denominator has limit $e^{1/4}$, and so the entire expression has the finite limit $e^{(N^2+N)/2}$ finishing step 3. Although I won't do all the algebra, similar calculations show that $\lim_n \mathbf{E}^{*n}\left[e^{N\omega(1)}\right] = e^{(N^2-N)/2}$ and $\mathbf{E}^n\left[e^{N\omega(1)}\right] =^n \left[e^{-N\omega(1)}\right] = e^{N^2/2}$.

Step 4. Recall the formula for the moments of the log-Normal distribution, and compare with the results of Step 3.

It is well known that the Nth moment of a log-Normal – that is, the expectation of X^N, where $X = e^{Z(\mu,\sigma^2)}$ and $Z(\mu,\sigma^2)$ is a standard Normal with mean μ and variance σ^2 – is $\exp(N\mu + N^2\sigma^2/2)$. This implies that

- Under the probability measure P, for which $\omega(1)$ is Normal with mean 0 and variance 1, $e^{N\omega(1)}$ is square-integrable (the expectation of its square is the $2N$ moment of the log-Normal), and $\mathbf{E}[e^{N\omega(1)}] = e^{N^2/2}$, which (by Step 3) is $\lim_n^n[e^{N\omega(1)}]$. That is

$$\lim_n \mathbf{E}^n[e^{N\omega(1)}] = \mathbf{E}[e^{N\omega(1)}].$$

- And since, under P, $\omega(1)$ has the same distribution as $-\omega(1)$,

$$\lim_n \mathbf{E}^n[e^{-N\omega(1)}] = \mathbf{E}[e^{-N\omega(1)}] = e^{N^2/2}.$$

- Under P^*, $\omega(1)$ is Normal with mean $-1/2$ and variance 1, so (combining the formula for the Nth moment with Step 3),

$$\lim_n \mathbf{E}^{*n}[e^{N\omega(1)}] = \mathbf{E}^*[e^{-N\omega(1)}] = e^{(N^2-N)/2}.$$

- Under P^*, $-\omega(1)$ is Normal with mean $1/2$ and variance 1, so (combining the formula for the Nth moment with Step 3),

$$\lim_n \mathbf{E}^{*n}[e^{N\omega(1)}] = \mathbf{E}^*[e^{-N\omega(1)}] = e^{(N^2+N)/2}.$$

Step 5. Apply the necessary half of Proposition 4.2 to conclude that, if f : $C[0,1] \to R$ is of the form

$$f(\omega) = \sum_{N=-m}^{M} \alpha_N e^{N\omega(1)},$$

then

$$\lim_{M \to \infty} \sup \left\{ \mathbf{E}^{*n}\left[f(\omega) \cdot 1_{\{f(\omega)>M\}}\right] ; n = 1, 2, \ldots \right\} = 0.$$

and similarly for $\mathbf{E}^n$.

Steps 3 and 4 establish convergence $\mathbf{E}^{*n}[f]$ to $\mathbf{E}^*[f]$, so this follows immediately from Proposition 4.2.

Step 6. Use the sufficiency half of Proposition 4.2 to finish the proof.

Suppose x is a nonnegative claim such that $x(\omega) \le f(\omega)$ for f taking the form in step 5. Then it is obvious that $x \cdot 1_{\{x \ge K\}} \le f \cdot 1_{\{f \ge K\}}$ and so, for each n and K,

$$0 \le \mathbf{E}^n\left[x \cdot 1_{\{x \ge K\}}\right] \le \mathbf{E}^n\left[f \cdot 1_{\{f \ge K\}}\right].$$

This immediately implies that

$$0 \le \lim_{M \to \infty} \sup \left\{ \mathbf{E}^{*n} \left[x \cdot 1_{\{x \ge M\}} \right]; n = 1, 2, \dots \right\} \le$$

$$\lim_{M \to \infty} \sup \left\{ \mathbf{E}^{*n} \left[f \cdot 1_{\{x \ge M\}} \right]; n = 1, 2, \dots \right\} = 0$$

and similarly for the P^n. Proposition 4.2 then implies that

$$\lim_{n \to \infty} \mathbf{E}^n [x] = \mathbf{E}[x] \quad and \quad \lim_{n \to \infty} \mathbf{E}^{*n} [x] = \mathbf{E}^* [x].$$

∎

Proof of Proposition 4.4

The problem is to maximize $\mathbf{E}[u(x(\omega))]$ subject to $\mathbf{E}^*[x(\omega)] \le W_0, x \in X$, where the constraint $x \ge 0$ may be added. Recall that p^* is the Radon–Nikodym derivative of P^* with respect to P, so $\mathbf{E}^*[x] = \mathbf{E}[p^*x]$.

(In what follows, a.s. is the abbreviation for *almost surely*; since P and P^* are probabilistically equivalent, a.s. means almost surely with respect to both probabilities.)

We start with necessity of the first-order, complementary-slackness conditions: if $x \ge 0$ is required,

$$u'(x^*(\omega)) \le \lambda p^*(\omega), \text{a.s.}$$

with equality if $x^*(\omega) > 0$, for some nonnegative λ. And if $x \ge 0$ is not required, then $u'(x^*(\omega)) = \lambda p^*(\omega)$ for some $\lambda \ge 0$.

First take the case where $x \ge 0$ is not imposed. Fix a candidate solution x. Since $p^* > 0$ a.s., we can look at the strictly positive random variable

$$r(\omega) = \frac{u'(x(\omega))}{p^*(\omega)}.$$

If this is (a.s.) constant, it gives the required λ, so assume it is not constant. Then there must exist values λ_1 and λ_2 with $\lambda_1 > \lambda_2 > 0$ such that the sets

$$A := \{\omega : r(\omega) \ge \lambda_1\} \quad and \quad B := \{\omega : r(\omega) \le \lambda_2\}$$

both have positive probability. Because u' is continuous, I can find λ_1', λ_2', and $\epsilon_o > 0$, such that $\lambda_1' > \lambda_2'$, and the sets

$$A' := \left\{ \omega : \frac{u'(x(\omega) + \epsilon)}{p^*(\omega)} \geq \lambda_1' \text{ for all } \epsilon < \epsilon_0 \right\} \quad \text{and}$$

$$B' := \left\{ \omega : \frac{u'(x(\omega) - \epsilon)}{p^*(\omega)} \leq \lambda_2' \text{ for all } \epsilon < \epsilon_0 \right\}$$

both have positive probability. Take subsets A'' of A' and B'' of B' of equal (strictly positive) P^*-probability, and consider modifying x as follows: On A'', replace $x(\omega)$ with $x(\omega) + \epsilon_0$, and on B'', replace $x(\omega)$ with $x(\omega) - \epsilon_0$. Since $P^*(A'') = P^*(B'')$, this change doesn't affect the P^* expectation of the claim, and the constraint continues to be satisfied. (Of course, x are modified remains square-integrable.)

However, the impact on the objective function is a strict increase. Note first that $1/p^*$ is dP/dP^*. So, on the set A'', the new versus the old integral is

$$\int_{A''} [u((x(\omega) + \epsilon_0) - u(x(\omega))] dP = \int_{A''} \frac{u((x(\omega) + \epsilon_0) - u(x(\omega))}{p^*(\omega)} p^*(\omega) dP$$

$$= \int_{A''} \frac{u((x(\omega) + \epsilon_0) - u(x(\omega))}{p^*(\omega)} dP^* = \int_{A''} \frac{\int_0^{\epsilon_0} u'(x(\omega) + \epsilon) d\epsilon}{p^*(\omega)} dP^*$$

$$\geq \int_{A''} \lambda_1' \epsilon_0 dP^* = \lambda_1' \epsilon_0 P^*(A'').$$

And, in similar fashion, on the set B'', the new versus the old integral is

$$\int_{B''} [u(x(\omega) - \epsilon_0) - u(c(\omega))] dP \geq -\lambda_2' \epsilon_0 P^*(B'').$$

Hence, as claimed, the impact on the objective function is no smaller than

$$\lambda_1' \epsilon_0 P^*(A'') - \lambda_2' \epsilon_0 P^*(B''),$$

which, since $P^*(A'') = P^*(B'')$ and $\lambda_1' > \lambda_2'$, is strictly positive. The candidate solutions x is not a solution.

Now consider the case where we impose the constraint $x \geq 0$. Part of the necessary conditions are that $\mathbf{E}^*[x] = W_0 > 0$, so $P(\{x > 0\} > 0$ is required. And, on the set where $x > 0$, $r(\omega) = u'(x(\omega))/p^*(\omega)$, r must be (a.s.) constant λ; the argument given for the unconstrained case shows this. So, with the constraint added, the only remaining way that x might violate the first-order, complementary-slackness conditions is if

$$P(\{x : x = 0 \text{ and } u'(x(\omega))/p^*(\omega) > \rho\}) > 0.$$

But, in this case, the argument given can be adapted: Increase x on a subset of the set in the previous display and decrease it on a set where $x > 0$.

This establishes necessity. The argument that the optimality conditions are sufficient is fairly standard, but I repeat it here for completeness: Again, begin with the case where the constraint $x \geq 0$ is not imposed. We suppose that x^* satisfies the first-order conditions $u'(x^*(\omega)) = \lambda p^*(\omega)$ a.s. as well as $\mathbf{E}^*[x^*] = W_0$, and we let x be any other claim from X that satisfies the budget constraint $\mathbf{E}^*[x] \leq W_0$. Since u is concave, for each ω we have the inequality

$$u(x) - u(x^*) \leq u'(x^*)(x - x^*).$$

Hence, since $u'(x^*) = \lambda p^*$, a.s.,

$$u(x, \omega) - u(x^*, \omega) \leq \lambda p^*(\omega)(x(\omega) - x^*(\omega)), \quad \text{a.s.}$$

Integrate over all of Ω with respect to P, and we get

$$\mathbf{E}[u(x) - u(x^*)] \leq \lambda \mathbf{E}[p^*(x - x^*)] = \lambda \mathbf{E}^*[x - x^*] \leq 0,$$

since $\mathbf{E}^*[x] \leq W_0 = \mathbf{E}^*[x^*]$. And if we have the constraint $x \geq 0$ (so the alternative to x^* must be nonnegative): We can repeat the previous argument, knowing that $u'(x^*)(x - x^*) \leq \lambda p^*(x - x^*)$ a.s., since if $x^* > 0$ we know that $u'(x^*) = \lambda p^*$, while if $x^* = 0$, we know that $\lambda p^* \geq u'(x^*)$, and (of course) $x - x^* \geq 0$, since $x \geq 0$ and $x^* = 0$.

There is one more (nonstandard) piece required for showing sufficiency. We have constrained x^* to be square integrable with respect to P

(so that it is integrable with respect to P^*), but we do not know (yet) that $u(x^*)$ is integrable with respect to P. Split $\mathbf{E}[u(x^*)]$ into two pieces: the integral on the set where $x^* \geq W_0$, and the integral over the set where $x^* < W_0$. Since $W_0 > 0$, $u(W_0)$ is finite, so to show that $u(x^*)$ is integrable, we must show that the integral over the first piece is less than $+\infty$ and that the integral over the second piece is greater than $-\infty$.

The first half is easy: For $x^* \geq W_0$, $u(x^*) \leq u'(W_0)(x^* - W_0)$, and the square-integrability of x^* is much more than we need. And, for the second half, in the unconstrained case, write

$$u(W_0) - u(x^*) \leq u'(x^*)(W_0 - x^*), \text{ or}$$
$$u(x^*) \geq u(W_0) - u'(x^*)(x^* - W_0) = u(W_0) - \lambda p^*(x^* - W_0),$$

which establishes integrability of $u(x^*)$ on the set $\{x^* \leq W_0\}$. As for the constrained case, the same inequality works if $\{x^* = 0\}$ has probability 0 (since, in this case, the first-order condition holds as an equality a.s.). We only need to worry about the possibility that $\{x^* = 0\}$ has positive probability. But, if it does, then $u(0)$ must be finite; since $u'(0) \leq \lambda p^*$ for any ω such that $x^* = 0$, $u'(0)$ cannot be ∞, and the fundamental theorem of calculus implies that $u(0)$ is finite. Integrability of $u(x^*)$ over $\{x^* \leq W_0\}$ is immediate.

Some Calculations for the General Binomial Model

Let ζ be a general two-element-support random variable, with mean 0. Specifically, let ζ have support $\{A, B\}$, where $A > 0 > B$. So that ζ has mean 0, is must be that

$$P(\zeta = A) = \frac{-B}{A - B}; \quad \text{hence,} \quad \mathbf{E}[\zeta^2] = A^2 \frac{-B}{A - B} + B^2 \frac{A}{A - B} = -AB.$$

In the fashion of Chapter 3, we imagine probability distributions P^n on $C[0,1]$ with support "jagged" paths that start at 0 and, over each time period k/n to $(k+1)/n$, rise linearly by $A/\sqrt{n}$ or fall by $B/\sqrt{n}$, with the uptick probability $-B/(A-B)$ and with the n increments independent of one another. By a standard application of Donsker's Theorem, $P^n \Rightarrow P$, where P here is Wiener measure on $C[0,1]$ but for a Brownian motion with drift 0 infinitessimal variance $-AB$. Obviously, there is a unique equivalent martingale measure P^*, equivalent to P, turning $\{e^{\omega(t)}\}$ into a martingale, which is Weiner measure for a Brownian motion with drift $AB/2$ and infinitessimal variance AB.

Per Chapter 2, for each n, there is a unique probability measure P^{*n} on $C[0, 1]$ equivalent to P^n and that turns $\{e^{\omega(k/n)}; k = 0, 1, \ldots, n\}$ into a martingale. The uptick probability π^{*n} (for each interval) must satisfy

$$\pi^{*n} e^{A/\sqrt{n}} + (1 - \pi^{*n}) e^{B/\sqrt{n}} = 1; \quad \text{hence,} \quad \pi^{*n} = \frac{1 - e^{B/\sqrt{n}}}{e^{A/\sqrt{n}} - e^{B/\sqrt{n}}},$$

with complementary probability $1 - \pi^{*n} = [e^{A/\sqrt{n}} - 1] / [e^{A/\sqrt{n}} - e^{B/\sqrt{n}}]$. To avoid writing so many $\sqrt{n}$s, fix n and write a for $A/\sqrt{n}$ and b for $B/\sqrt{n}$. Then under P^{*n}, the expectation of the increment over each time interval $[k/n, (k+1)/n]$ is

$$\frac{(1 - e^b)a + (e^a - 1)b}{e^a - e^b,} \tag{A1}$$

and, after much tiresome algebra, the variance of each increment is

$$\frac{\left(e^a + e^b - e^{a+b} - 1\right)\left(a - b\right)^2}{e^{2a} + e^{2b} - 2e^{a+b}}. \tag{A2}$$

The increments are, of course, i.i.d. A Taylor series expansion of the numerator of the expectation term is

$$-ab - \frac{ab^2}{2} + ab + \frac{a^2 b}{2} + o(1/n^2) = \frac{ab(a - b)}{2} + o(1/n^2),$$

while the denominator is

$$a + \frac{a^2}{2} - b - \frac{b^2}{2} + o(1/n^2) = (a - b)(1 + a/2 + b/2) + o(1/n^2).$$

As $n \to \infty$, a and b both are $O(1\sqrt{n})$, $a - b$ is also $O(1/\sqrt{n})$, and, hence, the $o(1/n^2)$ terms vanish, and the limit of (A1) is

$$\frac{ab}{2} = \frac{AB}{2}\frac{1}{n}.$$

By a similar (and much longer) algebraic exercise using Taylor series expansions of the numerator and denominator of (A2), the variance is

$$\left[-ab + o(1/n^2)\right] \cdot \left[\frac{(a-b)^2}{(a-b)^2 + o(1/n^2)}\right],$$

and passing to the limit in n gives $-ab = -AB/n$. From here, one applies the Lindeberg Central Limit Theorem to show that $\omega(1)$ under P^{*n} converges in distribution to a Normal with mean $AB/2$ and variance $-AB$. And, by an argument similar to one the Chapter 2 (possible because the Radon–Nikodym derivatives dP^*/dP and dP^{*n}/dP^n are both decreasing functions of $\omega(1)$), P^{*n} converges to Wiener measure adjusted to be a Brownian motion with drift $AB/2$ and instantaneous variance $-AB$, or P^{*n}, the equivalent martingale measure for the weak limit of the P^n.

The Radon–Nikodym derivative dP^{*n}/dP^n can be written down as a function of the uptick and downtick probabilities. And the general analysis of the Esscher Transform in Chapter 5 ensures that the Radon–Nikodym derivative dP^{*n}/dP^n converges to dP^*/dP.

(Asymptotic) Solutions of the Consumer's Expected-Utility Maximization Problem with CARA Utility

Consider an expected-utility-maximizing consumer whose utility function has constant absolute risk aversion; that is,

$$u(x) = -e^{-\lambda x} \quad \text{for } \lambda > 0.$$

Assume she has initial wealth W and faces the nth discrete-time model of a stock market from Chapter 5, where the variable ζ from which the model is built has bounded support (and mean 0 and variance 1).

Lemma A.1. The solution to the consumer's problem in this context, if she starts with wealth W, involves always investing a fixed amount of her wealth, $z_n(\lambda)$, in the risky asset, regardless of time, past events, and W, with the rest of her wealth held in the bond. This amount $z_n(\lambda)$ is the solution to the maximization problem

$$\textit{Maximize over } z \textit{ the value of } \hat{\mathbf{E}}\left[-\exp\left(-\lambda z\left[e^{\zeta/\sqrt{n}} - 1\right]\right)\right],$$

where $\hat{\mathbf{E}}[\cdot]$ means maximization over the distribution of ζ.

This is a "standard result" in the same sense as the "standard result" for CRRA utility functions provided on pages 141–2 and the proof is quite similar. Suppose that, at time $(n-1)/n$, the consumer has a portfolio with value V, and suppose that she chooses to invest z (in units of the bond) in the stock. Then the distribution of the value of her portfolio is the distribution of

$$V + \frac{z}{S((n-1)/n)} \times \left[S(1) - S((n-1)/n) \right],$$

where you should recognize this as the corresponding financial gains "integral." But this is

$$V + z \times \left[\frac{S(1)}{S((n-1)/n)} - 1 \right],$$

the distribution of which is the distribution of

$$V + z \times \left[e^{\zeta_{n-1}/\sqrt{n}} - 1 \right],$$

where $\{\zeta_k\}$ is an i.i.d. sequence of random variables, each with the distribution ζ. Hence, the consumer's expected utility if she invests z is

$$\hat{\mathbf{E}}\left[-\exp\left(-\lambda \left(V + z \times \left[e^{\zeta_{n-1}/\sqrt{n}} - 1 \right] \right) \right) \right],$$

where, as before, $\hat{\mathbf{E}}[\cdot]$ denotes expectation over the sequence $\{\zeta_k\}$. For this utility function, this expected utility can be rewritten

$$\hat{\mathbf{E}}\left[-e^{-\lambda V} \times \exp\left(-\lambda z \left[e^{\zeta_{n-1}/\sqrt{n}} - 1 \right] \right) \right] = e^{-\lambda V} \hat{\mathbf{E}}\left[-\exp\left(-\lambda \left[e^{\zeta_{n-1}/\sqrt{n}} - 1 \right] \right) \right].$$

The optimizing value of z is the solution in $z^n(\lambda)$ of the problem of maximizing $\hat{\mathbf{E}}\left[-\exp(-\lambda[e^{\zeta_{n-1}/\sqrt{n}} - 1]) \right]$. And if we define $\gamma^n(\lambda)$ as the constant $\hat{\mathbf{E}}\left[-\exp(-\lambda z_n(\lambda)[e^{\zeta_{n-1}/\sqrt{n}} - 1]) \right]$, the continuation value function at time $(n-1)/n$ is $-\gamma_n(\lambda)\exp(-\lambda V)$; the form of her problem at time $(n-2)/n$ is identical (up to this multiplicative constant), and so it is again optimal for her to choose at time $(n-2)/n$ to invest $z_n(\lambda)$ in the stock. And so on, back to time 0.   ∎

Note that in the problem

Maximize over z the value of $\hat{\mathbf{E}}\big[-\exp\big(-\lambda z[e^{\zeta/\sqrt{n}}-1]\big)\big]$,

the objective function is strictly concave and smooth in z, so we know that, if there is a solution, it is unique. And, since there is positive probability that $\zeta < 0$, there is positive probability that $e^{\zeta/\sqrt{n}} < 1$; the utility function is bounded above by 0, while it approaches $-\infty$ as the argument appraches $-\infty$. And so there exists a solution. Because $\hat{\mathbf{E}}[\zeta] > 0$, it follows that $\hat{\mathbf{E}}[e^{\zeta/\sqrt{n}}] > 1$, and therefore we know that the solution $z_n^*(\lambda) > 0$.

How does this solution $z_n^*(\lambda)$ behave, as $n \to \infty$? Approximate $e^{\zeta/\sqrt{n}} - 1$ using Taylor's Theorem in the exact form, and we get for each value of ζ that

$$e^{\zeta/\sqrt{n}} - 1 = \frac{\zeta}{\sqrt{n}} + \frac{\zeta^2}{2n} + \frac{\zeta^3}{6n^{3/2}}e^{\theta_\zeta/\sqrt{n}},$$

for some $\theta_\zeta \in [0, \zeta]$. And a Taylor series expansion of $e^{-\lambda zk}$ around $z = 0$ is

$$e^{-\lambda zk} = e^0 - \lambda k e^0 z + \frac{\lambda^2 k^2}{2}e^0 z^2 - \frac{\lambda^3 k^3}{6}z^3 e^{-\lambda k \phi_k z}$$
$$= 1 - \lambda k z + \frac{\lambda^2 k^2}{2}z^2 - \frac{\lambda^3 k^3}{6}z^3 e^{-\lambda k \phi_k z},$$

where $0 \le \phi_k \le 1$. Substitute the (exact) Taylor series expansion for $e^{\zeta/\sqrt{n}-1}$ for k in the expansion for $e^{-\lambda zk}$, adding a minus sign, and you get

$$-\exp\big[-\lambda z\big(e^{\zeta/\sqrt{n}} - 1\big)\big] = -1 + \lambda z\left[\frac{\zeta}{\sqrt{n}} + \frac{\zeta^2}{2n} + \frac{\zeta^3}{6n^{3/2}e^{\theta_\zeta/\sqrt{n}}}\right]$$

$$-\frac{\lambda^2 z^2}{2}\left[\frac{\zeta^2}{n} + \frac{\zeta^3}{n^{3/2}} + \zeta^4\left(\frac{1}{4n^2} + \frac{e^{\theta_\zeta/\sqrt{n}}}{3n^2}\right)\right] + \frac{\lambda^3 z^3}{6n^{3/2}} \times \psi(\zeta),$$

where $\psi(\zeta)$ is a multinomial in ζ and n whose value is uniformly bounded, because of the bound on the support of ζ. Now take expectations with respect to $\hat{E}$, noting that $\hat{E}[\zeta] = 0$ and $\hat{E}[\zeta^2] = 1$, and we get

$$\hat{E}\left[\left[-\exp\left[-\lambda z\left(e^{\zeta/\sqrt{n}} - 1 \right) \right] \right] \right.$$
$$= -1 + \frac{\lambda z}{2n}\left[1 + \frac{B_1}{n^{1/2}} \right] - \frac{\lambda^2 z^2}{2n}\left[1 + \frac{B_2}{n^{1/2}} \right] + \frac{\lambda^3 z^3}{6n^{3/2}} B_3 ,$$

where B_1, B_2, and B_3 are constants that are uniformly bounded in n, where the uniform bounds are because the support of ζ is bounded. Maximizing this (strictly concave) function in z is the same as maximizing the strictly concave function

$$\lambda z\left[1 + \frac{B_1}{n^{1/2}} \right] - \lambda^2 z^2\left[1 + \frac{B_2}{n^{1/2}} \right] + \frac{\lambda^3 z^3}{3n^{1/2}} B_3 ,$$

(I got rid of the constant -1 and multiplied through by n), which approaches pointwise the strictly concave function $z \to \lambda z - \lambda^2 z^2$, and does so uniformly on compact sets of z. So Lemma 5.3 (page 143) tells us that the unique maximizer $z_n(\lambda)$ of the consumer's problem in the nth discrete-time economy has as a limit the unique maximizer of the function $z \to \lambda z - \lambda^2 z^2$, which is the solution to $\lambda = 2\lambda^2 z$, or $z(\lambda) = 1/\lambda$ (which, as is known from the literature, is the solution to the consumer's problem for a consumer with CARA utility in the BSM economy).

Now we compute the expected utility for the consumer who, in each period, invests $z_n(\lambda)$ in the stock. The distribution of her final (consumption) portfolio is the same as the distribution of

$$W + \sum_{k=0}^{n-1} z_n(\lambda)[e^{\zeta_k/\sqrt{n}} - 1]$$

(this is her financial gains "integral"), where $\{\zeta_k\}$ is an i.i.d. sequence of random variables, each distributed as ζ. And, therefore, her expected utility is

$$\hat{E}\left[-\exp\left\{ -\lambda\left(W + \sum_{k=0}^{n-1} z_n(\lambda)[e^{\zeta_k/\sqrt{n}} - 1] \right) \right\} \right]$$

$$= \hat{\mathbf{E}}\left[-e^{-\lambda W}\prod_{k=0}^{n-1}\exp\left[-\lambda z_n(\lambda)[e^{\zeta_k/\sqrt{n}}-1]\right]\right],$$

which, because the sequence $\{\zeta_k\}$ is i.i.d, is

$$-e^{-\lambda W}\left(\hat{\mathbf{E}}\left[\exp[-\lambda z_n(\lambda)[e^{\zeta/\sqrt{n}}-1]]\right]\right)^n.$$

We now estimate $\hat{\mathbf{E}}\left[\exp[-\lambda z_n(\lambda)[e^{\zeta/\sqrt{n}}-1]]\right]$, using the Taylor series approximations from before:

$$\hat{\mathbf{E}}\left[\left[\exp\left[-\lambda z_n(\lambda)\left(e^{\zeta/\sqrt{n}}-1\right)\right]\right]\right]$$

$$= 1 - \frac{\lambda z_n(\lambda)}{2n}\left[1+\frac{B_1}{n^{1/2}}\right] + \frac{\lambda^2(z_n(\lambda))^2}{2n}\left[1+\frac{B_2}{n^{1/2}}\right] - \frac{\lambda^3(z_n(\lambda))^3}{6n^{3/2}}B_3,$$

which, substituting $1/(2\lambda)+o(1)$ for $z_n(\lambda)$, is

$$1 - \frac{1/2+\lambda o(1))}{2n}\left[1+\frac{B_1}{n^{1/2}}\right] + \frac{1/4+\lambda^2 o(1))}{2n}\left[1+\frac{B_2}{n^{1/2}}\right]$$
$$- \frac{1/(8n)+\lambda^3 o(1)}{6n^{3/2}}B_3,$$

which, after a massive collection of terms, is $1-1/(8n)+o(1/n)$. And, we conclude, the optimal expected utility attained by the consumer in the nth discrete-time economy has limit

$$\lim_n -e^{-\lambda W}\left(1-\frac{1}{8n}+o\left(\frac{1}{n}\right)\right)^n = -e^{-\lambda W-1/8}.$$

We end by checking that this is the expected utility garnered by the consumer in the limit, continuous-time, BSM economy. In that economy, markets are complete, and so we can solve the consumer's problem as maximization of her expected utility subject to a single budget constraint. Per Proposition 4.4, the first-order condition for her solution is

$u'(x^*(\omega)) = \gamma/e^{\omega(1)/2+1/8}$, where γ is the multiplier on her wealth constraint, or (for this utility function)

$$\lambda e^{-\lambda x^*(\omega)} = \frac{\gamma}{e^{\omega(1)/2+1/8}} \quad \text{or} \quad e^{-\lambda x^*(\omega)} = -\frac{\gamma}{\lambda e^{\omega(1)/2+1/8}}.$$

Hence, her expected utility is

$$\mathbf{E}\left[-e^{-\lambda x^*(\omega)}\right] = -\mathbf{E}\left[\frac{\gamma}{\lambda e^{\omega(1)/2+1/8}}\right] = \frac{\gamma}{\lambda} e^{-1/8} \mathbf{E}\left[e^{-\omega(1)/2}\right].$$

Since $-\omega(1)$ has the same distribution as $\omega(1)$, $\mathbf{E}\left[e^{-\omega(1)/2}\right] = e^{1/8}$ (the variance of $\omega(1)/2$ is $1/4$), and so we conclude that her expected utility is $-\gamma/\lambda$.

Go back to the first-order condition and rewrite as

$$\gamma = \lambda e^{-\lambda x^*(\omega)} e^{\omega(1)/2+1/8}.$$

Taking logs on both sides, we have

$$\ln(\gamma) = \ln(\lambda) - \lambda x^*(\omega)/2 + \omega(1) + 1/8 \quad \text{or}$$

$$\lambda x^*(\omega) = \ln(\lambda) - \ln(\gamma) + \omega(1)/2 + 1/8.$$

But since $\mathbf{E}^*[x^*(\omega)] = W$ (her wealth), taking expectations on both sides gives

$$\lambda W = \ln(\lambda) - \ln(\gamma) - 1/4 + 1/8 \quad \text{and so} \quad e^{\lambda W} = \frac{\lambda}{\gamma} e^{-1/8}.$$

Hence, her expected utility at her optimal solution in the BSM world, which is $-\gamma/\lambda$, is $-e^{-\lambda W - 1/8}$. It does indeed check.

References

Arrow, K. J. (1964). "The Role of Securities in the Optimal Allocation of Risk-bearing," *Review of Economic Studies*, Vol. 31, 91–6. (Originally appeared in French in 1953, published in *Econométric*, CNRS, Paris.)

Bernardo, A., and O. Ledoit (2000). "Gain, Loss, and Asset Pricing," *Journal of Political Economy*, Vol. 108, 144–72.

Billingsley, P. (1999). *Convergence of Probability Measures*, 2nd edn, New York: John Wiley & Sons.

Black, F., and M. Scholes (1973). "The Pricing of Options and Corporate Liabilities," *Journal of Political Economy*, Vol. 81, 637–59.

Cochrane, J., and J. Saa-Requejo (2000). "Beyond Arbitrage: 'Good-Deal' Asset Price Bounds in Incomplete Markets," *Journal of Political Economy*, Vol. 108, 79–118.

Cont, Rama (2019). Private communication.

Cox, J., and C. Huang (1989). "Optimal Consumption and Portfolio Policies when Asset Prices Follow a Diffusion Process," *Journal of Economic Theory*, Vol. 49, 33–83.

Cox, J., and S. A. Ross (1976). "The Valuation of Options for Alternative Stochastic Processes," *Journal of Financial Economics*, Vol. 3, 145–66.

Cox, J., S. A. Ross, and M. Rubinstein (1979). "Option Pricing: A Simplified Approach," *Journal of Financial Economics*, Vol. 7, 229–63.

Dalang, R., A. Morton, and W. Willinger (1990). "Equivalent Martingale Measures and No-Arbitrage in Stochastic Securities Market Model," *Stochastics and Stochastic Reports*, Vol. 29, 185–201.

de Finetti, B. (1931). "Sul significato soggettiva della probabilità," *Fundamenta Mathematicae*, Vol. 17, 298–329.

Delbaen, F., and W. Schachermayer (1994). "A General Version of the Fundamental Theorem of Asset Pricing," *Mathematische Annalen*, Vol. 300, 463–520.

_____(2006). *The Mathematics of Arbitrage*. Berlin: Springer Finance.

Duffie, D. (2001). *Dynamic Asset Pricing Theory*, 3rd edn, Princeton, NJ: Princeton University Press.

Duffie, D., and P. Protter (1992). "From Discrete to Continuous Time Finance: Weak Convergence of the Financial Gain Process," *Mathematical Finance*, Vol. 2, 1–16.

Esscher, F. (1932). "On the Probability Function in the Collective Theory of Risk," *Skandinavisk Aktuarietidskrift*, Vol. 15, 175–95.

Föllmer, H. (1978). Private communication.

Föllmer, H., and D. Sondermann (1986). "Hedging of Non-Redundant Contingent Claims," in *Contributions to Mathematical Economics in Honor of Gerard Debreu*, Hildenbrand and Mas-Colell (eds.), Amsterdam: North-Holland, 205–23.

Fudenberg, D., and D. Levine (2009). "Repeated Games with Frequent Signals," *Quarterly Journal of Economics*, Vol. 124, 233–65

Goldman, M. B., H. Sosin, and M. Gatto (1979). "Path Dependent Options: "Buy at the Low, Sell at the High," *Journal of Finance*, Vol. 34, 1111–27.

Guesnerie, R., and J.-Y. Jaffray (1974). "Optimality of Equilibrium of Plans, Prices, and Price Expectations," in J. Dreze (ed.), *Allocation Under Uncertainty, Equilibrium, and Optimality*. London: Macmillan, 71–86.

Hakansson, N. (1970). "Optimal Investment and Consumption Strategies Under Risk for a Class of Utility Functions," *Econometrica*, Vol. 38, 587–607.

Harrison, J. M., and D. M. Kreps (1979). "Martingales and Arbitrage in Multiperiod Securities Markets," *Journal of Economic Theory*, Vol. 20, 381–408

Harrison, J. M., and S. R. Pliska (1981). "Martingales and Stochastic Integrals in the Theory of Continuous Trading," *Stochastic Processes and their Applications*, Vol. 11, 215–60.

_____(1983). "A Stochastic Calculus Model of Continuous Trading: Complete Markets," *Stochastic Processes and their Applications*, Vol. 15, 313–16.

He, Hua (1991). "Optimal Consumption-Portfolio Policies: A Convergence from Discrete to Continuous Time Models," *Journal of Economic Theory,* Vol. 55, 340–63.

Hubalek, F., and W. Schachermayer (1998). "When Does Convergence of Asset Processes Imply Convergence of Option Prices?," *Mathematical Finance,* Vol. 8, 385–403.

Jakubowski, A., J. Ménin, and G. Pagès (1989). "Convergence en loi des suites d'integrales stochastiques sur l'espace D^1 de Skorohod," *Probability Theory and Related Fields,* Vol. 81, 111–37.

Kabanov, Y., and D. Kramkov (1994). "Large Financial Markets: Asymptotic Arbitrage and continguity," *Theory of Probability and Applications,* Vol. 39, 222–28.

Karatzas, I., and S. Shreve (2014). *Brownian Motion and Stochastic Calculus,* 2nd edn, Berlin: Springer.

Kemeny, J. G. (1955). "Fair Bets and Inductive Probabilities," *Journal of Symbolic Logic,* Vol. 20, 263–73.

Klein, I., and W. Schachermayer (1997). "Asymptotic Arbitrage in Non-Complete Large Financial Markets," *Theory of Probability and Its Applications,* Vol. 41, 780–88.

Kramkov, D., and W. Schachermayer (1999). "The Asymptotic Elasticity of Utility Functions and Optimal Investment in Incomplete Markets," *Annals of Applied Probability,* Vol. 3, 904–50.

Kreps, D. M. (1981). "Arbitrage and Equilibrium in Economies with Infinitely Many Commodities," *Journal of Mathematical Economics,* Vol. 8, 15–35.

_____(1982). "Multiperiod Securities and the Efficient Allocation of Risk: A Comment on the Black–Scholes Option Pricing Model," in *The Economics of Information and Uncertainty,* John J. McCall, ed., Chicago, IL: The University of Chicago Press.

_____(2013). *Microeconomic Foundations: Choice and Competitive Markets,* Princeton, NJ: Princeton University Press.

Kreps, D. M., and W. Schachermayer (2019). "Asymptotic Synthesis of Contingent Claims in a Sequence of Discrete-Time Models," Stanford Graduate School of Business Research Paper No. 3795. Available at SSRN: https://ssrn.com/abstract=3402645.

Kurtz, T., and P. Protter (1991a). "Weak Limit Theorems for Stochastic Integrals and Stochastic Differential Equations," *Annals of Probability*, Vol. 19, 1037–70.

_____(1991b). "Characterizing the Weak Convergence of Stochastic Integrals," *The Proceedings of the Durham Symposium on Stochastic Analysis*, 255–60.

Le Gall, J.-F. (2016). *Brownian Motion, Martingales, and Stochastic Calculus* (English translation), Berlin-Heildelberg: Springer-Verlag.

Luenberger, D. (1969). *Optimization by Vector Space Methods*, New York: John Wiley & Sons.

Merton, R. (1969). Lifetime Portfolio Selection under Uncertainty: The Continuous-Time Case," *Review of Economics and Statistics*, Vol. 51, 247–57.

_____(1971). "Optimal Consumption and Portfolio Rules in a Continuous-Time Model," *Journal of Economic Theory*, Vol. 3, 373–413.

_____(1973a). "The Theory of Rational Option Pricing," *Bell Journal of Economics and Management Science*, Vol. 4, 141–83.

_____(1973b). "An Intertemporal Capital Asset Pricing Model," *Econometrica*, Vol. 41, 867–87.

_____(1975). "Theory of Finance from the Perspective of Continuous Time," *Journal of Financial and Quantitative Analysis*, Vol. 10, 659–84.

_____(1977). "On the Pricing of Contingent Claims and the Modigliani–Miller Theorem," *Journal of Financial Economics*, Vol. 5, 241–9.

Novshek, W. (1985). "Perfectly Competitive Markets as the Limits of Cournot Markets," *Journal of Economic Theory*, Vol. 35, 72–82.

Radner, R. (1972). "Existence of Equilibrium of Plans, Prices, and Price Expectations, *Econometrica*, Vol. 40, 289–304.

Ross, S. A. (1977). "Return, Risk, and Arbitrage," in I. Friend and J. Bicksler (eds.), *Risk and Return in Finance*, Cambridge: Ballinger, 189–218.

Royden, H. (1968). *Real Analysis,* 2nd edn, London: The Macmillan Company.

Sadzik, T., and E. Stacchetti (2015). "Agency Models with Frequent Actions," *Econometrica,* Vol. 83, 193–237.

Schachermayer, W. (2010). "The Fundamental Theorem of Asset Pricing," *Encyclopedia of Quantitative Finance,* Vol. 2, 792–801.

____(2019). Private communication.

Sharpe, W. F. (1978). *Investments,* Englewood-Cliffs, NJ: Prentice-Hall.

Shimony, A. (1955). "Coherence and the Axioms of Confirmation," *The Journal of Symbolic Logic,* Vol. 20, 1–28.

Shreve, S. (2004). *Stochastic Calculus for Finance, Vols. I and II.* Berlin: Springer.

Stricker, Ch. (1990). "Arbitrage et Lois de Martingale," *Annales de l'Institut Henri Poincaré – Probabilites et Statistiques,* Vol. 26, 451–60.

Williams, R. J. (2006). *Introduction to the Mathematics of Finance.* Providence, RI: American Mathematical Society.

Author Index

Subject Index

Econometric Society Monograph Series *(continued from page ii)*

D. M. Kreps & K. F. Wallis (eds.), *Advances in Economics and Econometrics: Theory and Applications, Seventh World Congress, Vols. I, II, & III*, 1997

R. Guesnerie, *A Contribution to the Pure Theory of Taxation*, 1995

C. Sims (ed.), *Advances in Econometrics, Sixth World Congress, Vols. I & II*, 1994

H. White, *Inference, Estimation and Specification Analysis*, 1994

J.-J. Laffont (ed.), *Advances in Economic Theory, Sixth World Congress, Vols. I & II*, 1992

W. Härdle, *Applied Nonparametric Regression Analysis*, 1990

A. Roth & M. Sotomayor, *Two-Sided Matching*, 1990

T. Lancaster, *The Econometric Analysis of Transition Data*, 1990

L. G. Godfrey, *Misspecification Tests in Econometrics*, 1989

H. Moulin, *Axioms of Cooperative Decision-Making*, 1988

T. Bewley (ed.), *Advances in Economic Theory, Fifth World Congress, Vols. I, II, & III*, 1987

C. Hsiao, *Analysis of Panel Data*, 1986

J. Heckman & B. Singer, *Longitudinal Analysis of Labor Market Data*, 1985

A. Mas-Colell, *The Theory of General Economic Equilibrium: A Differentiable Approach*, 1985

R. J. Bowden & D. A. Turkington, *Instrumental Variables*, 1985

B. Peleg, *Game Theoretic Analysis of Voting in Committees*, 1984

F. M. Fisher, *Disequilibrium Foundations of Equilibrium Economics*, 1983

J.-M. Grandmont, *Money and Value*, 1983

G. Debreu, *Mathematical Economics*, 1983

G. S. Maddala, *Limited Dependent and Qualitative Variables in Econometrics*, 1983

W. Hildenbrand (ed.), *Advances in Economic Theory*, 1983

W. Hildenbrand (ed.), *Advances in Econometrics*, 1983